FOREWORD

T O BORROW FROM DICKENS, these are the "best of times" as well as "the worst of times." Anyone who loves Christ and has his or her head screwed on straight could find a reason to smile and cheer yet only moments later to sigh and cry. Our mixed-up world has spawned a strange-looking, out-of-balanced Body.

On the one hand, today's evangelical church scene makes many of us sit up and take notice. Growth is somewhere between rapid and phenomenal . . . and prosperity is unparalleled. There are more "mega churches" than at any other time in our nation's history. Pastoral conferences and seminary classrooms include frequent references to personal creativity and cultural relevance. Who could argue with such excitement and openness?

On the other hand, when the church of Jesus Christ is placed alongside the Scriptures for comparison, the triangles aren't anywhere near congruent. Discerning minds know that we're in trouble . . . *serious trouble.*

True commitment is at an all-time low. Unashamed greed and materialism abound. In some parts of the country there are as many divorces within the church as without. Lifestyles of infidelity, workaholism, parental neglect, and selfishness are both accepted and justified. Let's face it, the distinctions between a believer's lifestyle and an unbeliever's are now blurred. I heard recently that the church needs to lower its expectations . . . we should "get real" and relax our out-of-date standard.

Some—dare I say, most?—simply shrug and yawn as they mumble, "Well, it's the sign of the times. Christ's coming can't be that far away."

But there are a few of us who refuse to buy that rationalization. With prophet-like courage and zeal, they call us back to the basics. They remind us that those who are followers of Jesus Christ should reflect the lifestyle of Jesus Christ. In today's terms, they challenge us to walk the talk.

Such prophets are not only rare, they are right.

My longtime friend, Gene Getz, is one of them. I am grateful he has the guts to stand against the tide as he turns our heads, points to the statements and the principles of scriptural truth, and exhorts us to re-examine *The Walk* that God intended for His people. As a pastor for over thirty years— and now as a seminary president—I applaud his efforts to take us back to the New Testament to measure our ministry by the divine standard instead of yielding to the feel-good philosophy and theories of our times.

Dr. Getz is no novice in church planting and pastoring growing churches. Long before church-growth gurus roamed the landscape, he was thinking creatively and working diligently in innovative methods. He was engaged in teaching the truths he dug from the treasures of God's Book as well as modeling them week after week. The man speaks and writes, therefore, from hands-on experience as he builds a solid foundation on biblical principles mixed with a refreshing freedom in form and structure. In this, his latest volume, the needs of a fast-approaching twenty-first century culture are addressed in a manner that makes good sense while remaining true to the original blueprint set forth in the first century. Any book that accomplished that incredible feat, gets my vote!

Because this is one of those, I commend it to you. Pace yourself as you read *The Walk*. Take your cue from its title and refuse to race through the pages. Keep your Bible nearby so you can check the references as you enjoy the scenery of each chapter. Don't allow your mind to drift. Force yourself to think deeply . . . think creatively . . . think theologically.

That's the least we can do since our times have given us their worst and Gene Getz has given us his best.

— Chuck Swindoll

gene a. getz
THE WALK

gene a. getz
THE WALK

GROWING INTO THE FULLNESS OF CHRIST

BROADMAN
&HOLMAN
PUBLISHERS

Nashville, Tennessee

© 1994, 1999, 2000 by Gene A. Getz
All rights reserved
Printed in the United States of America

0-8054-2139-4

Published by Broadman & Holman Publishers, Nashville, Tennessee

Dewey Decimal Classification: 262
Subject Heading: CHURCH \ CHRISTIAN LIFE
Library of Congress Card Catalog Number: 94-21333

Unless otherwise stated all Scripture citation is from the New King James Version, copyright © 1979, 1980, 1982, Thomas Nelson, Inc., Publishers, used by permission.

Originally published with a different subtitle in hardcover (1994) and paperback (1999) but no longer available. Previously the Library of Congress has cataloged these editions as follows:

LIBRARY OF CONGRESS CATALOGING-IN-PUBLICATION DATA
Getz, Gene A.
    The walk : the measure of spiritual maturity / by Gene A. Getz ; foreword by Chuck Swindoll
        p. cm.
    ISBN 0-8054-6157-4 (hc)
    ISBN 0-8054-1870-9 (pbk.)
    1. Church renewal. 2. Christian life. I. Title.
BV600.2.G45   1994
262'.001'7—dc20
                                                        94-21333
                                                        CIP
ISBN 0-8054-2139-4

1 2 3 4 5   04 03 02 01 00

CONTENTS

A PERSONAL JOURNEY

I BEGAN MY WRITING MINISTRY WHILE a professor at Moody Bible Institute in Chicago. In each instance, I deliberately set out to author several books. However, when I accepted the invitation to teach at Dallas Theological Seminary in the fall of 1968, I had a fascinating new experience.

A BOOK I NEVER PLANNED TO WRITE

The book I never intended to write is entitled *Sharpening the Focus of the Church.* Challenged by my students at Dallas Theological Seminary to take a fresh look at what the New Testament really teaches regarding what God intended the church to be, they became a part of a dynamic process of interacting with Scripture and surfacing supracultural principles that can help us measure the effectiveness of our present church structures.

A CHURCH I NEVER PLANNED TO START

The end result of this writing experience was destined to impact my life dramatically. Not only did I write a book I had never planned to write, but I started a church that I never planned to start—the first Fellowship Bible Church. A small group of families challenged my wife and me to launch this church, utilizing the principles I had outlined in *Sharpening the Focus of the Church.* Their desire was to go back to basic biblical principles and allow the forms and structures to emerge that would best help us carry out the Great Commission in our present cultural situation.

A VOCATIONAL CHANGE I NEVER PLANNED TO MAKE

We accepted this invitation with the understanding that we'd simply help launch this new work and then I'd get on about my business of being a seminary professor. However, this church planting effort led to another decision I had never planned to make. Our new church grew so quickly and dramatically that I had to face a very important question—"Should I continue to serve full-time in the academic world or become totally involved at the local church level?"

After wrestling with this issue for a period of time, I decided to leave the very secure sacred halls of learning as a full-time tenured professor and become a full-time pastor. To this point in my professional career, I had devoted twenty years (thirteen years at Moody Bible Institute and seven years at Dallas Theological Seminary) to preparing people to serve Jesus Christ in the local church. However, I often smile and with "tongue in cheek" share that I then proceeded to spend the next 20 years learning how! The facts are that serving as a church planting pastor has been one of the greatest and most challenging learning periods in my ministry life. It's one thing to dispense theory in the classroom. It's yet another to put this theory into practice. Though some of my experiences have been intensely painful, in retrospect those difficult challenges provided me with my most significant and profitable learning opportunities. Though this was in many respects a much more uncomfortable ministry journey, I've never regretted my decision to make this vocational change. Incidentally, I still teach part-time at Dallas Theological Seminary, particularly in their doctor of ministries program. But hopefully, I'm bringing a new level of reality to the classroom—one that grows out of my daily "wall-to-wall" experiences as a pastor.

A CHURCH PLANTING EXPERIENCE I NEVER ENVISIONED

Planting the first Fellowship Church in November of 1972 led to more unexpected pastoral experiences. I've had the unique privilege of launching and pastoring two additional churches in the Dallas metroplex. During this same period of time, I've helped start a number of other branches and "sister" churches in the Dallas area as well as in other parts of the United States.

Several of us launched the church I presently pastor in 1981—Fellowship Bible Church North in Plano, Texas—a far north suburb in the Dallas area, classified as one of the fastest growing cities in the United States. A great challenge lies before us in carrying out the Great Commission of our Lord Jesus Christ.

A TIME FOR PERSONAL REFLECTION

As I reached my 37th year in full-time ministry—over half of those years as a pastor—I was challenged one day while reading a book by George Barna entitled *The Power of Vision* to begin to ask myself some very specific and penetrating questions. I wanted to get to know myself better—to learn more about who I really am! I also began to reflect on my ministry environment—which certainly includes the people I minister to, who they are, and where they are in their own relationship with God. And in asking that question about others, I had to ask that very personal question of myself. What is the status of my personal relationship with God?

It was during this soul searching process that I began to ask the Holy Spirit to reveal to me what He really wanted for the church that I presently pastor. What was God's plan for all of us? In short, I asked God for a vision for our people—a vision they could embrace and own as God's vision for all of us!

It was during these times of intense scriptural study and prayer that my mind and heart began to focus on the importance of *modeling*—being an example to others of what God really intends His church to be! Could this be God's specific will and vision for our church? After all, I had spent a number of years attempting to plant churches that reflected New Testament principles. Was it time to evaluate in a new and fresh way where I was in this process and, at the same time, to help my fellow leaders and the people I presently pastor at Fellowship Bible Church North to develop a passion as well as a unique strategy to model these concepts to others?

As I reflected on these questions, I believe the Holy Spirit also directed my thoughts to a scriptural affirmation—something Paul wrote to the Thessalonians, commending them for their corporate example. First, Paul wrote—"You became followers of us and of the Lord." Then he commended these believers for becoming *"examples* [or a model] to all in Macedonia and Achaia who believe" (1 Thess. 1:6–7).

This scriptural verification reassured me that these thoughts were indeed from God—not just the result of my own mental and emotional projections and desires. This kind of goal can certainly be motivated by self-interest. In order to check my motives, I openly and very specifically shared this personal process with my lay leadership team as well as my fellow staff pastors. Taking seriously the Proverb—"In the multitude of counselors there is safety" (Prov. 11:4), together we prayed and sought God's wisdom. And together, we began to experience a oneness of heart and mind that confirmed that God indeed had made His will known to us![1]

DEVELOPING A SENSE OF OWNERSHIP

My next step was to represent this "oneness" of conviction among our leadership team by sharing this process with our whole congregation. With input from our pastoral and lay leadership team, I began to unfold this vision, to our people through a series of messages, looking particularly at passages of scripture and biblical principles that outline what God intends every church to be!

One principle stands out above all the rest. *To become a model to others means to begin with ourselves*—being that model in our "own Jerusalem"— not only through our church at large, but in our families, our marriages and our personal lives. It was exciting to see people begin to develop a keen sense of ownership—that this vision was indeed *their* vision—one that also applied to their own personal Christian experience.

MEASURING OUR SPIRITUAL MATURITY

It was during my presentation of these messages that Greg Vaughn, a good friend and a member of our church, began to personalize these principles in his own life. Having been in visual media production for a number of years, he asked if I would be willing to do a series of video messages on one of the most basic of all New Testament church principles—measuring our spiritual maturity in Christ. Greg's own personal vision was to have me present a series of biblical concepts on this subject that were universal, normative and supracultural—in short, principles every church anywhere in the world could use to evaluate their walk with Jesus Christ. It was also his idea to approach various key leaders in the Christian world to introduce and close out each video presentation. I'm indeed grateful to those who responded and also consented to introduce each chapter in this book (see Acknowledgment section).

After once again consulting my ministry team, I consented to do this project. I determined to do a fresh study of the New Testament, focusing particularly on Paul's church planting ministry as recorded by Luke in the Book of Acts and in the letters he wrote to these churches. Paul, more than any other New Testament leader and author, outlines and explains God's plan for measuring maturity, both at the corporate and personal level. Perhaps his concern for all churches is best expressed in his letter to the Ephesians: "I, therefore, the prisoner of the Lord, beseech you to walk worthy of the calling with which you were called" (Eph. 4:1).

My personal prayer is that this study will help you—professional pastor or lay person—to look first at your own spiritual walk and to determine the extent to which you measure up to "the measure of the stature of the fullness of Christ." Second, it is my prayer you will then be able to lead your church to reflect Christ's life in their walk together as a corporate body of believers. The facts are, this is where I began in my own personal experience—and, would you believe, I ended up writing another book I never intended to write!

ACKNOWLEDGMENTS

I WANT TO PERSONALLY THANK the following key Christian leaders who consented, not only to participate in the video project—"The Measure of Spiritual Maturity"—but, to write an introduction to each of the following chapters:

- Dr. John F. Walvoord, who as president of Dallas Theological Seminary, encouraged me greatly in my initial endeavors in biblical research on the first-century churchs.

- Stephen Olford, who I consider one of my greatest models in my pastoral and preaching ministry.

- Bill and Vonette Bright, whose vision for reaching the world with the Gospel at times overwhelms me.

- Josh McDowell, whose boldness for Christ and boundless energy challenge me to greater heights in the ministry.

- Max Lucado, whose literary and pastoral talents serve as a great inspiration and challenge.

- Bruce Wilkinson, who alone has made my seminary teaching a highlight in my life since Walk Through the Bible grew out of Bruce's master's thesis I had the privilege of supervising.

- Charles Stanley, whose commitment to Jesus Christ and steadfast endurance in the ministry challenge me daily to never turn to the "right" or to the "left".

- Joseph Stowell, who serves as president of Moody Bible Institute, the school that laid the biblical and theological foundations upon which I've built my life and ministry.

- Luis Palau, whose evangelistic ministry and compassion for the lost remind me regularly why the Church exists in this world.

- Norm Wright, whose example as a husband and father and whose burden to help others in this arena has challenged me over the years.

- Tony Evans, who, as one of my students at Dallas Theological Seminary, became the first full-time missionary we sent out from the first Fellowship Bible Church—resulting in Oak Cliff Bible Fellowship and its sister organization, Urban Alternative.

- I need to express my deep gratitude to Chuck Swindoll for taking time out of a very busy schedule as president of Dallas Theological Seminary to write the foreword to this book. Chuck's solid biblical teaching on Insight for Living has captured my interest and generated ideas for my own teaching and radio ministry.

I also want to thank several key people whose suggestions actually precipitated this project and whose constant encouragement enabled me to complete it. First, I want to thank Greg Vaughn, president of Grace Products Corporation and an active member of Fellowship Bible Church North, who personalized our vision—"To model (be an example) to people everywhere what God intends His church to be!" Without Greg's challenge to prepare the video series, "The Measure of Spiritual Maturity," I would not have tackled this writing project.

I also want to thank Chuck Wilson from Broadman & Holman Publishers and Mike Hyatt from Wolgemuth & Hyatt, Inc. who approached me about this writing project and made it possible for me to broaden my ministry opportunities through this unique publishing enterprise.

I want to express deep appreciation to my executive assistant, Iva Morelli and to her secretary, Randi Bengtson, for the many sacrificial hours they spent typing this material for both the video project and this published manuscript.

There are many others to whom I am deeply indebted for encouraging me to complete this project—the total staff at Fellowship Bible Church North and in the Center for Church Renewal, as well as the Fellowship Bible Church North body at large. Without these wonderful people, I would not have had the inspiration to tackle this rather enormous video and writing project.

Last, but by no means least, I want to thank my wonderful wife, Elaine, who has always encouraged me beyond measure in projects such as this by standing beside me as my loyal helpmate, my prayer partner, and my best friend.

GOD WANTS TO USE YOUR CHURCH!

T HROUGHOUT CHURCH HISTORY, GOD has used individual Christians to serve as key leaders and certain churches to become strategic centers of influence in carrying out the Great Commission. In the New Testament world, Peter and John as well as Paul and Barnabas stand out as these kinds of leaders. The Jerusalem church was this kind of church, as well as the church in Antioch of Syria and the church in Ephesus.

On the other hand, there were many churches in the New Testament world that we know little about and yet these churches and their pastoral leaders will stand out in eternity as dynamic examples of faithfulness to Jesus Christ. They penetrated their communities with the Gospel message and demonstrated what it means to "walk worthy of the calling with which they have been called" (Eph. 4:1).

Following the first century, church history has continued to illustrate this divine principle for nearly 2,000 years. And it's still true today. God is using certain leaders and certain churches in an unusual way to penetrate the world with the message of faith, hope, and love (1 Cor. 13:13). Some of these churches are well known in the evangelical world—and even in the world at large. Some are known only to a few, and some are basically known only to God—but their legacy is being carefully recorded by Jesus Christ Himself who knows all about their faithfulness.

Unfortunately, the opposite is also still true—just as it was in New Testament days and throughout church history. There are many churches—large and small—that are not measuring up to what God had in mind. The problem lies—not with our Lord Jesus Christ or the culture in which the church exists—but with our failure to become what God intended the church to be! This is certainly illustrated in the penetrating letters written to the seven churches in Asia (Rev. 3,4). Most of these churches had unique weaknesses and Jesus Christ Himself challenged them to "repent" and to "hear what the Spirit says to the churches" (Rev. 2:5,7,11,16,17,29; 3:3,6,13,22).

A PERSONAL CHALLENGE

What about you? And what about your church? Though your sphere of influence, both personally and corporately, may be localized and limited from a human point of view, remember that God measures success by a different standard than many people measure success today. He honors faithfulness based on the way we carry out His instructions (Matt. 25:14–13). But He also holds us accountable based on what He has provided in the way of talents and resources. To those He has given much, He requires much (1 Cor. 4:2; Luke 12:48b).

Hopefully this study on spiritual maturity will motivate you and your church—no matter what your cultural challenges or no matter what your size—to "dream the most possible dream" and to become all that God wants you to become. We must remember that He "is able to do exceedingly abundantly above all that we ask or think, according to the power that works in us" (Eph. 3:20).

While preparing this manuscript, I had the opportunity to speak at a retreat center to a rather large group of men in Canada. Though sponsored by Men Alive—a parachurch ministry—the conference was planned primarily by a committee from a relatively new church in Brockville, Ontario. Together, these men had spent an entire year praying and planning for this conference.

As I delivered my messages and interacted with the men on this planning committee and rubbed shoulders with their pastor, I became aware of a dynamic church that is making a difference in people's lives. Though I've ministered at many conferences, I sensed an unusual presence of the Holy Spirit. I experienced it as I delivered my messages and in the way the men listening responded to the Scriptures.

As the conference ended, the chairman of this committee shared with all of us seven prayer requests that these men had been praying about for nearly a year. God had answered every request. It was then I began to really understand why this conference was unique.

Following this Friday-Saturday conference, I was invited to speak on Sunday to the church body where the planning group worshipped. This experience only confirmed the observations I've just made. Here is a church, little known by the populous—and certainly almost unknown in the United States—that is penetrating its community with the Gospel of Jesus Christ. It is dynamic and alive and very well known by the Lord Jesus

Jesus Christ. It is dynamic and alive and very well known by the Lord Jesus Christ! It did not take long to conclude that here is a church that is definitely in the process of measuring up "to the stature of the fullness of Christ" (Eph. 4:13).

A "Worthy Walk"

The purpose of this book is to help you and your church—wherever you may be located in this world—to reflect the image of Jesus Christ in your personal and corporate walk and to become all that He intended you to be. My primary source is the New Testament, with a particular focus on Paul's strategy for planting churches and assisting those churches to become mature. And since it is my conviction and that of my publisher, that the Scriptures are inspired by God, our prayer is that you will respond to the challenge issued by Jesus Christ Himself so many years ago—"he who has an ear, let him hear what the Spirit says to the churches" (Rev. 2:7,11,17,29; 3:6,13,22). With this in mind, let's "set the stage" for our study.

The Pauline Strategy A Foundational Perspective

The apostle Paul's unique calling to carry the gospel beyond Jerusalem, Judea, and Samaria and "to the end of the earth" (Acts 1:8); and to build the church by reaching Gentiles for Christ, stands out clearly in the unfolding of New Testament revelation. This calling came directly from Jesus Christ, but was affirmed by others (Acts 9:15) and recognized by the other apostles (Gal. 2:7–10). It is also affirmed in biblical church history. Most of what Luke recorded in the Book of Acts, beginning with Paul's conversion in chapter 9, focuses on the ministry of this dynamic and dedicated apostle.

Paul's unique calling is also verified and illustrated by the number of letters he wrote which are included in the New Testament. Therefore, the broad framework for this book focuses on the Pauline strategy—the way Paul and his coworkers carried out the Great Commission. However, within this broader perspective, we'll focus on a specific aspect of Paul's objectives and strategy—namely, that every church he planted or came in contact with would grow and mature and measure up to "the stature of the fullness of Christ" (Eph. 4:13).

PAUL'S HOME-BASED CHURCH

After several years of intense preparation following his dramatic conversion to Jesus Christ on the road to Damascus (Acts 9:1–19; Gal. 1:15–18), Paul's ministry to the Gentiles began in a concentrated way in Antioch of Syria, where disciples of Christ were first called "Christians" (Acts 11:26). Joining his friend Barnabas, he helped establish what was to become one of the most strategic and influential churches in the first century world.

Primarily a Gentile church (Acts 11:19–21), this group of believers established a beachhead for expanding the ministry of the gospel to the pagan world. It was here that Paul and Barnabas were commissioned by the Holy Spirit to carry out this great task (Acts 13:1–3).

PAUL'S FIRST MISSION

On Paul's first missionary journey, he and Barnabas established churches in southern Galatia (Acts 13:1–14:28). After successfully planting churches in Antioch of Pisidia, as well as in Iconium, Lystra and Derbe, Paul and Barnabas circled back to help these new believers become established in their faith (see figure 1). And to make sure that each church would

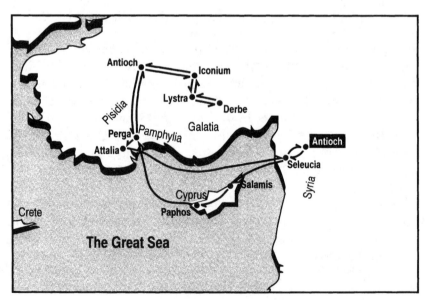

Figure 1: Paul's First Journey

continue to grow spiritually, Paul and Barnabas appointed mature leaders in each church who could shepherd and teach these new believers (Acts 14:21–23).

After returning to Antioch of Syria, Paul and Barnabas helped resolve the great law and grace debate in Jerusalem (Acts 15:1–35). During this same period, they filled their days "preaching and teaching the word of the Lord" in Antioch—their home-based church. It is my personal opinion that it was also during this time frame that Paul wrote his first letter, the Epistle to the Galatians.

PAUL'S EXPANDED MISSION

During this stay in Antioch, Paul developed an intense desire to revisit the churches he and Barnabas had launched on their first journey. This decision indicates his commitment to helping Christians become mature. He was not satisfied with merely preaching the Gospel and leading people to Christ. Unless a dynamic church was established in the faith, he felt his task was only half finished—and indeed it would have been. Consequently, Paul with Silas, a new missionary companion, "went through Syria and Cilicia, *strengthening the churches*" (Acts 15:41).

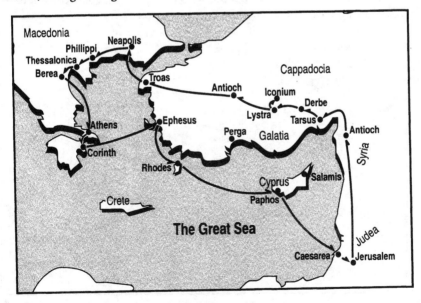

Figure 2: Paul's Second Journey

When Paul and Silas reached Lystra, Timothy joined the missionary team and together these men expanded the ministry into Europe where some of the most prominent churches mentioned in the New Testament were planted and established—the churches in Philippi, Thessalonica, and Corinth (See figure 2).

PAUL'S BEACHHEAD IN EPHESUS

After spending at least a year and a half in Corinth, Paul once again returned to minister in his home church in Antioch of Syria, stopping briefly in Ephesus but promising to return (Acts 18:11–22). But true to form, Paul again became burdened to follow up his evangelistic and church planting efforts. Consequently, he launched his third journey traveling throughout "the region of Galatia and Phrygia . . . *strengthening all the disciples*" (Acts 18:23).

It was also on this journey that he established another beachhead in Ephesus. He returned to this key Asian city as he had promised, and for two years, he taught "daily in the school of Tyrannus" (Acts 19:9). As a result of this concentrated effort, Paul established a strong and dynamic corporate witness which resulted in churches being established throughout Asia (Acts 19:26). Many people who came to this great commercial

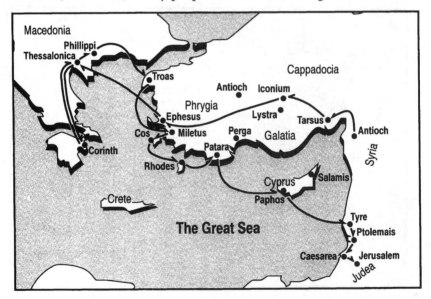

Figure 3: Paul's Third Journey

center to do business and to worship in the temple of Diana were converted to Jesus Christ and returned to their home towns and established churches of their own. No doubt this helps explains the founding of the six other churches in Asia mentioned in the Book of Revelation (Rev. 1:11).

PAUL'S LETTERS

In this brief overview of Paul's personal, "face-to-face" traveling ministry, it's very apparent that this New Testament church planter was dedicated to not only lead people to Christ, but to establish these new believers in the faith and to help them to "walk worthy" of their great calling (Eph. 4:1)—measuring up to "the stature of the fullness of Christ" (Eph. 4:13).

But Paul, under the leadership of the Holy Spirit, developed another follow-up technique. He penned letters to many of these churches—epistles that today make up a great portion of the New Testament. These letters give us unusual insight into the spiritual status of these churches at the time Paul wrote these letters. Furthermore, these epistles are filled with important insights as to how God measures the maturity level of local churches, as well as how to produce and develop this kind of maturity. In essence, these insights help us understand not only our wonderful position in Christ, but how to measure up "to the stature of the fullness of Christ."

Though the focus in this book highlights the Pauline strategy in evangelism and church planting, we will also draw upon the totality of the New Testament for insights regarding producing and measuring spiritual maturity. Consequently, the Jerusalem model—the first church we encounter in the New Testament and a church founded several years before Paul's conversion to Christianity—is used as a dynamic example and a frame of reference for learning how to produce churches that are maturing in Jesus Christ. But, as we will see, it is Paul's church planting efforts described in the Book of Acts and especially the content in his subsequent letters to these churches that help us understand more fully how to become a church that reflects the Jerusalem model, particularly as it functioned during its early years of existence.

Dr. John F. Walvoord

I FIRST MET DR. GENE GETZ OVER twenty-five years ago when, as president of Dallas Theological Seminary, I interviewed Gene and subsequently asked him to join the faculty of the seminary after a distinguished career on the faculty of Moody Bible Institute. As a professor, first in the Christian Education Department and later in Pastoral Ministries, his teaching has been characterized by a deep love for the church of Jesus Christ and an intense dedication to discover what the Scriptures teach about the local church and how it should function as a dynamic witness in various cultures of the world. It was this keen interest that motivated him to begin his extensive writing in the area of practical ecclesiology and which eventually led him out of the classroom as a very competent full-time professor and into a unique, innovative, and creative church planting ministry.

Being able to combine his professorship with planting and pastoring churches has given Gene a unique ability to blend both theory and practice. The chapter you are about to read is refreshing and challenging, particularly during a period of time that is often characterized by an emphasis on building great churches through pragmatic and culturally relevant approaches but often neglecting to build firmly on biblical principles that will produce Christ-like maturity. Gene rightly takes us back to the Scriptures that certainly place an emphasis on *quality* rather than *quantity* when it comes to measuring the effectiveness of the church.

Though Gene has planted and pastored some large and growing churches in Dallas, and at the same time built these churches on creative and culturally relevant approaches, I have personally observed that he has emphasized Paul's goal —to build up the body so as to reflect "the stature of the fullness of Christ" (Eph. 4:12b–13). The results are evident in the lives of many of those who have come to Christ and have been discipled in the faith.

This chapter entitled "Holy and Without Blemish" focuses that goal and sets the stage for the chapters to follow that flesh out what true maturity is in the local church. Beginning with John's wedding metaphor and the marriage supper of the Lamb in Revelation 19 where Jesus Christ is revealed to have united with His perfect bride (the church) at the rapture, Gene then takes us from heaven back to earth, correlating John's wedding metaphor with Paul's marriage metaphor in Ephesians chapter 5 where Jesus Christ's ultimate goal for the church was to present "to Himself a glorious church not having spot or wrinkle or any such thing, but that it should be *"holy and without blemish"* (Eph. 5:25–27). As I state in my own commentary on Revelation, "The present work of sanctification of the church must be distinguished from justification."[1]

It is my opinion that John was referring to the process of becoming conformed to the image of Jesus Christ following conversion when he specifically identified the bride's purity as "the righteous acts of the saints" (Rev. 19:8b). This is what Paul also had in mind when he encouraged the Ephesian believers to "to measure up to the stature of the fullness of Christ" (Eph. 4:13).

As you read this chapter carefully, I am confident you will develop a new appreciation for what Paul had in mind when he wrote to the Ephesians and said — "I, therefore, the prisoner of the Lord, beseech you to *walk worthy* of the calling with which you were called" (Eph. 4:11).

ONE

HOLY AND
WITHOUT BLEMISH

I, therefore, the prisoner of the Lord, beseech you to *walk*
worthy of the calling with which you were called.
— Ephesians 4:1

H AVE YOU EVER STOPPED TO WONDER why you are here in this world or what life is all about? Sometimes we get so busy carrying out the responsibilities and routines of life, we forget to even ask these questions. We get so involved in meeting our needs that we simply lose focus. We cannot "see the forest for the trees," and sometimes we even lose our way!

In this book, I would like to demonstrate from Scripture that life is not a series of haphazard events and relationships or accidents. God has a marvelous plan—an eternal plan—and if you know Jesus Christ as your personal Lord and Savior, you are a part of this marvelous unfolding plan.

To understand this plan, I want to take you on an exciting spiritual journey. On this journey, you'll discover how you fit into God's great eternal plan. You'll learn more fully what God's will is for you personally. But, more than that, you'll learn what God's plan is for that unique group of people you associate with—your spiritual family—that body of people God calls His church.

These studies focus our "walk with Christ"—in essence, the way we measure our spiritual maturity. All that we look at in Scripture will relate to this theme. We must not forget that God has called us and placed us in His body to conform our lives to the image of Jesus Christ. And we must not forget that our spiritual walk with Christ is not just an individual and personal experience. It also involves marvelous reality described in Scripture—the body of Christ. God's plan is that we "walk together," demonstrating oneness of heart and mind and the holiness and righteousness of Jesus Christ (John 13:34–35; 17:20–23; Rom. 12:1–2; 15:5–6; Eph. 4:1–6).

Our foundational passage of Scripture in this study is Ephesians 4:1–16. As we launch our study with this passage and then look at other passages in the New Testament, we'll reflect on this wonderful section of Scripture rather frequently. It is indeed an "anchor" passage for understanding God's plan for His church corporately and locally. And it's particularly important in understanding our "walk with Christ" and the way we can measure our spiritual maturity, both personally and as a corporate body.

In the first half of his Ephesian letter, Paul described our "calling" in Christ. He reminded these New Testament Christians—and all of us as believers—that "He chose us in Him [Christ] before the foundation of the world" (Eph. 1:4a). However, God had a wonderful purpose in mind for His body, the Church— "that we should be holy and without blame before Him in love" (Ephesians 1:4b). Elaborating on "our calling" and "our position in Christ" in chapters 1–3, Paul transitioned to "our walk with Christ" beginning in chapter 4. He beseeches us to "walk worthy" of the calling to which we have been called (Eph. 4:1).

GOD'S PLAN FOR PRODUCING SPIRITUAL MATURITY

Beginning in verse 11 of chapter 4, Paul outlined God's specific plan for enabling all of us to become a mature church. First, Paul specified the leaders Christ appointed to launch and lead the church. Second, he described these leaders' basic responsibility. Third, Paul outlined what should result when these leaders function as they should—the specific goal of our study together.

- Christ's Appointed Leaders

And He Himself [Jesus Christ] gave some to be apostles, some prophets, some evangelists, and some pastors and teachers. (Eph. 4:11)

- These Leaders' Basic Responsibility

For the equipping of the saints for the work of ministry. (Eph. 4:12a)

- The Results

For the edifying of the body of Christ, till we all come to the unity of the faith and the knowledge of the Son of God, to a perfect man, *to the measure of the stature of the fullness of Christ* [emphasis mine, both here and throughout the remainder of the book whereever italics are used with scriptural quotations]. (Eph. 4:12b–13)

A CORPORATE PERSPECTIVE

To fully understand this plan, we must not focus only on our individual walk with Christ. You are you, and I am who I am—but to comprehend God's plan for our lives personally, we must see ourselves as part of a family—a "household"—that unique group of people that God calls His church—His Body (Eph. 2:19–22). We must understand God's plan for corporate growth and corporate maturity. This indeed is the emphasis of the New Testament and without this understanding and without this experience, we will not (and we cannot) measure up to "the stature of the fullness of Christ" as disciples—at least not to the extent that God intended. We need the context of the body of Christ to grow spiritually where "every joint supplies" and "every part does its share." This is what "causes growth of the body for the edifying of itself in love" (Ephesians 4:16).

AN ETERNAL PERSPECTIVE

At one point in time, this unique family concept was called a mystery (Ephesians 3:3). But that mystery has been revealed—from beginning to end—and viewed from God's eternal perspective, it becomes one of the most wonderful and glorious realities in the universe.

I remember when I first arrived in New York City to work on my doctorate at New York University. I had never been there before, and I felt lost in a mass of concrete and humanity with endless streets and rail systems. To gain perspective, I took the elevator to the top of the Empire State Building—at the time the tallest building in the world—and viewed that great city in every direction. When I descended once again to the streets and folded into the millions of people going in what appeared to be a thousand different directions, from that point forward I always knew where I was—or at least I knew how to find out where I was— and how to find my way to my predetermined destination.

To understand God's plan for His family more fully, allow the Holy Spirit to transport you in your thinking to the very end of time. Perch with me for a few moments on the very edge of eternity, and from that vantage point look back at God's plan for your life—and mine—from an eternal perspective.

JOHN'S VISION

Nearly two thousand years ago, Jesus Christ spoke to the apostle John who was exiled on the island of Patmos. In some respects, perhaps he also felt somewhat lost and confused as to how he fit into God's eternal plan. He had devoted his life to carrying out the Great Commission—making disciples of all nations, baptizing those disciples and teaching them everything Jesus Christ had taught him. And now here he was in exile on a lonely island in the Mediterranean Sea. At this point in time, tradition tells us that all of his fellow apostles had literally given their lives for the cause of Jesus Christ.

It was there that Jesus Christ spoke directly to John and said, "Come up here, and I will show you things which must take place after this" (Rev. 4:1). John's vantage point was far more spectacular than a view from a skyscraper overlooking a great city.

At that moment, he was transported—not bodily—but in his mind into the future. With the eyes of his heart he could see prophetically God's marvelous eternal plan for all mankind unfolding. It was an awesome revelation.

THE OLD TESTAMENT HALL OF FAITH

Much of what John saw initially involved God's judgments on the earth. But beyond those judgments, John saw a beautiful scene which he describes metaphorically in Revelation chapter 19. In his vision, John saw a great multitude of people lifting their voices in praise to the Almighty God. Though we are not told specifically who was in that enormous crowd, we can be confident that Abel stood out among the rest as he offered his personal sacrifice of praise. After all, he is the first Old Testament saint listed in the Hebrew "Hall of Faith" (Heb. 11:4).

Enoch, who never experienced physical death, would certainly be shouting his own "hallelujahs" (Heb. 11:5–6). Noah perhaps knelt before God, lifting his hands to his Creator and Savior (Heb. 11:7). Abraham, Isaac, and Jacob may have stood arm-in-arm, lifting their voices with words of adoration and thanksgiving (Heb. 11:8–10). And their wives—Sarah, Rebekah, Leah, and Rachel—would certainly also be worshipping Jesus Christ, the Son of God (Heb. 11:11).

Joseph would also stand out in this great multitude, just as he did on earth when he wore his coat of many colors (Heb. 11:22). And Moses' face would be radiant, just as it was when he descended from Mount Sinai or after he emerged from the tent of meeting where he had experienced God's holy presence (Heb. 11:23–29; Ex. 33:12–23; 34:29–35).

Perhaps one of the most exciting aspects of this great scene will be to see Joshua standing beside Rahab the harlot . . . and her family. Millenniums before, she had exclaimed to the two spies who visited her house, "The

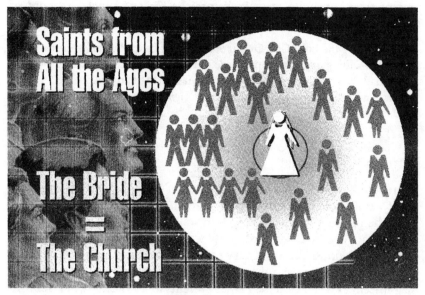

Figure 1.1: John's Vision

LORD your God, He is God in heaven above and on earth beneath" (Josh. 2:11). And as she stood in this great future throng, she certainly personalized that statement of honor and adoration, calling the Lord her God as well (Heb. 11:30–31).

THE SAINTS OF ALL AGES

Others who are listed in the Old Testament "Hall of Faith" will also be there (11:32–40). But they will be few compared with the size of the multitude that the apostle John witnessed in his vision. The number seemed endless, representing saints from "all nations, tribes, peoples, and tongues" (Rev. 7:9). And the sounds that emanated from the depth of their collective hearts and souls rent the air and resounded so loudly that John described it as if it were "the sound of many waters and as the sound of mighty thunderings"—a virtual Niagra Falls a thousand times over (Rev. 19:6).

Today, New Age voices fantasize about "harmonic convergence." However, their false hopes and empty dreams pale against the backdrop of the true "oneness and unity" that will one day be revealed through this great multi-racial and diverse body of people as they with one heart and voice present their corporate message before the King of Kings and Lord of Lords:

> Alleluia! For the Lord God Omnipotent reigns! Let us be glad and rejoice and give Him glory, for the marriage of the Lamb has come, and His wife has made herself ready. And to her it was granted to be arrayed in fine linen, clean and bright, for the fine linen is the *righteous acts of the saints*. (Rev. 19:6b–8).

THE BRIDE OF CHRIST

I remember so clearly my daughter Robyn's wedding. Relatively speaking, it was a rather large celebration—with nearly 1,000 people attending. I had the privilege of giving her away, walking down the aisle as Robyn, dressed in a beautiful, spotless white wedding gown, made her glorious entrance. Obviously, it was a very moving experience for me. After all, I was her father. However, no earthly wedding will ever be as glorious and magnificent as when God the Father presents to Jesus Christ, His Son, His eternal bride—the church.

In actuality, John saw two groups of people in his vision (see figure 1.1). First, there was the larger group—all of those who were "called to the marriage supper of the Lamb" (Rev. 19:9)—the saints of all ages. The second group is identified as the "wife" or "bride" of Christ—clearly the church. In describing this scene, the Holy Spirit inspired John to select a beautiful metaphor to illustrate those who, at this moment, occupied "center stage" in God's scheme of things, a "bride" who had adorned herself for her bridegroom—the Lord Jesus Christ. As Merrill C. Tenney has stated, "The marriage of the Lamb is certainly figurative of the ultimate union of Christ with His people." And even though "the word 'church' is not used here, the bride can scarcely mean anything else."[2]

THE "MYSTERY REVEALED"

What John saw prophetically was indeed a grand culmination of the great "mystery" that was revealed first and foremost to the apostles and New Testament prophets. Paul wrote rather extensively about this divine mystery in his letter to the Ephesians (Eph. 3:2–6).

He testified that God had chosen him—unworthy though he was—"to make all people see what is the fellowship of *the mystery*, which from the beginning of the ages has been hidden in God who created all things through Jesus Christ" (3:9). God's intent, Paul stated, was that "the mani-

Figure 1.2: The Seven Churches of Asia

fold wisdom of God might be made known *by the church* to the principali-
ties and powers in the heavenly places, according to the eternal purpose
which He accomplished in Christ Jesus our Lord" (Eph. 3:10–11). Though
this great mystery was unveiled in the first century, it has now been
prophetically and ultimately unveiled in John's vision as both Jew and
Gentile believers stand "face to face" with their blessed Savior (1 Cor.
13:12). Attending this wedding banquet are the saints of all ages, rejoicing
and praising God as they participate in this glorious eternal moment.

Paul's Marriage Metaphor

The apostle Paul also used a similar metaphor to describe the relationship between Christ and the church. However, Paul went beyond a "wedding celebration" to draw on the subsequent and ongoing relationship between a husband and a wife. In so doing, he expanded the metaphor. Paul likened a "husband" to "Jesus Christ" and the "wife" to the "church," and in so doing stated Jesus Christ's ultimate goal for the church:

> That He might present it to Himself a glorious church, not having spot or wrinkle or any such thing, but that it should be holy and without blemish. (Eph. 5:27)

When John's wedding metaphor and Paul's marriage metaphor are merged together, a major truth stands out in bold relief—the concept of "holiness" and "righteousness." The great multitude in John's vision shouted: "The marriage of the Lamb [Jesus Christ] has come, and His wife [the church] has made herself ready" (Rev. 19:7b). That readiness is then described as being dressed in "fine linen, clean and bright" (19:8a)—which, wrote John— "is the righteous acts of the saints" (19:8b). In this glorious, future scene described in John's vision, the bride of Christ stands before Jesus Christ reflecting what Paul described in Ephesians as Christ's goal for the church—"A glorious church, not having spot or wrinkle or any such thing, but that she should be holy and without blemish" (Eph. 5:27).

The Seven Churches Of Asia

When John received his revelation on the island of Patmos, most of what he saw and described was yet to be. But Jesus Christ's initial instructions to John involved the present. He was to describe what he was about to see and hear by writing it on a scroll and sending it "to the seven churches" in Asia (Rev. 1:11, see figure 1.2).

These churches were groups of people who comprised local bodies of believers. They were geographical in nature, and each church was different in terms of their walk with Christ and the extent to which these believers measured up "to the stature of the fullness of Christ." In fact, some who claimed to be Christians and a part of these "local churches" were not believers at all. They were Christians "in name only."

Jesus' special message to each of these seven churches in Asia certainly represents the strengths and weaknesses of local churches of all time and in every culture of the world (Rev. 2:1—3:22). Not surprisingly, one of the major emphases in these little epistles focuses on what it means or does not mean to "walk worthy" of our calling in Christ and the extent to which Christians truly "measure up to the stature of the fullness of Christ."

A LOOK BACK

At this point, let's go back about thirty years—before John, in his vision, heard Jesus speak directly to the church in Ephesus. Let's look at the "anchor" passage we referred to earlier—in a letter written to the church in Ephesus by the apostle Paul. The goal Jesus Christ has for His church, wrote Paul, is to produce "a mature" body of believers that "walks worthy" of Christ's calling and measures up to His stature. Jesus Christ is our example, our model, our standard for spiritual maturity. We are to walk as He walked.

Interestingly, to illustrate the mature church, Paul changed his metaphor from the "bride" or "wife" to "manhood;" that is, to become a "perfect man" (Eph. 4:13). No doubt Paul chose this metaphor in this context to illustrate that our example is "the perfect man," Christ Jesus. We, as a body of believers, are to become like Him.

Paul used other forms of this same metaphor to illustrate that we are to conform to the image of Jesus Christ. In fact, in verse 14 of this same passage in Ephesians he states that it is God's will that "we no longer be children" (Eph. 4:14). Paul also identified the Corinthians as "babes" or "infants" in Christ—Christians who had not grown very much in their spiritual journey. And the apostle Peter used the same metaphor when he encouraged new Christians—"as newborn babes"—to "desire the pure milk of the word" in order to grow and mature (1 Pet. 2:2).

"THE STATURE OF THE FULLNESS OF CHRIST"

When God chose us to be Christ's bride, He had an ultimate purpose in mind—that we would "be holy and without blame before Him in love" (Eph. 1:4). Paul made this point very clear in his opening words to the Ephesians.

God also had a plan for this to happen. It is true that all believers experience positional righteousness and holiness when we are justified by faith in Jesus Christ (Rom. 5:1). Personally and collectively, we have a new identity. We are "in Christ" and He is in us (Col. 1:25–28). God views us as perfect the moment we truly believe because of Christ's atoning sacrifice. But attaining the "righteous acts of the saints" described in John's vision is both a divine and human process. It is true that we are God's "workmanship, created in Christ Jesus for good works, which God prepared beforehand that we should walk in them" (Eph. 2:10). But it is also true that this process depends on our obedience to Jesus Christ's commands (John 15:10).

THE BUILDING METAPHOR

In Paul's letter to the Corinthians, he used another metaphor to describe the importance of becoming spiritually mature as a collective body of believers. In this letter, he emphasized the importance of constructing a building that is built on a proper foundation. In this metaphor the foundation is Jesus Christ (1 Cor. 3:11).

Paul made it very clear in this passage that there will be Christians in heaven whose works will be burned up because they have not been obedient to Jesus Christ. They "will be saved, yet so as through fire" (1 Cor. 3:15). Their reward will be eternal life. But correlating and mixing the building metaphor with the one John used in describing his apocalyptic vision—their "wedding garments" will no doubt lack the same quality of those who have responded to God's grace by being "zealous for good works" (Titus 2:14). Their "building materials" will be "wood, hay, straw" rather than "gold, silver, precious stones" (1 Cor. 3:12). "The fire," Paul wrote, "will test each one's work, of what sort it is. If anyone's work which he has built on it endures, he will receive a reward. If anyone's work is burned, he will suffer loss; but he himself will be saved, yet so as through fire" (1 Cor. 3:13–15). Though it sounds crude, John's wedding metaphor indicates that there will be Christians standing before Jesus Christ without garments at all!

Paul's point is clear: There will also be a time in the future when all believers will be judged for the way they have lived their lives while here on earth. The Scriptures identify this as the "judgment seat of Christ" (Rom. 14:10; 2 Cor. 5:10). This experience will not involve our salvation; rather, it involves our rewards for faithful living and service. Some of us will receive no crowns whatsoever because we have fallen short—far short—of measuring up to "the stature of the fullness of Christ" (Eph. 4:13).

At this point, there is a truth I cannot explain satisfactorily. The Scriptures seem to teach that rewards will be both for individual Christians and for churches, particularly as we look at Jesus Christ's messages to the seven churches in Revelation (Rev. 2–3). Our Christian walk will be judged both as individuals and as a corporate body of believers. However, I do not need to understand how all of this will happen in order to endeavor to "walk worthy" of my calling in Christ as an individual believer, as well as to do all I can to enable the church I both lead and am a unique part of to "measure up to the stature of the fullness of Christ." As a pastor particularly, I want the people I shepherd to reflect Jesus Christ and to "walk worthy" of their great calling—just as Paul wanted the Ephesians to live this kind of lifestyle, both in a personal and a corporate level.

AN AWESOME RESPONSIBILITY

In this same passage of Scripture in the Corinthian letter, Paul made a statement that is startling, and in context, has a primary application to those of us who are leaders in the church. Here, he used "the temple" metaphor to illustrate the body of Christ. "Do you not know," Paul queried, "that you [as a body] are the temple [church] of God and that the Spirit of God dwells in you [as a body]? If anyone defiles the temple [church] of God, God will destroy him. For the temple [church] of God is holy, which temple [church] you are" (1 Cor. 3:16–17).[2]

On the surface, it may appear that here Paul is writing to individual Christians. In actuality he's writing to both a local church (the Corinthians) and to individual leaders who are defiling or destroying this temple.

In my own church-planting experience, I worked with a young man who became a trusted friend and fellow pastor. In fact, I trusted him so completely that I turned over to him the reigns of leadership to be my successor in a large church I had helped start and build from the ground up. At the same time, I left that homebase church to start our fifth branch work in Dallas. Unknown to me, this young pastor had problems in his marriage. Affected by these problems, he began to falter as a spiritual leader. He also began to manifest attitudes and actions that were definitely out of the will of God.

Unfortunately, while all of this was happening, he sought the advice of others, some of whom were themselves carnal Christians. They encouraged him to fight for his position using lying and false accusations to achieve this goal.

As a result, confusion reigned. Innocent people were deceived. Ultimately, the church split and left a number of Christians wounded and disillusioned. And some even turned their back on God.

This story has a very sad ending. Today, as I write these words, this young man still languishes in prison. Subsequent to the church split, this young pastor disintegrated spiritually and morally. He was even charged with attempted rape.

Not only did he suffer the results of personal disintegration, his family also self-destructed, which has been one of the most painful results of his sin. Though he has confessed that sin and I believe he has truly repented, all that he worked for in building his life has been destroyed—getting a theological education, having three beautiful children, and being involved in ministry.

When this happened, a friend of mine—at that time, a fellow seminary professor—directed my thoughts to these verses stated by Paul to the Corinthians— "If anyone defiles [destroys] the temple of God, God will destroy him. For the temple of God is holy, which temple you are" (1 Cor. 3:17).

Though this warning is directed to all Christians, it is particularly applicable to those of us who are leaders—pastors, elders and deacons— who are responsible to lead the church to maturity. We are to build the church, not destroy it! It's a sacred trust! Thus, Paul wrote to the Ephesians and charged them—and us—to endeavor "to keep the unity of the Spirit in the bond of peace" (Eph. 4:3).We must remember, he wrote, that "there is one body and one Spirit, just as you were called in one hope of your calling; one Lord, one faith, one baptism; one God and Father of all, who is above all, and through all, and in you all" (Eph. 4:4–6).

A WALK WORTHY

Paul charged the Ephesians to "walk worthy" of their special calling (Eph. 4:1). Again, this is a corporate exhortation—a challenge as a body of believers "no longer to walk as the rest of the Gentiles walk" (Eph. 4:17), but to "walk in love" (Eph. 5:2) and to "walk as children of light" (Eph. 5:8). In summary, he challenged the Ephesians to "walk circumspectly, not as fools, but as wise, redeeming the time because the days are evil" (Eph. 5:16).

This book is designed to help all of us evaluate our Christian walk and commitment to Jesus Christ and His church. It is designed to help all of us evaluate our own level of maturity—as individuals, yes, but more than that—as local bodies of believers. As stated earlier, Paul used the metaphor of the "perfect man," to describe a "body" of believers who become this "perfect man"—reflecting the man Christ Jesus. Though we will never measure up completely until we are transformed into His image and stand before Him "face to face" as His "perfect bride," we are to be consistently involved in this process of becoming more and more conformed to the stature of Jesus Christ.

Using various New Testament churches in the next four chapters, we want to look at our faith, our hope, and our love—as a church—when measured by God's standard. As we go deeper into this study, we'll use the church in Jerusalem as a dynamic model to measure:

- Our commitment to learning and practicing God's truth as revealed in the *Word of God.*

- Our commitment to *prayer*—that divine means whereby God's power can be released to enable us to be the churches God wants us to be.

- Our commitment to *Koinonia*—the degree to which we are maintaining a dynamic fellowship with God and with one another as we participate in each other's lives.

- Our commitment to being *generous Christians* who use their material possessions to glorify God and to build the kingdom of God.

- Our commitment to *reaching others* for Jesus Christ with the wonderful message of salvation.

- Our commitment to *building strong families* in a world where the family is disintegrating and under serious attack.

- Our commitment to *growing spiritually as individual Christians* in order that each of us may contribute our part to the overall spiritual maturity in our particular local churches.

MEASURING OUR WALK

As we conclude, let me leave you with several final questions:

1. Are you ready to mature in Jesus Christ and to "walk worthy" of your calling? What experiences in your life have led you to this conclusion?

2. Are you ready to learn what it means to measure up to the stature of the fullness of Christ? What do you think it means at this point in your walk?

3. How do you see your church in light of this command? Are you ready to do your part in helping your church become this kind of church?

Dr. Stephen Olford

I WAS FIRST INTRODUCED TO GENE GETZ through his books. In fact, I was so impressed with his exposition of the Word of God, and particularly what the New Testament teaches about the local church, that I invited Gene to lecture at the Stephen Olford Center for Biblical Preaching in Memphis, Tennessee.

As I listened to Gene Getz open the Scriptures, I was fascinated by his ability to distinguish absolute, enduring, and transcultural principles in the Word of God from what is non-absolute, temporary, and cultural.

What impressed me the most, however, was his exposition of 1 Corinthians chapter 13. From this passage, he demonstrated how Paul's use of the trilogy of "faith, hope, and love" (verse 13) serves as a key to understanding the Pauline Epistles—particularly in terms of measuring the maturity level of the local church. Frankly, in all of my study of Scripture, I had not seen "faith, hope, and love" as God's standard for measuring spiritual conformity to the fullness of Christ— for individual Christians as well as the corporate life of the local church. I then understood more fully Dr. Griffith Thomas' statement that, " 'faith, hope, and love' constitute both the doctrine and the duty of the local church for all time."

I am thankful for Gene Getz and his commitment to the Word of God and the work of God. Whether he speaks or writes, he is an annointed messenger "for such a time as this."

Please read this chapter carefully. Taken seriously, the truth in this chapter can dramatically change both your personal life and the life of your church.

THE MEASURE
OF A CHURCH

This I say, therefore, and testify in the Lord, that you
should *no longer walk* as the rest of *the Gentiles walk.*
— Ephesians 4:17

I F THE APOSTLE PAUL SAT DOWN TO WRITE to your church—or
my church—how would he begin the letter? What would he thank
God for? What would he mention first?

There are a lot of ways churches are measured today, usually in terms
of success. The most prominent are numerical growth, building projects,
well-orchestrated services, contemporary music, need-oriented messages, a potpourri of activities, mission outreach, organizational effi-
ciency, management styles, etc. Interestingly, all of these things are noteworthy—and most are even important—but this is not what Paul and
other New Testament writers thanked God for in their letters to New
Testament churches. Rather, they were thankful for the degree of *faith,
hope,* and *love* that existed in those churches.

To illustrate this point, look carefully at Paul's first letter to the Corinthians—a letter written to a church that has historically been classified as
a very immature church—at least at the time Paul wrote this first letter. In
fact, even today a "Corinthian" is defined by Webster as a "profligate man."

Paul first referred to faith, hope, and love in the Corinthian letter at the
end of chapter 13—a verse that has probably become one of the most often
quoted verses among Christians and non-Christians alike (1 Cor. 13:13).
In fact, when I was studying English literature in college a number of years
ago, I did a research paper on the term "charity"—the old English word
for "love" translated from the Greek word, *agape.* My professor—though
schooled in literature—admittedly had little in-depth knowledge of the

English Bible. Nevertheless, he was very familiar with 1 Cor. 13:13 as translated in the King James New Testament:

> And now abides faith, hope and charity, these three; but the greatest of these is charity.

I remember how surprised my professor was when he discovered that the term "charity" was a much broader concept than the way Christians use their material possessions. Today, of course, most people know the difference because of updated translations which use the term "love."

We may smile at my professor's lack of knowledge—even as a professor of English literature. I have discovered that even though 1 Corinthians

Figure 2.1

13:13 is one of the most memorized and often quoted verses in the Bible, many believers—including church leaders—do not understand that Paul used faith, hope, and love—and especially love—to measure the degree to which a local church reflects the image of Jesus Christ. Thus it is very important to understand when and where Paul first used these "words" in this letter. It's also important to note the context of these words, not only in the Corinthian letter but in other letters Paul wrote to various churches (see figure 2.1).

PAUL'S THESSALONIAN LETTERS

Figure 2.2

To understand more fully what Paul had in mind when he used these three words in the Corinthian letter, let's compare the way he used these words in some of his other letters. Note again that his use of faith, hope, and love is the first time Paul used these words as a trilogy in this epistle to the Corinthians (see figure 2.1), and in so doing, he used them more toward the end of the letter rather than at the beginning. He did this in several epistles (see figures 2.2 and 2.3). For example, note how he began his first letter to the Thessalonians, a letter he probably wrote on his second missionary journey while stationed in Corinth: "We give thanks to God always for you all, making mention of you in our prayers, remembering without ceasing your work of *faith, labor of love, and patience of hope* in our Lord Jesus Christ in the sight of our God and Father" (1 Thess. 1:2–3).

Ephesians

1:15, 16, 18...Faith, Love & Hope

Figure 2.3

In his second letter to the Thessalonians, Paul followed a similar pattern: "We are bound to thank God always for you, brethren, as it is fitting, because your *faith grows exceedingly,* and *the love of every one of you all abounds* toward each other, so that we ourselves boast of you among the churches of God" (2 Thess. 1:3–4).

COMPARING THESE TWO INTRODUCTIONS

When these two "introductions" to the Thessalonian letters are compared, even casually, several similarities become very apparent.

First, when Paul remembered these Christians in his prayers, he was thankful for what was happening in their lives.

Second, his "thanksgiving" focused on the qualities of faith, hope and love.

Third, he described these qualities and how they were reflected in the Thessalonian church. In his first introduction, he referred to their "work of faith, their labor of love, and their patience of hope." In the second letter, he stated that their "work of faith" was growing and their "labor of love" was increasing.

Fourth, when Paul thanked God for faith, hope, and love in the New Testament churches, he used the plural pronoun "you" and "your." Though clear in the Greek text, it is not clear in English since we use identical words to express "singleness" or "corporateness" and we determine the meaning of these pronouns from the context in which we use the words. For example, I might say "to you" as an individual— "I thank God for *your walk* with Christ." However, I might stand before a large audience and make the same statement—"I thank God for *your walk* with Christ." However, when speaking to more than one individual, the word "your" takes on a much more significant meaning. I am now referring to corporate growth among a group of believers that can be measured by observing their Christian walk as they relate to God and interact with one another.

In nearly all instances in the New Testament, Paul used these pronouns in a corporate sense to describe faith, hope, and love. In fact, it is difficult to measure growth in these areas apart from seeing these qualities manifested among Christians as they relate to God and to one another as a corporate unit.

Measurable Growth

Perhaps one of the most significant differences between these "introductions" in the Thessalonian letters is that when Paul wrote the second letter, the Thessalonian believers had already grown significantly in their Christian walk, particularly in reflecting "faith" and "love." In several months time, they had made significant progress spiritually. According to Paul, there was a measurable difference. Their faith had grown "exceedingly" and their love had abounded toward each other (2 Thess. 1:3–4). Furthermore, Paul was actually boasting about their spiritual growth among other churches (2 Thess. 1:4). This indicates the extent to which Paul was pleased when a body of believers matured in these areas of their lives.[1]

Paul's Twin Epistles

Approximately ten years after Paul wrote to the Thessalonians, he wrote two additional letters that also clearly focus on the qualities of faith, hope, and love. Evidently written while Paul was under house arrest in Rome, they are sometimes identified as "twin epistles." This is understandable since much of what Paul wrote to the Colossians is repeated and expanded in his letter to the Ephesians.

1 Corinthians
1:4-7...Grace Gifts

Figure 2.4

Colossians

Paul's "introduction" to his epistle to the Colossians is very similar to his "introduction" in his first letter to the Thessalonians (see figure 2.4). Though his main source of information regarding the spiritual growth of this church came from his co-worker, Epaphras (Col. 1:4,7–8), he nevertheless prayed for them diligently and thanked God for their maturity in Christ. More specifically, he wrote (note again the use of plural pronouns to reflect the corporate manifestation of these qualities):

> We give thanks to the God and Father of our Lord Jesus Christ, praying always for you, since we heard of *your faith* in Christ Jesus and of *your love* for all the saints; because of *the hope* which is laid up for you in heaven, of which you heard before in the word of the truth of the gospel. (Col. 1:3–5)

Figure 2.5

EPHESIANS

Paul's "introduction" to the letter to the Ephesians is also similar (see figure 2.5). However, there are two differences. First, Paul does not refer to these concepts until several paragraphs into the letter to the Ephesians (in contrast to the placement in the Thessalonian and Colossian letters). Second, the fact that he prayed that these believers might grow in their hope is a very significant observation in terms of their spiritual needs. Thus, Paul wrote:

> Therefore I also, after I heard of your faith in the Lord Jesus and your love for all the saints, do not cease to give thanks for you, making mention of you in my prayers: . . . that you may know what is the hope of His calling. (Eph. 1:15–16,18)

THE CORINTHIAN LETTER

We've already noted Paul's use of the terms faith, hope, and love in the Corinthian letter. As pointed out, he did not refer to these concepts until near the end of the letter (see figure 2.6) when he said:

"And now abide faith, hope, love, these three; but the greatest of these is love" (1 Cor. 13:13).

A CLOSER LOOK

Why this difference? Why didn't Paul begin this letter to the Corinthians in the same way he opened his letters to the Thessalonians, the

Figure 2.6

Colossians, and Ephesians? And, why didn't he thank God for the Corinthians' faith, hope, and love?

The answer to these questions lies in understanding the degree to which this church (at the time Paul wrote this letter) measured up—or should we say, did not measure up—"to the stature of the fullness of Christ." They were certainly not "walking worthy" of their calling. They were walking more like the "Gentiles walked," rather than walking in love and in the light of Jesus Christ (Eph. 4:17). This becomes increasingly clear as you look at the context of Paul's first letter to the Corinthian church. Stated more succinctly, the Corinthians were not demonstrating to any great extent, if at all, the qualities of faith, hope, and love. They were walking in the flesh and not according to the Holy Spirit.

A COMPARISON

When introducing his letter to the Corinthians, Paul took an entirely different approach. Rather than thanking God for faith, hope, and love; he thanked God for God's grace in these believers' lives (see figure 2.7). However, it is very important to note that Paul was not referring here to

God's grace which had resulted in their salvation apart from works (see Eph. 2:8–9). Rather, he was attesting to the "grace-gifts" that had been sovereignly bestowed on the Corinthians by the Holy Spirit. The context itself clarifies what Paul meant: "I thank my God always concerning you for the *grace of God* which was given to you by Christ Jesus, that you were enriched in everything by Him in all utterance and all knowledge, even as the testimony of Christ was confirmed in you, so that *you come*

Figure 2.7

short in no gift" (1 Cor. 1:4–7).

Here Paul associated God's "grace" with the gifts of the Holy Spirit. Just as their salvation had come by God's grace apart from works, so they had received the gifts of the Holy Spirit by God's grace. They had not earned them nor worked for them. In fact, there is no evidence they ever asked for or sought these gifts. Rather, they were sovereignly given by God according to His desire and His will in the matter (see also Heb. 2:3–4).[2]

However, in spite of their giftedness, Paul quickly reminded the Corinthians that they had not grown in their Christian lives, even during the eighteen months he had spent ministering to them in Corinth. At the very

moment he wrote this letter, Paul still identified them as infants in Christ. They fell far
short of "measuring up to the stature of the
fullness of Christ" (see figure 2.8). By telling
the Corinthians they were "behaving like mere
men," he in essence, was saying they were walking—not like Christians—but like unsaved
Gentiles who had given themselves over to the
lusts of the flesh (Eph. 4:17). Thus, Paul wrote:

1 Corinthians

3:1-3...Carnal, Babes & Mere Men

Figure 2.8

> And I, brethren, could not speak to you as to
> spiritual people but as to carnal, as to babes
> in Christ. I fed you with milk and not with
> solid food; for until now you were not able to receive it, and even now you
> are still not able; for you are still carnal. For where there are envy, strife, and
> divisions among you, are you not carnal and behaving like mere men? (1
> Cor. 3:1–3)

Here Paul used the same metaphor he used when he wrote to the
Ephesians. His goal, which was God's goal, was that believers "should no
longer be children," but rather grow up and become mature adults—
Christians who measure up to "the stature of the fullness of Christ" (Eph.
4:13–14).

Against this backdrop—comparing Paul's use of the words faith, hope,
and love in his other epistles—we can now comprehend more quickly and
meaningfully what he meant when he wrote the paragraphs contained in
1 Corinthians chapter 13.

THE GREAT LOVE CHAPTER

As we've already noted, Paul began this letter to the Corinthians by
thanking God for their "grace gifts." The first three verses of chapter 13
returns to this theme. By implication, he acknowledged their possession
and use of these gifts, but reminded them that without love, these gifts
were meaningless. In essence, he was saying: "Yes, you have more gifts than
any church in the New Testament world, but because you lack love, your
gifts are basically useless and certainly do not reflect Christ-like maturity."

Making his point to these believers, Paul used a very tactful grammatical
technique. He applied this truth to his own life, putting himself in their
place. Consequently, he used a personal pronoun—a powerful communication technique. In essence, here is what Paul said:

THEIR GIFTS: NOT A MARK OF MATURITY (1 COR. 13:1–3)

13:1   *Though I speak with the tongues of men and of angels* [as you do,
        Corinthians, more than any other church], *but have not love* [as
        you certainly don't, Corinthians], *I have become as sounding
        brass or a clanging cymbal* [the sound of your speaking gifts is as
        "noise without true meaning."](see 1:7; 12:10,28; 14:1–25 for
        Paul's references to their gifts).

13:2   *And though I have the gift of prophecy, and understand all mys-
        teries and all knowledge* [as you certainly do, Corinthians], *and
        though I have all faith, so that I could remove mountains, but have
        not love* [as you have demonstrated that you don't], *I am nothing*
        [the way you are using these gifts is a meaningless exercise in
        God's sight.] (see 1:5; 12:10; 12:28; 14:1–3,39 for references to
        these gifts).

13:3   *And though I bestow all my goods to feed the poor, and though I
        give my body to be burned, but have not love* [as you don't,
        Corinthians], *it profits me nothing.* [The way you are using your
        gifts is of no value in God's sight.]

At this juncture, we can imagine how the Corinthians were reacting to
these indictments on their giftedness—what they thought was a measure
of their spirituality. The most painful reality would be to hear Paul say they
had no love. Their natural reaction would be to rationalize—to question—
Paul's conclusions regarding their lack of love.

Paul anticipated this reaction, and he then proceeded to demonstrate a
literary technique that must have left them breathless, if not speechless.
Within the space of four verses, he reviewed sequentially (chapter by
chapter) all of the major issues he had examined in the first twelve chapters
of this letter—issues and problems that demonstrated unequivocally why
he concluded they were not demonstrating love in their church.

THEIR LOVE: THEY HAD VERY LITTLE (1 COR. 13:4–6)

13:4a   *Love suffers long and is kind; love does not envy.* [Earlier, Paul had
        said, "For you are still carnal. For where there are envy, strife,
        and divisions among you, are you not carnal and behaving like
        mere men [that is, non-Christians" (1 Cor. 3:3).]

13:4b   *Love does not parade itself, is not puffed up.* [Earlier, Paul had said,
        "Therefore let no one glory in men, then each one's praise will

come from God, . that none of you may be puffed up on behalf of one against the other . . . Why do you glory as if you had not received it? . . . Now some are puffed up, as though I were not coming to you" (1 Cor. 3:21; 4:5–7,18).]

13:5a   *[Love] does not behave rudely.* [Earlier, Paul had said, "It is actually reported that there is sexual immorality among you. . . . And you are puffed up. . . . Your glorying is not good. . . . There-fore when you come together in one place, it is not to eat the Lord's Supper. For in eating, each one takes his own supper ahead of others; and one is hungry and another is drunk" (1 Cor. 5:1–2,6; 11:20–21).]

13:5b   *[Love] does not seek its own, is not provoked.* [Earlier, Paul had said, "Dare any of you, having a matter against another, go to law before the unrighteous, and not before the saints? . . . But brother goes to law against brother, and that before unbelievers! . . . No, you yourselves do wrong and defraud, and you do these things to your brethren!" (1 Cor. 6:1,6,8)]

13:5c; *[Love] thinks no evil; does not rejoice in iniquity, but rejoices in*
6a   *the truth* [Earlier, Paul had said, "Do you not know that your bodies are members of Christ? Shall I then take the members of Christ and make them members of a harlot? Certainly not! . . . For you were bought at a price; therefore glorify God in your body and in your spirit, which are God's" (1 Cor. 6:15,20).]

13:7a   *[Love] bears all things.* [Earlier, Paul had said, "But beware lest somehow this liberty of yours becomes a stumbling block to those who are weak" (1 Cor. 8:9).]

13:7b   *[Love] believes all things.* [Earlier, Paul had said, "Am I not an apostle? Am I not free? Have I not seen Jesus Christ our Lord? Are you not my work in the Lord? If I am not an apostle to others, yet doubtless I am to you. For you are the seal of my apostleship in the Lord" (1 Cor. 9:1–2).][3]

13:7c   *[Love] hopes all things.* [Later, Paul says, "And if Christ is not risen, your faith is futile; you are still in your sins! Then also those who have fallen asleep in Christ have perished. If in this life only we have hope in Christ, we are of all men the most pitiable" (1 Cor. 15:17–19).]

13:7d *[Love] endures all things.* Following this summary of chapters 1 through 12, and even projecting ahead to chapter 15, Paul once again returned to their focus—their giftedness—and reminded them that their gifts were merely temporal and a means to develop spiritual maturity. They had allowed their supernatural gifts of grace to become an "end" in themselves and to become expressions of arrogance and disunity. Paul then explained why love is the greatest of all Christian virtues—even greater than faith and hope.

A BIBLICAL GOAL: PURSUE FAITH, HOPE, AND LOVE (1 COR. 13:8–13)

13:8a *Love never fails.* But whether there are prophecies, they will fail [your prophecy gifts are temporal whereas love is eternal];

Figure 2.9: Their Present Condition is Carnality

"That He might present her to Himself a glorious church, not having spot or wrinkle or any such thing, but that she should be holy and without blemish." (Eph. 5:27)

Figure 2.10: Their Eternal Condition

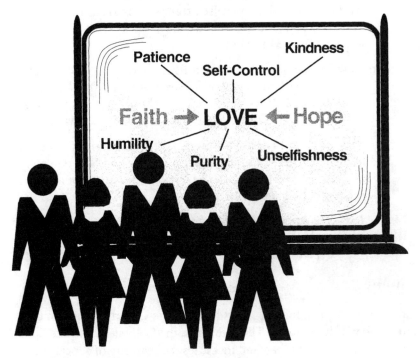

Figure 2.11: Their Condition If They Became a Mature Church

13:8b   *whether there are tongues, they will cease* [your tongue gifts are temporal whereas love is eternal];

13:8c   *whether there is knowledge, it will vanish away* [even your knowledge gifts are temporal whereas love was and is eternal].

13:9   *For we know in part and we prophesy in part.* But when that which is perfect [your total transformation into the image of Christ] *has come, then that which is in part* [the temporal] *will be done away.*[4]

13:10   *When I was a child, I spoke as a child* [as you Corinthians were doing], *I understood as a child* [as you are doing], *I thought as a child* [as you are doing]; *but when I became a man* [when Paul, himself, began to measure up to the stature of the fullness of Christ], *I put away childish* [or immature] *things* [such as focusing on the gifts of the Spirit he has just outlined in 1 Cor. 13:1–3].

13:12a *For now we see in a mirror dimly* (see figure 2.9), *but then face to face* (see figure 2.10) Corinthians, your corporate lifestyle is a poor reflection of Christ as you look into the mirror of God's truth, but someday you will be translated into His presence and there will be no mirror for you will see Jesus Christ "face to face" and you will be like Him].

13:12b *Now I know in part* (see again figure 2.9) [your knowledge of God is limited], *but then I shall know just as I also am known* (see again figure 2.10) [you will have full knowledge when you are transformed into His image and each will have a new body].

13:13   *And now* [God's desire for these believers in their present situation on earth] *abide faith, hope, love, these three; but the greatest of these is love (see figure 2.11)[which was the element most missing among them].*

14:1a   *Pursue love [you should not pursue gifts but rather love, the greatest thing which you lack almost completely].*

A FINAL WORD

Hopefully, this quick look at Paul's letter to the Corinthians when compared with his letters to the Thessalonians, the Colossians and the Ephesians has demonstrated that God measures the maturity of a local church by the degree of faith, hope, and love expressed and reflected by its members. In essence, this is the kind of corporate lifestyle that demonstrates the extent to which a body of Christians "measures up to the stature of the fullness of Christ." This indicates the extent to which they are walking according to the Spirit rather than according to the flesh (Gal. 5:19–26).

Certainly, God's will is that each believer in a corporate body reflect these qualities. However, it is possible for a church to demonstrate faith, hope, and love—even though in any given church there will be immature believers (new Christians), carnal Christians (those who live after the flesh rather than the Spirit), and even "natural" or unsaved people (particularly those who are seeking God). In fact, any church that is really impacting the world will include these three groups of people. But at the same time, if the church as a whole is growing in faith, hope, and love; the overall image of that church will be a reflection of Jesus Christ and His lifestyle.

Furthermore, there is no better place for those who lack faith, hope, and love to grow and mature in these areas of their lives than mingling with and observing Christians who are walking in the light and measuring up to the stature of the fullness of Christ. In fact, this is God's ideal context for discipleship to take place—within a functioning body that is "building itself up in love as each member participates in the growth of the church." (paraphrase of Eph. 4:16)

I would like to end where I began—with a question. If the apostle Paul sat down to write a letter to your church, how would he begin the letter? What would he thank God for?

As a pastor, this is a question I attempt to ask myself. I also try to focus this question for our total leadership team and for all those in our congregation. In fact, when we built our facility in Plano, Texas, a couple in our church donated a beautiful stained glass window above our baptistry and behind the pulpit which features in bold relief the words Faith, Hope, and Love.

This beautiful window reminds all of us constantly that our building is not the church. The church in the New Testament always refers to the people of God. It's only as we, as a body of Christians, grow together in Jesus Christ that we will truly reflect faith, hope, and love. And that is a true measure of a church!

MEASURING OUR WALK

1. How would Paul begin a letter to your church?

2. What would he thank God for about your fellowship?

CHRIST'S LETTER TO THE
CHURCH IN PERGAMOS

A Contemporary Paraphrase of Rev. 2:12–17

Dear Brothers and Sisters:

I am well aware that you are living in the center of Satan's territory. Occult practices are everywhere. Demonic worship and ritual abuse is rampant. Even some of your own children have become victims of those who claim to be Christians but are secretly worshipping Satan. However, as a body of believers, you have remained true to me. You have not renounced your faith in me—in spite of the fact that your dear brother Antipas was secretly murdered because of his strong witness.

But I must warn you that there are some in your congregation that are subtly undermining the faith of others by teaching that it's all right to dabble in the world—for example, to attend theaters that feature elicit sexual activity. And it may surprise you that some are renting adult movies and viewing them in the privacy of their own homes.

There are also some of your number that are worshipping at the shrine of materialism, caught up in making money in dishonest and unethical ways. You must warn these people and disassociate yourself from them if they do not turn from their sinful activities. If you don't deal with their sin, I will have to, and this will make it more difficult for all of you. Please take my warnings seriously.

He whose words can penetrate
to the dividing of soul and spirit,

Jesus Christ

Dr. Bill Bright

THE BIBLE CLEARLY TEACHES THAT without faith it is impossible to please God (Heb. 11:6). For over forty years, I have traveled many miles to all the major countries of the world and every continent, and in my travels I have talked to many millions of people. In the process, I have observed many demonstrations of faith. I have been deeply moved again and again and challenged by what I see among believers in other cultures in terms of their faith. In many respects, it must be similar to what happened to people who became believers in the New Testament world.

In this chapter entitled "Measuring Our Faith," Dr. Gene Getz takes us back to the New Testament church for illustrations of faith—true biblical faith—and demonstrates how these believers lived out their faith in unusual ways in spite of some very difficult challenges. In turn, these biblical examples give us principles that are cross-cultural and applicable to Christians wherever we live in the world. Read carefully! These biblical truths can change your life and the life of your church.

THREE

MEASURING OUR FAITH

So we are always confident, knowing that while we are at
home in the body we are absent from the Lord. For we
walk by faith, not by sight.

— 2 Corinthians 5:6–7

T HE LATE DR. FRANCIS SCHAEFFER once asked a very penetrating and convicting question. He wondered if we removed
every reference to faith in the Bible—particularly with respect to
releasing God's power through supernatural means—would it really make
any difference in the way Christians live their lives?

Dr. Schaeffer's question reminds me of my friend, Jeannie, a single
woman from America who taught school in Iran during the days when the
Shah was deposed. When the Ayatollah Khomeini took over, persecution
that had already begun under the Shah intensified throughout the country.
As you might expect, Christians were a particular threat to Islamic funda-
mentalism. For example, if an Islamic son decided to follow Jesus Christ,
his own father would hire assassins to first reason with his son. If there was
no response, they would beat him. If there was still no response, they would
take his life.

When Khomeini took the reins of power, the radical groups were
unrestrained and intensified persecution by also hiring assassins who
would mark all of the doors where Christians lived. The door to Jeannie's
home was marked as well with a black X. Day and night she lived with the
threat of having her home bombed and burned—and with the continual
fear of being killed. Through it all, however, God gave her a marvelous
sense of His presence and His peace.

One of the most tragic events—from a human point of view—involved
Jeannie's pastor, himself a convert from the Muslim religion. He had been
warned not to continue to share the message of Jesus Christ with the
Iranian soldiers in the hospital down at the local base in Tehran. But, in

spite of these threats, he felt compelled to preach the Good News to his Iranian brothers, just as Peter and John did in Jerusalem. And then it happened—just as it happened to John the Baptist, Stephen, James, and eventually to Peter and Paul. The pastor became a martyr for the cause of Christ. Khomeini's assassins entered his church office and took his life— literally severing his head from his body.

Jeannie recounts with deep emotion how she came on the horrible scene in the church office shortly after her pastor was killed—just like the apostle James (Acts 12:1–2). She also can recount how time and again God enabled her to trust Him in the midst of some very difficult and frightening experiences. In many respects, Jeannie and her Iranian brothers and sisters in Christ exemplify the kinds of faith that Paul talked about when he wrote to New Testament Christians and commended them for their faith in the midst of intense persecution.

Faith Is Foundational

In determining the degree to which a group of believers—in any culture— measure up to the stature of the fullness of Christ, faith stands out in Scripture as foundational.

First, faith is a part of that great trilogy—faith, hope, and love (1 Cor. 13:13).

Second, faith is always mentioned first when these three concepts appear together. Note Paul's introductions in his letters to the Thessalonians, the Colossians, and the Ephesians:

- "We give thanks to God always for you all . . . remembering without ceasing *your work of faith.*" (1 Thess. 1:3)

- "We are bound to thank God always for you . . . because *your faith grows exceedingly.*" (2 Thess. 1:3)

- "We give thanks to the God and Father of our Lord Jesus Christ . . . since we heard of *your faith* in Christ Jesus." (Col. 1:3–4)

- "Therefore I also, after I heard of *your faith* in the Lord Jesus Christ . . . do not cease to give thanks for you." (Eph. 1:15–16)

Third, faith is not just personal and individual. In fact, most references Paul made to faith in his letters to various churches as a means for measuring maturity is related to "corporate faith"—the way faith is expressed by a body or group of believers. This is why Paul used plural pronouns (you, your) in the introductions outlined above.

THREE DIMENSIONS OF FAITH

Before looking at "faith" as a means of measuring our maturity in Christ, it's important to understand the various ways this concept is used in the New Testament.

A MEANS OF SALVATION

Faith that brings salvation is a watershed issue in the history of Christianity. Martin Luther, of course, stands out as a symbol of man's struggle with this truth. Born and reared in a context that emphasized "salvation by works," he gradually and dramatically learned, from his own personal and direct study of the Scriptures, that all are saved by faith and faith alone. His discovery and his outspoken and bold propagation of this truth rocked the whole religious world, resulting in reverberations even to this very moment in history.

Paul's letter to the Romans was particularly instrumental in opening Luther's eyes to this great truth. In the first four chapters of this epistle, Paul developed a careful and logical argument—using both Old and New Testament examples—to demonstrate that righteousness come "by faith" (Rom. 1:17; 3:22,28–30; 4:5,9,11,13,22–23). Thus, Paul concluded in Romans 5:1 with these words:

"Therefore, since we have been justified through faith, we have peace with God through our Lord Jesus Christ."[1]

A BODY OF TRUTH

The word *faith* is also used by New Testament writers to refer to a system of beliefs. In these instances, what people believe is called "*the* faith." For example, on one occasion in Jerusalem, Luke recorded that "the number of the disciples multiplied greatly in Jerusalem, and a great many of the priests were *obedient to the faith*" (Acts 6:7). Heretofore, many of these priests zealously opposed and rejected the teachings of the apostles that Jesus Christ was the true messiah, the promised one who was crucified, buried, resurrected, and who ascended to the right hand of God the Father. However, when they were obedient to *the faith*," they embraced the doctrines of Christianity.[2]

Today, we still use the concept of "faith" in this way. For example, I've been asked—and I'm sure you have too— "What is your faith?" Or, "To what faith do you belong?" In these instances, people are referring to our "denominational" background or to our particular religious affiliation. In essence, however, they are referring to what we believe.

A GROWING CHRISTIAN EXPERIENCE

When New Testament writers used the word "faith" as a means of measuring maturity in Christ, they were referring to what happens in peoples' lives *after* they respond *"by* faith" to *"the* faith." This kind of "living" faith is a verification of true conversion to Jesus Christ. This is why James wrote that "faith by itself, if it does not have works, is dead" (James 2:17).

THE THESSALONIAN EXAMPLE

Faith that produces works among Christians is visible, and consequently, discernable and measurable. Thus Paul, in his letter to the Thessalonians, thanked God for their "work of faith" (1 Thess. 1:2–3), and later in his second letter wrote:"We are bound to thank God always for you, brethren, as is fitting, because *your faith grows exceedingly"* (2 Thess. 1:3).

When Paul secretly left the city of Thessalonica because of intense persecution (Acts 17:5–10), he was desperately concerned about the effect the persecution he left behind would have on these new believers. Would they continue to be strong in their faith? Would Satan sidetrack them and destroy the work he and his fellow missionaries had begun?

When Paul arrived at Athens, his anxiety level was so intense that he and Silas sent Timothy back to Thessalonica. Later—when Timothy had returned with a good report—he penned these words, reflecting on his own concerns and subsequent actions:

> But now that Timothy has come to us from you and brought us good news of *your faith* and love . . . therefore, brethren, in all our afflictions and distress we were comforted concerning you by *your faith.* (1 Thess. 3:6–7)

MEASURABLE ASPECTS OF FAITH

What were some of the visible and measurable aspects of their growing faith?

First, those who had been converted out of paganism and idolatry had not returned to their idolatrous and immoral lifestyles (1 Thess. 1:8–10). In fact, by the time Paul wrote his first letter, their faith had become known all over Macedonia, and was even being talked about in the neighboring country of Achaia (1 Thess. 1:5–7).

Second, these believers reflected their growing faith by continuing to serve Jesus Christ in spite of persecution. They had not turned their backs on God and denied that they knew and loved Him. This is certainly inherent in the encouraging report Timothy brought back to Corinth and shared with Paul and Silas. Thus, Paul responded with these glowing words: "For now we live, if you stand fast in the Lord" (1 Thess. 3:8).

Third, the Thessalonians also reflected their "growing faith" with their generous and unselfish attitudes toward their material possessions. No doubt these believers were among the "Macedonians" whom Paul commended for their generosity, even in the midst of poverty. They had given even "beyond their ability" (2 Cor. 8:1–4).[3]

One real mark of a true and growing faith is being willing to share material blessing with those who have physical needs—especially when we are giving that which we really need ourselves. Dr. Charles Ryrie underscores this point in his book *Balancing the Christian Life*. He states:

> How we use our money demonstrates the reality of our love for God. In some ways, it proves our love more conclusively than depth of knowledge, length of prayers or prominence of service. These things can be feigned, but the use of our possessions shows us up for what we really are.[4]

THE SOURCE OF FAITH

This kind of faith is not something we conjure up on our own. It is not rooted in some kind of "positive thinking" that is based on humanistic teaching—such as, "whatever the mind of man can conceive and believe it can achieve." Because we're made in the image of God, all of us are capable of developing a strong sense of self-confidence, enabling us to achieve great things. But the ultimate source of biblical faith is God, His glorious riches and His incomparable power. And the means for releasing this kind of faith is the supernatural presence of the person of the Holy Spirit in each of our lives as well as in the corporate lives of Christians who are bonded together in Jesus Christ.

Our source of faith is powerfully illustrated in Paul's prayer for the Christians in Ephesus:

For this reason I bow my knees to the Father of our Lord Jesus Christ, from whom the whole family in heaven and earth is named, that He would grant you, according to the riches of His glory, to be strengthened with might through His Spirit in the inner man, that Christ may dwell in your hearts *through faith.* (Eph. 3:14–17a)

LESSONS FOR US ALL

Paul's prayer for the Ephesians teaches us several things about "living faith." First, we should pray the same prayer for ourselves and for all of the people in our church. In short, we should pray that God's Holy Spirit will release God's power in our lives, resulting in more faith to do what God wants us to do. This is why Paul culminated his prayer with this grand doxology—"Now to him who is able to do exceedingly abundantly above all that we ask or think, according to the power that works in us" (Eph. 3:20).

When I asked my good friend, Dr. Bill Bright, founder and president of Campus Crusade International, to reflect on the subject of this chapter, he gave this encouraging testimony—

I have great hope for the church because I've sensed in an unprecedented way—certainly in this century—there is a mighty movement of God to pray. Many Christians are praying in ways they've never dreamed of until these last few years. . . I anticipate revival to come to America because of the incredible volume of prayer that is saturating the communities of our country.

Second, Paul's prayer teaches us not only that we are saved by grace through faith, but also that when Jesus Christ comes into our lives, He wants to reveal His presence moment by moment and day by day, living His life through us and accomplishing the very things He asks us to do. This, I believe, is what Paul meant when he prayed that "Christ may dwell in your hearts through faith" (Eph. 3:17).

A young woman in our church named Bunnie, was diagnosed with breast cancer. So certain that the visible lump in her breast was malignant, the doctors decided to operate as soon as possible.

Being Canadian, she returned home where most of her family were non-Christians. Having some time to think and pray and study the Word of God, she looked up every reference to faith in the New Testament. Though she observed that God never promised to always heal, nevertheless she noticed that faith was always present when God did choose to heal, either in the life of the person healed or in the lives of others who were concerned—or in the lives of both.

Consequently, Bunnie contacted a number of fellow Christians in several churches and asked them to pray—not for specific healing, but that she could simply live a life of faith, realizing and experiencing the presence of the indwelling Christ as she faced this traumatic experience. She did pray specifically that God might allow the doctors to be successful and that she might have a few more years to enjoy life on this earth. Most importantly, she prayed that her non-Christian family would observe her faith in Jesus Christ as she faced the reality that lay before her.

On the day the operation was scheduled, she awoke, prepared herself, and headed for the hospital. At this juncture, the lump was still visible and very apparent. When she arrived at the hospital, she entered the examining room and waited for her doctor who was scheduled to do the operation. When he arrived, he made final preparations, examining once again the lump in her breast. To his amazement—and Bunnie's too—the lump had totally disappeared—sometime between the time she had gotten up that morning and the time she arrived at the hospital. It was gone—with only one explanation. God chose to honor Bunnie's life of faith and the faith of her friends. In so doing, God chose to heal her completely.

Bunnie firmly believes that one of the primary reasons God chose to heal her was to demonstrate faith to her unsaved family, thus enabling these loved ones to "see Christ dwelling in her heart and in the hearts of her Christian friends by faith." All this happened because God's power was released through prayer and the presence of the Holy Spirit in Bunnie's life and in the lives of her friends. I will never forget my telephone conversation with Bunnie following this experience—she in Canada and I in Dallas. What an illustration of God's responding sovereignly to the power of living faith!

Third, this kind of faith defeats Satan. This is why Paul exhorted the Ephesian Christians—who had been heavily into the occult before their conversions to Jesus Christ—to take "the shield of faith" with which they would "be able to quench all the fiery darts of the wicked one" (Eph. 6:16; see also Acts 19:19).

Fourth, biblical faith is not blind faith. It is based on reality.

Let me try to illustrate this point. When my son, Kenton, was in college, he was a member of a Colorado downhill racing team. On one occasion he was competing in Northwest Montana. The top of the mountain was so foggy that the racers could not even see the first gate. And once they went through the first gate, they couldn't see the second gate.

It may appear that to leave the top of a mountain going through fog at speeds up to eighty miles an hour is not only "blind faith" but absurd. Actually, it was neither.

Before these racers began their downhill journey at breakneck speeds, they had carefully "scoped the slope." They knew the placement of every set of gates. They knew the texture of the snow. They also knew the contour of the slope and its many variations. In fact, Kenton always made it a habit to actually memorize the slope during trial runs so that he could ski the mountain in his mind before actually leaving the starting gate.

But another area of faith is involved in this kind of racing. These racers had faith in their ability to negotiate turns. They had faith in their overall skills to race at top speeds and yet not panic and lose control. They had faith in their equipment—particularly that their bindings would hold their weight and not release under stress. At the same time, they had faith that these bindings would release and set them free from their skis should they get into trouble.

In many respects, this illustration helps us to understand true biblical faith. When the apostle Paul prayed for the Ephesians that they might have a deep, abiding and on-going faith; he knew beyond a shadow of a doubt that Jesus Christ is who He said He is! Not only had Paul met Jesus Christ face to face on the road to Damascus, but he had joined hands with Peter and John and the other apostles who had witnessed Christ's life, death, resurrection, and ascension.

Today, our Christian faith is based on the testimony of numerous eye witnesses plus thousands of documents that were written by men who lived with Jesus Christ continually for three-and-a-half years. They saw Him work miracles and they heard Him teach. Later, they recorded their experiences in writing, which forms the bulk of the New Testament. This literature is composed of documents that can be verified as accurate and authentic more than any other historical records that exist. Christian faith is not blind faith! [5]

THAT KIND OF FAITH

I began this chapter by referring to my friend Jeannie and her family of Iranian believers who lived in the midst of Islamic persecution. Their faith enabled these Christians to stand firm, even when their pastor was killed because he continued to preach the Gospel after being warned to stop. And, of course, this pastor's faith enabled him to continue to preach the Good News and to later face his assassins without flinching or retreating.

This kind of faith also enabled Jeannie to secretly adopt two little Iranian twin boys who were born to an Iranian woman out of wedlock—in itself, an act punishable by death. And, of course, had Jeannie been found out, she too would have been guilty. Her faith enabled her to face the risk of being discovered. Her faith enabled her to feed them and care for them when, as newborns, they were ill and nearly died—and were destined for a garbage can. Her faith caused her to call out to God for help when, humanly speaking, there didn't seem to be any help. And her faith enabled her to experience miracle after miracle, culminating in one of the greatest miracles of all—to be able to escape from the country and return to the United States with her two little adopted baby boys who at this writing are teenagers and worship each Sunday in our church.

Jeannie is a constant reminder to me and to those who know her well that faith is a true mark of spiritual maturity. Many times she demonstrated that "we walk by faith, not by sight" (2 Cor. 5:7). Her demonstration of faith during these difficult days also reminds me of Dr. Schaeffer's penetrating question. If we removed every reference to faith in the Bible—particularly with respect to releasing God's power through supernatural means—would it really make any difference the way I live my life as a pastor? Would it really make any difference in the way the people I pastor live their lives? Would it make any difference in the way we manifest faith as a corporate body of believers? I would hope so—but sometimes I wonder.

Dr. Henrietta Mears, one of the greatest Christian women of our century, was used greatly by God. She had a profound impact on Bill Bright, for it was in her home that he came to Christ and launched the ministry of Campus Crusade. Billy Graham has testified that no woman outside of his mother has had a greater impact on his life. In addition, thousands of young people came to Christ and hundreds have gone into Christian service because of her ministry in their lives. Yet, when Dr. Mears came to the end of her life, someone asked her what she would do differently if she had life to live over again. Her response was quick and to the point— "I would simply believe God more!"

Many of us—Lord willing—have many years ahead of us. We have opportunities to measure our faith—right now—in the present. With the nobleman of old who approached Jesus one day, let us also cry out to God—"Lord, I believe! Help my unbelief!" (Mark 9:24).

MEASURING OUR WALK

1. What evidence of faith is in your life?

2. How would you describe your faith?

CHRIST'S LETTER TO THE
CHURCH IN PHILADELPHIA

A Contemporary Paraphrase of Rev. 3:7–13

Dear Brothers and Sisters:
What a joy all of you bring to my heart! You have served me faithfully. You have used every opportunity to share the story of my death and resurrection with those around you. Even when you have been weakened by the attacks of Satan and his evil forces, you've remained true to my Word and you've not denied my name.

Because of your faithfulness to me, I will bring judgment on those who claim to be religious but who are hypocrites and deceivers. They will eventually be humbled before you. They will even admit how much I have loved you!

Furthermore, because of your faithfulness, I will protect you in a special way during some rather intense and difficult days that are coming to your community. I will give you strength to endure.

As I close this epistle, I must remind you to keep looking for my coming. Be sure to keep your eyes fixed on me. Do not turn to the right or to the left. And when I come, I will reward you. You will be a pillar in my eternal kingdom. When you are discouraged, please reread this letter.

The One who is holy and true,

Jesus Christ

Mr. Josh McDowell

RECENTLY I INTERVIEWED A MAN who is very influential in youth culture. I asked him to describe young people today. He said, "We have a youth culture without hope." How ironic to describe American youth in this way—youth whose country was once built on the bedrock principles of Judaism and Christianity as reflected in the Old and New Testaments.

Consider Russia. For years the Russians lived under atheistic Communism. Now they have been freed from this bondage. But there is only one phrase to describe most of the people in Russia. They are without hope. When you introduce these people to the truth about Jesus Christ, those who accept this message discover hope.

We need to remind ourselves that empires come and go. Philosophies are believed and then denied. Societies develop and then they self-destruct. It seems to be happening in our own American culture. There is one thing that has been consistent , however, for two thousand years, and that is the hope we can have in Jesus Christ. This is why I am so thankful that Gene Getz included this chapter in his book. As you will see, hope defined biblically is the way to measure our maturity in Jesus Christ—not only as individual Christians but as local churches.

FOUR

MEASURING OUR HOPE

As you have therefore received Christ Jesus the Lord, so
walk in Him, rooted and built up in Him and established
in the faith.

— Colossians 2:6–7a

B
EGINNING WITH THE FIRST CENTURY—and periodically
throughout church history—Christians all over the world have
had to face intense persecution. And because of their hope in Jesus
Christ, by faith they have faced that persecution victoriously, even in the
face of death.

A DYNAMIC TWENTIETH-CENTURY ILLUSTRATION

I met Kefa Sempangi several years ago. He founded and pastored the 14,000
member Redeemed Church in Uganda when Idi Amin held control of this
country as a ruthless dictator. Kefa and his family escaped death by the
narrowest of margins and fled to America where I had the privilege of
meeting him—and then reading his book entitled *A Distant Grief.*

From the very beginning of Amin's reign of terror, his primary target
was the Christian church. Here's Kefa's graphic account:

All of his victims suffered unspeakably. They were tortured and humiliated
in front of families and friends. They were dismembered, decapitated, made
to eat their own flesh. Their bodies were fed to crocodiles or left unburied
in streets and forests. Perhaps worst of all, an entire generation of Uganda
children was growing up having nothing but suffering, horror, and terror.[1]

Easter Morning—1973

In telling his story, Kefa shares one remarkable and miraculous event regarding the way Christians in Uganda faced their persecutors with undying faith. One such amazing event took place Easter morning, 1973. By nine o'clock, over seven thousand people had gathered. They had come from miles around. When the compound was filled, people climbed trees and sat on roof tops. Hundreds simply stood in the streets.

That morning, Kefa preached on the "Suffering of Jesus Christ." He spoke of how Christ triumped over evil and how He experienced victory over death. He spoke on the power of Christ's resurrection.

At 12:30 p.m., Kefa tried to close the service, but the people refused to leave. They encouraged him to rest and then to come back and preach again—which he did. When he returned, he preached another three hours and closed the service as the sun was going down.

Face To Face With Amin's Assassins

After Kefa had pushed his way through the crowd and finally arrived at the place where he was staying, he noticed that several men had entered the room and closed the door behind them. They were Amin's assassins. At this juncture, a remarkable thing happened. The tallest of the men, pointing his rifle in Kefa's face, told him that they were going to kill him but that Kefa could say some final words. Kefa could only stare at him in utter shock and unbelief. Fear gripped his soul. He knew these men were on a serious mission from Amin himself.

And then suddenly, he regained his composure and uttered words that could only have come from God's supernatural guidance. He responded:

"I do not need to plead my own cause. I am a dead man already. My life is dead and hidden in Christ. It is your lives that are in danger, you are dead in your sins. I will pray to God that after you've killed me, He will spare you from eternal destruction."

Suddenly, the hatred visible in these men's faces changed to curiosity. Directed to drop their rifles by their leader, he asked if Kefa would indeed pray for them—right then. Amazed and as bewildered as his enemies, Kefa began to pray for their eternal salvation.

When Kefa completed what was a very simple and direct prayer, Amin's men turned to leave, assuring him of their protection. In fact, these men later became believers and eventually assisted Kefa and his family to escape from Uganda.

"By Life Or By Death"

That evening as Kefa drove home, he was deeply puzzled but had joy in his heart. He felt that he had passed from death to life and that he could now speak in one mind with the apostle Paul who wrote to the Galatians:

I have been crucified with Christ; it is no longer I who live, but Christ lives in me; and the life which I now live in the flesh I live by faith in the Son of God, who loved me and gave Himself for me. (Gal. 2:20)

What motivates followers of Jesus Christ to face this kind of oppression so triumphantly? The answer to this question focuses on a believer's eternal hope in Jesus Christ. They realize that this earth is not their real home. Rather, they view themselves as strangers and aliens passing through. Their real abode is in heaven.

This realization is what motivated Paul to write to the Philippians from a Roman prison and to say, "For to me, to live is Christ, and to die is gain" (Phil. 1:21). He knew that if his natural life was taken by a Roman soldier, he had eternal life—a supernatural life—in heaven. "For we know," he wrote to the Corinthians, "that if our earthly house, this tent, is destroyed, we have a building from God, a house not made with hands, eternal in the heavens" (2 Cor. 5:1).

Paul's First Letter To The Thessalonians

Again, the term hope appears in the three-word "trilogy" used by New Testament writers to measure the degree to which Christians measure up to the stature of the fullness of Christ.

Paul's Introduction

Once again, note how Paul opened his first letter to the Thessalonians:

We give thanks to God always for you all, making mention of you in our prayers, remembering without ceasing your work of faith, labor of love, and *patience of hope* in our Lord Jesus Christ in the sight of our God and Father. (1 Thess. 1:2–3)

Here Paul described the Thessalonian Christians' "hope" with the term "*patience* of hope." Other translations describe this concept as "*steadfastness* of hope" (NAS) or as "*endurance* inspired by hope" (NIV). All of these words help us to understand what Paul had in mind when he originally penned this letter. Our Christian "hope," of course, is closely aligned with our faith. Thus, Paul wrote to the Colossians—"As you therefore have received Christ Jesus the Lord, so walk in Him, rooted and built up in Him and *established in the faith*" (Col. 2:6–7a).

PERSECUTION IN THESSALONICA

As we've noted in the previous chapter on the subject of faith, the Thessalonian believers faced unusual persecution. Even while Paul and his fellow missionaries—Silas and Timothy— were in Thessalonica, the religious community that opposed the gospel staged a vicious riot, attacked the homes of believers, and dragged them before the city magistrates (Acts 17:5–9). The hatred became so intense and life-threatening that some of the leaders in the church helped Paul, Silas, and Timothy to escape from Thessalonica at night, where they went on to Berea (17:10).

TIMOTHY'S POSITIVE REPORT

Even after these New Testament missionaries left Thessalonica, the persecution continued. Consequently, when they eventually arrived in Athens, Paul sent Timothy back to check on these new believers. Timothy's subsequent report brought intense joy to Paul's heart when he discovered they were standing "fast in the Lord" (1 Thess. 3:8). In fact, everywhere Paul went throughout Macedonia—and even when he arrived in Corinth in Achaia—people everywhere were talking about the way these Thessalonian Christians were continuing in the faith and patiently waiting for the second coming of Jesus Christ (1 Thess. 1:9–10).

Here we see how "faith" and "hope" were closely linked in the lives of the Thessalonians.

- Their faith enabled them to believe and trust God in the midst of their trials and tribulations.

- Their hope of eternal life and the second coming of Jesus Christ provided a sense of security, steadfastness, endurance, and patience in the midst of their difficulties.

WHAT HAPPENS TO BELIEVERS WHO DIE BEFORE CHRIST RETURNS?

Though these believers were doing well—in spite of persecution—Timothy did report on one problem in conjunction with their hope. Even though Paul had spent considerable time teaching these believers those glorious truths regarding the second coming of Christ, some were still confused regarding what happens to believers who die before Jesus Christ comes again. Evidently, some of their Christian friends had already passed away since Paul's initial ministry in Thessalonica. They were very concerned about their loved ones' eternal destiny. What happened to them when they died?

This may seem like a very elementary question to most of us who have been taught the Bible, but we must remember that many of these people had been converted out of pagan religions. Even those Greeks who had become proselytes to Judaism before these missionaries arrived would have had a very limited understanding of these great eschatological truths.

PAUL'S ANSWER

As a result of Timothy's report, Paul wrote his first letter to the Thessalonians, and among other things, addressed the question raised by some of the Thessalonians regarding those who had already died. He did not want them to "sorrow as others who have *no hope*" (1 Thess. 4:13). Rather, he wanted them to know that if those who died believed in the death and resurrection of Jesus Christ, they would go to be with Jesus Christ immediately. Paul underscored this point when he wrote to the Corinthians and told them that his preference was that he might be away from his body and at home with the Lord (2 Cor. 5:8).

The point, however, that Paul was making to the Thessalonians was that when Christ returned, those who had died in Christ would return with Him be united to a new body and they would be taken up with all of those who are still alive in Christ (1 Thess. 4:14–18).

PERSONALIZING THIS TRUTH

I had the wonderful privilege of speaking at my dad's funeral. He died at age seventy-eight, doing what he loved most—driving the tractor on the family farm in Indiana. He suffered a heart attack, and the tractor swerved off into some pine trees. My mother found him still sitting on the tractor seat with his hands quietly resting on his lap. He was leaning back, simply looking toward heaven.

I vividly remember walking into the funeral home. When I first saw him, my heart was instantly filled with grief. Tears welled up in my eyes, and I found it difficult to accept the fact that he was no longer alive.

But as I passed through those initial hours of grief, I remembered what we had talked about so often when we were together—the hope we both had in Jesus Christ. My grief began to subside as I realized that my father was no longer residing in his body. He had gone to be with Christ, which Paul said, was "far better" than to remain on earth (Phil. 1:23).

As my hand touched his, I realized I was only touching a lifeless body—the "house" he had lived in for seventy-eight years. That very moment, my father was in heaven with Jesus. In the midst of my own tears, I was sure he was in that place where there were no tears—only eternal joy and happiness. Some day God would bring him "with Jesus" to take all those who are alive to be with the Lord forever. Together the "dead in Christ" and "those who are alive and remain" would be "caught up together with them in the clouds to meet the Lord in the air" (1 Thess. 4:14–17). My dad's soul and spirit would be reunited with his body—a new body. Once again we would be able to converse together, but this time in the presence of the Lord.

At that moment, this great truth made all the difference in the world for me and my whole family and for all of our loved ones who had gathered to honor my father's homegoing! That experiential knowledge and understanding also enabled me to calmly stand before all of them the next day and preach my father's funeral message. My text was from 1 Thessalonians, chapter 4:13–18. That day I announced with all certainty that my dad had gone home to be with the Lord Jesus Christ. We need not grieve like those who have *no hope!* These truths enabled me to sense personal comfort and encouragement—but also to comfort everyone who knew and loved my father (1 Thess. 4:18).

PAUL'S MESSAGE OF HOPE

Paul helped the Thessalonian Christians to understand these wonderful truths regarding our hope in Jesus Christ. We not only have hope if we're still alive when Christ returns, but we also have hope should we die before Christ comes again. Consequently, Paul ended his letter, in a sense, where he began the letter—by urging them to put "on the breastplate of faith and love, and as a helmet the *hope of salvation*" (1 Thess. 5:8).

PAUL'S SECOND LETTER TO THE THESSALONIANS

HAS THE "DAY OF CHRIST" ALREADY COME?

After the Thessalonians had received Paul's first letter, someone evidently claimed to have had a "prophecy" indicating that the "day of Christ had come." Someone else claimed to have heard a "reliable teacher" indicate the same thing. And it seems that someone else actually claimed to have seen a "letter" from Paul himself teaching the same doctrine.

When Paul received this report, he set the record straight in his second letter:

> Now, brethren, concerning the coming of our Lord Jesus Christ and our gathering together to Him, we ask you, not to be soon shaken in mind or troubled, either by spirit or by word or by letter, as if from us, as though the day of Christ had come. Let no one deceive you by any means. (2 Thess. 2:1–3a)

A Different Introduction

Paul's reference to their being "shaken" or "troubled" explains why he began his second letter with a different introduction. In his first letter, he thanked God for their "work of faith, labor of love and patience of hope" (1 Thess. 1:3). But, in this second letter, he thanked God that their faith was growing and that their love was increasing, but he did not mention their hope (2 Thess. 1:3).

In view of Paul's words in chapter 2, verses 1–3, we can now understand why he commended these believers in two areas—faith and love—and then proceeded to reestablish them in their hope. He reassured them that "the day of Christ"—that period of God's judgment on earth—had not come (2 Thess. 2:3–17). Therefore, they could, as Paul later wrote to the Christians in Crete, continue "looking for the blessed hope and glorious appearing of our great God and Savior Jesus Christ" (Titus 2:13).

Paul's Letter To The Ephesians

Paul's Introduction

When Paul wrote his letter to the Ephesians, he first of all described their "calling in Christ" (Eph. 1:1–14). He then thanked God for their "faith in the Lord Jesus" and also thanked God for their "love for all the saints" (Eph. 1:15–16). However, he did not thank God for their hope. Rather, he prayed that they might "know *what is the hope* of His calling" (Eph. 1:18).

Why this approach? The answer is similar as to why Paul varied his "introduction" in his second letter to the Thessalonians. However, rather than correlating their "lack of hope" with their faulty view regarding Christ's second coming—as he did in his second letter to the Thessalonians—he correlated "hope" with the Ephesians' "calling" and "heavenly position" in Jesus Christ—in essence, their eternal salvation.

THE HISTORICAL AND THEOLOGICAL CLIMATE

In order to understand why Paul shifted his approach, we need to understand the historical and theological climate that existed in Ephesus and in the surrounding regions. You will remember that Paul set up a beachhead in this great city where he spent time "reasoning daily in the school of Tyrannus" (Acts 19:9). He continued this ministry "for two years, so that all who dwelt in Asia heard the word of the Lord Jesus, both Jews and Greeks" (Acts 19:10).

Many who came to Ephesus to do business and to also worship in the great temple of Diana became Christians. Evidently, these new believers went back to their hometowns with the gospel message and started churches in their own communities. This is why it appears that Paul's letter to the Ephesians was a circular letter to the churches throughout Asia. Paul's frequent reference to the "universal church" rather than to a particular local church in this letter helps verify the broader purpose Paul had in mind when he penned this epistle.

A CULTURAL AND RELIGIOUS MIX

Note also that many of those who came from all over Asia and who responded to the Gospel were "both Jews and Greeks" (Acts 19:10). Consequently, those who heard the Ephesian letter read in their churches had come from both a "God-centered" religious background (Judiasm) as well as a "gods-centered" religious background (paganism).

This cultural and religious mix created some unusual problems in these local churches. Generally speaking, there are always difficulties when we attempt to mix people from different social and ethnic backgrounds. However, the problem is intensified when those mixed communities consist of individuals who represent strong religious cultures that vary greatly in terms of attitudes, values and doctrines.

This happened in the churches in Asia, but especially in the "mother church" in Ephesus. This helps explain why Paul, rather than beginning the letter by thanking God for their faith, hope and love, focused on the following great doctrinal truths:

- Election (Eph. 1:3-4)

- Sanctification(Eph. 1:4b)

- Predestination(Eph. 1:5)

- Redemption(Eph. 1:7)

- Security in Jesus Christ(Eph. 1:13–14)

This also explains why Paul then thanked God for their "faith in the Lord Jesus" and their "love for all the saints" (Eph. 1:15), but then proceeded to pray that they might "know what is the *hope of His calling*" (Eph. 1:18).

One of Paul's main concerns was that the Gentile believers in Ephesus and throughout Asia realize that even though they were "aliens from the commonwealth of Israel and strangers from the covenants of promise, having no hope and without God in the world," they were now one with all of those in Israel who had also put their faith in Jesus Christ (Eph. 2:12–16).

Being "one body in Christ" is also a theme that runs throughout the whole of the Ephesian letter (Eph. 1:10; 2:14,16,21–22; 3:6; 4:4-6,13,16). Paul taught that all believers who have this wonderful hope and eternal calling form "one body" in Jesus Christ, no matter what their cultural, ethnic, or religious background. Paul was adamant about this when he wrote to the Galatians:

> For there is neither Jew nor Greek, there is neither slave nor free, there is neither male nor female; for you are all one in Christ Jesus. (Gal. 3:28)

We all have the same hope—eternal life in Jesus Christ.

Measuring Our Hope

What does it really mean to have this kind of hope in Christ? How is it recognizable and measurable?

Steadfastness And Stability In Jesus Christ

We have already noted in Paul's letters to the Thessalonians that hope is related to our view of the second coming of Jesus Christ. We know that He is coming someday and we also know that if we are still alive when He comes, we will go to be with Him forever. We will be delivered from this present earth and we will receive glorified bodies. We will see Christ "face to face" (1 Cor. 13:12).

But we also know that if we die before Christ comes, we can also reflect the same sense of security as the apostle Paul when he wrote to the Corinthians—"We are confident, yes, well pleased rather to be absent from the body and to be present with the Lord" (2 Cor. 5:8).

I once had a conversation with several Christians who were really distressed over the direction of our society, so much so that they were frightened and scared. Somewhat naively and unintentionally, I accentuated their anxiety when I informed them that I believed that things were going to get much worse!

I will never forget one woman's response. "Oh!" she said. "You don't believe God would ever allow that to happen in America, do you?"

"Yes!" I responded, "I believe He might—and I believe He will if we don't repent and turn back to God. Why shouldn't He?" I questioned. In other words, why would God spare us when He has judged every nation on earth that has turned and departed from His eternal will?

I then attempted to turn the conversation toward a positive direction by informing this group of Christians that our *hope* must not be in what we have on this earth—our possessions, our freedoms, our economic opportunities. Rather, our hope must be in the One who is the "same yesterday, today, and forever"—Jesus Christ! (Heb. 13:8). This world is not our real home; we are just strangers passing through. And while we are here, we are to be light and salt (Matt. 5:13–16). As Paul wrote to the Philippians, we are to "shine as lights in the world, holding fast the word of life" (Phil 2:15–16).

How, then, should a Christian reflect this kind of hope? We must not allow the direction of our society to create a sense of insecurity in our lives. It is natural for us to become concerned, but to allow this concern to turn into fear and panic and even anger is to allow ourselves to fix our eyes on our changing environment rather than on the unchanging Christ. At this point Peter's words to Christians who were living in the midst of intense persecution should become real in our lives:

> Blessed be the God and Father of our Lord Jesus Christ, who according to His abundant mercy has begotten us again to a *living hope* through the resurrection of Jesus Christ from the dead, to an inheritance incorruptible and undefiled and that does not fade away, reserved in heaven for you, who are kept by the power of God through faith for salvation ready to be revealed in the last time. (1 Peter 1:3–5)

ASSURANCE AND SECURITY IN JESUS CHRIST

Peter's promises certainly lead to another way in which our hope can be measured—which relates directly to Paul's concern for the Ephesians and the other churches in Asia. It has to do with who we are in Christ because of His death, burial and resurrection. Paul wanted these believers to know that the same power that raised Jesus Christ from the dead and seated Him at God's "right hand in the heavenly places," is the very same power that has "raised us up together" with Christ and "made us sit together in the heavenly places in Christ Jesus" (Eph. 1:20; 2:6). This is why Paul began his letter to the Ephesians by saying—"Blessed be the God and Father of our Lord Jesus Christ, who has blessed us with every spiritual blessing in the heavenly places in Christ" (Eph. 1:3). And this is why he ended his opening remarks by reminding them that they "were sealed with the Holy Spirit of promise," which guarantees their inheritance (Eph. 1:13–14).

Paul wanted these Christians—and Christians of all time—to know that eternal life does not begin when Jesus Christ returns, or when we die prior to Christ's return. Eternal life begins for us the moment we believe and respond by faith to the message of the Gospel. At that point, God sees us as not only "called" and "justified," but also "glorified" (Rom. 8:30). That is why Paul culminated this great section in his letter to the Romans with this glorious personal testimony:

> For I am persuaded that neither death nor life, nor angels nor principalities nor powers, nor things present nor things to come, nor height nor depth, nor any other created thing, shall be able to separate us from the love of God which is in Christ Jesus our Lord. (Rom. 8:38–39)

All true believers—no matter what our ethnic or religious background, no matter what our language or our color, no matter where we live on the face of the earth or at what point we have lived in history—all of us become equal people at the foot of the cross. Equally we are sinners, but equally we are "heirs of God and joint heirs with Christ" (Rom. 8:17). Together, we can reflect that hope to the whole world.

I grew up in a religious community where I was taught that I could not know for sure that I had eternal life. It was only as I tried to live a good life that I believed that I might just make it to heaven. Needless to say, my Christian life was a "roller coaster" existence.

How I felt and lived was reflected in the whole church. Funerals were often sad occasions. People were not taught to share the good news of Jesus Christ with others. In reality, we didn't know what that good news really was—not in its fullness—and so we had little to share with others. Consequently, we were not prepared—as Peter said we should be—to "always be ready to give a defense to everyone" who asked us to explain the reason for *our hope* in Jesus Christ (1 Peter 3:15).

It took me several years, even as a Christian, to understand this kind of hope . . . and to be able to share it openly and freely with others. But thankfully, several men and women like Aquila and Priscilla with Apollos in Ephesus, took me "aside and explained . . . the way of God more accurately" (Acts 18:26). What a difference it has made in my life—and in the churches I have served.

Godly And Righteous Living

Paul, in his letter to Titus, emphasized that Christians who have hope in Christ are affected in the way they live their Christian lives. Thus he wrote:

> For the grace of God that brings salvation has appeared to all men, teaching us that, denying ungodliness and worldly lusts, we should live soberly, righteously and godly in the present age, *looking for the blessed hope* and glorious appearing of our great God and Savior Jesus Christ. (Titus 2:11–13)

The apostle John emphasized the same truth when he wrote:

> Beloved, now we are children of God; and it has not yet been revealed what we shall be, but we know that when He is revealed, we shall be like Him, for we shall see Him as He is. And everyone who has *this hope* in him purifies himself, just as He is pure. (1 John 3:2–3)

The Rest Of The Story

I began this chapter with a dynamic story of hope—the story of Kefa Sempangi. But as I close out this chapter, let me share the rest of the story.

Kefa and his family continued to experience one miracle after another and eventually they escaped from Uganda since Amin's assassins were committed to taking their lives. But again and again they escaped by a narrow margin.

They eventually arrived in Philadelphia where Kefa attended seminary. The warm reception they received from believers brought continual healing to their lives. However, as they settled into life here in the United States—with all of its comforts and blessings, Kefa openly shared that he noticed unique changes taking place in his life. He wrote:

"In Uganda, Penina and I read the Bible for hope and life. We read to hear God's promises, to hear His commands and obey them. There had been no time for argument and no time for religious discrepancies or doubts.

"Now, in the security of a new life and with the reality of death fading from mind, I found myself reading Scripture to analyze text and speculate about meaning. I came to enjoy abstract theological discussions with my fellow students and, while these discussions are intellectually refreshing, it wasn't long before our fellowship revolved around ideas rather than the work of God in our lives.

"The biggest change came to my prayer life. In Uganda I had prayed with a deep sense of urgency. I refused to leave my knees until I was certain I had been in the presence of the resurrected Christ. Now, after a year in Philadelphia, the urgency was gone. When I prayed publicly, I was more concerned to be theologically correct than to be in God's presence. Even in private, my prayers were no longer the helpless cries of a child. They were spiritual tranquilizers, thoughts that made no contact with anything outside themselves. More and more, I found myself coming to God with vague requests for gifts I did not expect.

"One night, I said my prayers in a routine fashion and was about to rise from my knees when I heard the convicting voice of the Holy Spirit.

"Kefa, who were you praying for? What is it you wanted? I used to hear the name of children in your prayers, the names of friends and relatives."

A Lesson For Us All

This penetrating question by the Holy Spirit to Kefa is particularly relevant to those of us who live in cultures where we have so many resources and opportunities to achieve remarkable and almost unbelievable goals. After all, we are taught by precept and example that we can achieve almost anything we set our minds to—particularly if we think positively. In this sense, our faith and hope are in ourselves.

This reality hit me in a new way one day when my wife, Elaine, and I had the oportunity to visit the Grand Hyatt Hotel in Maui, Hawaii. Located on fifteen hundred acres of beautifully landscaped property overlooking the Pacific, it stands as an incredible and almost unimaginable monument to man's ability to design and create something magnificent and beautiful. As one well-known man in the hotel industry said—"This is the ultimate creation as a resort hotel by mankind on earth during this century."

But in some respects, beautiful buildings are eclipsed by man's accomplishments when it comes to investigating and exploring space. Landing men on the moon—and everything thereafter—has dazzled our minds in terms of scientific achievements.

All of these great accomplishments, however, pale in terms of what God has created—and can do. As Paul wrote, God is "able to do exceedingly abundantly above all that we ask or think, according to the power that works in us" (Eph. 3:20). Unfortunately, men and women today seldom consult God for wisdom and assistance when it comes to goal achievements. We put our hope in our human resources. Sadly, this mentality has also spilled over into the church and has dulled our spiritual sensitivities. We often lose sight of our heavenly destination.

Do not misunderstand! God wants us to be responsible human beings. We must not be presumptuous or selfish. We must not be guilty of having "faith in faith" or "hope in hope." But, as George Barna states, God does want us "to dream the most possible dreams." And those possibilities are enormous—even in this life—when they grow out of sound scriptural guidelines, promises and principles.

MEASURING OUR WALK

1. How does your hope measure up to the standard described in this chapter?

2. What steps can you take to strengthen your hope?

CHRIST'S LETTER TO THE CHURCH IN SMYRNA

A Contemporary Paraphrase of Rev. 2:8–11

Dear Brothers and Sisters:

I know that you are facing serious difficulties because of those who hate me. I also know that you are suffering physically because of those in your city who won't offer you jobs because you're Christians. But may I remind you that you are rich in faith and love—and beyond that, you have a glorious inheritance in heaven that will never fade away. You have eternal hope! And, you will stand out as bright and shining stars when I reward you at my judgment seat. In the meantime, don't allow Satan to defeat you. Resist him and he will flee from you. The persecution you are facing will not last long. And remember, I will never leave you nor forsake you. Please believe and rest in what I'm saying.

The One who died and rose again,

Jesus Christ

A PERSONAL WORD FROM

Mr. Max Lucado

I WOULD LIKE TO ASK YOU A REALLY important question. What is the greatest treasure in life? What is the one thing that matters more than anything else? You look around the world and you see people answering that question by the way they live their lives. Some people think the greatest treasure is power—they want to be in control, they want to be at the top, they want to be seen. Others think the greatest treasure is prestige—they want to have their names in lights: they want everybody to recognize them when they walk past. Many think the greatest treasure in life is possessions, something they can drive, something they can put in the bank, something they can live in or wear.

Well, folks, all of these answers are wrong—dead wrong! The Bible tells us that the greatest treasure in life is not prestige, it's not power, it's not a possession. The greatest treasure is love. Dr. Gene Getz, my friend and fellow Bible teacher, addresses this topic in this chapter entitled "Measuring Our Love." As only he can do, he's going to take us right into the Scriptures and remind us that faith, hope, and love abide, but the greatest of these is love (1 Cor. 13:13).

FIVE

MEASURING OUR LOVE

Therefore be followers of God as dear children. And *walk in love*, as Christ also has loved us and given Himself for us, an offering and a sacrifice to God for a sweet-smelling aroma.

— Ephesians 5:1–2

O NE DAY I PICKED UP A COPY OF A book written by Dr. Francis Schaeffer entitled *The Mark of a Christian*. Few books have touched my life like this one. Once I began reading, I could not put it down.

The book contained a very simple exposition of Christ's words to His disciples, as recorded by John: "A new commandment I give to you, that you love one another; as I have loved you, that you also love one another" (John 13:34).

The apostles—being Jewish—all knew about "the old commandment:" It was the law of Moses—the Ten Commandments which represent the essence of the Old Testament law given at Mt. Sinai. However, Jesus wanted His disciples to know that He had come to fulfill the law by giving His life to redeem sinful humanity (John 3:16).

When Paul penned his letter to the Romans, he underscored and reinforced what Jesus taught His men that day in the Upper Room. He wrote:

For the commandments, "You shall not commit adultery," "You shall not murder," "You shall not steal," "You shall not bear false witness," "You shall not covet," and if there is any other commandment, are all summed up in this saying, namely, "You shall love your neighbor as yourself." Love does no harm to a neighbor; therefore love is the fulfillment of the law." (Romans 13:9–10)

When I asked Max Lucado to illustrate this kind of love taught by Jesus, he responded with this experience: "The best example of love that I can think of occurred at the death of my own father. I remember a lady who was a distant relative of our family. She drove six hours to get to the funeral. She walked in the house and went immediately into the kitchen and began washing the dishes. I didn't even know she was there. She straightened up everything and helped prepare for the meal. She came to the funeral. After the funeral, she came back and did the dishes again, got in her car and went home. As far as I know, she never said a word. She never introduced herself. But when I looked around, I realized that love had been in our house."

THE GREATEST OF THESE IS LOVE

When Paul wrote to the Corinthians and said, "And now abide faith, hope, and love, these three" he also made it very clear that "the greatest of these is love" (1 Cor. 13:13). As Henry Drummond once wrote—keying off this Pauline statement—love is the "greatest thing in the world."

Without question, love is the greatest mark of maturity when it comes to measuring the spiritual vitality of a church. The facts are that there is so much said in the New Testament about this quality of maturity that it's virtually impossible to include all that could be said in a single chapter of a book. The sheer volume of references to "biblical love" in itself demonstrates why "the greatest of these is love" (1 Cor. 13:13).

We have already noted that when Paul wrote to the Thessalonians, the Colossians and the Ephesians, he introduced these letters by thanking God for this quality (1 Thess. 1:3; 2 Thess. 1:3; Col. 1:4; Eph. 1:15). Other letters focused the same concern. Writing to the Philippians, Paul said, "And this I pray, that your *love* may abound still more and more" (Phil. 1:9). And when he wrote to Timothy in Ephesus, he reminded him that his instructions and commandments were for one major purpose—to produce "*love* from a pure heart" (1 Tim. 1:5). And returning, once again, to our "anchor" passage in Ephesians chapter 4, we need to remind ourselves that the process of measuring up to the stature of the fullness of Christ involves "speaking the truth in *love*" to one another—which Paul says—"causes growth of the body for the edifying of itself in *love*" (Eph. 4:15–16). Thus, love should be the ultimate goal for every church! We are to walk in love, just as Christ loved us!

God Is Love

There is a unique and divine reason why Paul—when comparing love with faith and hope—wrote that "the greatest of these is love." This mark of maturity is related to the very essence of who God is. As John states—"God is love" (1 John 4:8,16).

This certainly does not mean that our Creator is some immaterial force called "love"—some eternal principle that is operating in our universe. Though a common idea in various religions, this is not a biblical concept. Rather, to state that "God is love" means that the very essential nature of God—the living, personal God—is love. As He is "light" (1 John 1:5) and "Spirit" (John 4:24), He is also "love." And New Testament writers teach that Jesus Christ is a personification of that love (1 John 4:9).

The concept of love is also deeply rooted in the Old Testament. On one occasion, an expert in the Law of Moses tried to trap Jesus with a question, "Teacher, which is the great commandment in the law?" Jesus' reply jolted him. He said, "You shall love the Lord your God with all your heart, with all your soul, with all your mind."

As Jesus continued to answer this man's question, He added a second commandment, "You shall love your neighbor as yourself." And then the Lord astounded these men by saying: "On these two commandments hang all the law and the prophets" (Matt. 22:34–40).

With this answer, Jesus zeroed in on these religious leaders' weakness. They could not be good Jews unless they loved both God and their fellow men. To top it off, Jesus emphasized that burnt offerings and sacrifices were meaningless to God without love (Mark 12:33).

The directive to "love your neighbor as yourself" appears at least eight times in the New Testament, approximately half in the Gospels, and half in the Epistles. Our neighbors, of course, include not only our fellow Christians, but our unsaved friends and associates as well.

Directives "To Love"

To love others is one of the most repeated exhortations in the whole New Testament. This should not surprise us since "love is the fulfillment of th law." It appears no less than fifty-five times—*as a direct command.* Not some of the following, which are representative of the total picture:

- But I say to you, love your enemies, bless those who curse you, (good to those who hate you, and pray for those who spitefully u you and persecute you" (Matt. 5:44).

As Christians, we are not only to love those who love us, but we are also to love those who hate us. Jesus Christ, of course, set the great example when, from the cross, He prayed for those who were taking His very life (Luke 23:34).

This is a convicting exhortation and example from Jesus Christ. In chapter 1, I shared a true story about a young man who became my associate pastor. After launching a new church, I eventually turned this growing and dynamic work over to him to be the senior pastor as my wife and I began a new church in another part of Dallas. Unknown to me, this young man allowed serious sin to take root in his life. To cover up his own wrongdoing and failures, he began to make false accusations about me and influenced a number of other people to do the same. My entire family was desperately hurt by what happened.

Eventually, this man's wrongdoing led him into a desperate situation, resulting in a serious crime. At this writing, he is completing his ninth year in a state prison. His wife divorced him and his children have also forsaken him—and the Lord. He is a brokenhearted man.

While this was happening, I was faced with one of the greatest challenges I have ever faced in life. Could I love this man who had turned against me and had become my enemy, even after I had entrusted him with a great responsibility and opportunity? Though I experienced a great deal of hurt and anger, God enabled me to forgive him and to love him. Though my feelings fluctuated, particularly during and after the time I was being falsely accused, I chose to do all I could to love him as Christ loved me.

Though I was the primary target of his false accusations, I began to correspond with this man on a regular basis. When I had opportunity to visit him in prison, I did so. And another pastor, who was also desperately hurt by this man, has made more visits to the state prison than any other person I know.

Today, because of God's supernatural grace in my life, my feelings are filled with compassion for this man, so much so that I pray that somehow, someday, God might once again use this very talented individual to carry out His purposes in this world.

Has this been easy? No. But can we do less when Jesus loved us even when we were walking out of His will? Furthermore, His will is that we love even those who despise us, and if we are willing and if we seek His help, He will give us His divine and supernatural strength to carry out this directive.

- "A new commandment I give to you, that you love one another; as I have loved you, that you also love one another" (John 13:34).

This specific directive to "love one another," which we looked at earlier, appears at least fifteen times in the New Testament—approximately five times in the Gospels and ten times in the Epistles. It refers specifically to loving relationships within the body of Christ.

This is a much easier commandment to obey, especially if love is mutual and reciprocal. However, not all people that say they are Christian believers are loving Christians.

When I was in college, my roommate and I were in ministry together. Sadly, this young man developed a reputation among his fellow Christians as being "unlovely"—though no one seemed willing to confront him with his inappropriate attitudes and actions. Unfortunately, everyone was talking among themselves—but not to him.

For me, it was doubly difficult because we occupied the same living quarters. Furthermore, the more I tried to act lovingly toward him, the more he seemed to do things to provoke me.

Eventually, I confronted this young man with his behavior. Though an intensely emotional experience, I did so literally with tears and sadness, hurt and frustration. Though I was angry, God seemingly enabled me to communicate that anger in the context of compassion and concern.

Following this confrontation, it seemed this man actually enjoyed seeing me in this state of mind. However, the real changes came in his life several years later when he wrote me a letter thanking me for that day. He admitted he knew then that I was right in what I had communicated, but he said, "I could not admit it at that time." He then asked for forgiveness.

- "And now abide faith, hope, love, these three; but the greatest of these is love. Pursue love" (1 Cor. 13:13–14:1a).

The way of love is a philosophy of life—a Christian philosophy of life. It gives a central focus to all that we do. It is living as Christ lived. The Corinthian Christians were following the way of selfishness and carnality. Some were competing with each other in using their God-given abilities and gifts to humiliate each other and elevate themselves. Paul exhorted them to make their prime objective the "way of love"—not the "way of competition and selfish behavior." They were to actively *pursue* this quality of life.

In the two previous illustrations, I had to make a choice. In both situations, my fleshly nature cried out to retaliate, to get even, to return hurt for hurt. However, as I repeatedly began to move in that direction, I could not get away from my responsibility as a Christian. I was to "pursue love"—even though it was difficult. Ultimately, God enabled me to be victorious, just as He has promised.

- "Let all that you do be done with love" (1 Cor. 16:14).

Everything a Christian does is to be done from a love motive. "All that you do" is a very inclusive concept, but it is the Christian way of life. There are no exceptions. Anything that is *not* done in love is out of the will of God. Paul admonished the Corinthians that even when they were taking a stand against false doctrine, they were to do it with an attitude of love.

- "For you, brethren, have been called to liberty; only do not use liberty as an opportunity for the flesh, but through love serve one another" (Gal. 5:13).

A life of service is another hallmark of the Christian way of life. Again, Jesus set the supreme example when He said: "For even the Son of Man did not come to be served, but to serve, and to give His life a ransom for many" (Mark 10:45).

Saint Francis of Assisi captured this thought beautifully in his simple prayer: "O divine master, grant that I may not so much seek to be consoled as to console, to be understood as to understand, to be loved as to love; for it is in giving that we receive, it is in pardoning that we are pardoned, and it is in dying that we are born to eternal life."

While putting this material together in this book, I asked Dr. Bill Bright to share a personal experience about his own life. He responded with this testimony: "I'm a businessman by training and profession. Before I became a Christian, I signed thousands of contracts in my secular vocation. One day my wife and I signed the greatest contract that anyone could ever sign. In Romans chapter 1, Paul said: 'This letter is from Paul, Jesus Christ's slave, chosen to be a missionary sent out to preach God's good news.' My wife, Vonette, and I chose in 1951 to sign a contract relinquishing all of our claims to Jesus Christ and we became His slaves. And I want to tell you the greatest thing that ever happened to me was that day of total, absolute, irrevocable commitment to the Lordship of Christ. And all these years, as Vonette and I have walked with Him—almost fifty years—it has been one joyful, exciting adventure being a slave and a servant of Jesus Christ. Our desire has been to be conformed to His image, seeking to do His will in everything we think and say."

I am thankful for Bill and Vonette's example. It fleshes out in such a beautiful way what Paul wrote in Galatians: "Through love, serve one another." Furthermore, no one will question how God has used this couple to impact the world for Jesus Christ.

- "I, therefore, the prisoner of the Lord, beseech you to have a walk worthy of the calling with which you were called, with all lowliness and gentleness, with longsuffering, bearing with one another in love" (Eph. 4:1–2).

As stated earlier, not all Christians are easy to love. But Paul made it clear that we are to love all believers nevertheless. And this calls for humility, gentleness, and above all patience and forbearance.

Bill Bright shared another experience with me. He stated that the greatest lesson he had ever learned was the importance of love. During a time of great crisis in his personal life and ministry a number of individuals in whom he entrusted major responsibilities betrayed those trusts. In this time of crisis God showed him how to love these men. He did so by faith. In conjunction with that experience, Bill stated, "The command to love God with all our hearts, souls, mind and strength, our neighbors as ourselves, our enemies which our Lord has truly commanded us to do is impossible. But the command to love associated with the promise to love and the promise in God's Word that if we ask anything according to His will, He hears and answers."

- "But, speaking the truth in love, we may grow up in all things into Him who is the head—Christ—from whom the whole body, joined and knit together by what every joint supplies, according to the effective working by which every part does its share, causes growth of the body for the edifying of itself in love" (Eph. 4:15–16).

Even when Christians speak the truth, calling for correction in the lives of others, it is to be done in love. Paul made this very clear to Timothy in his instructions regarding how to communicate to the people who were opposed to the truth: "And a servant of the Lord must not quarrel but be gentle to all, able to teach, patient, in humility correcting those who are in opposition" (2 Tim. 2:24–25).

- "My little children, let us not love in word or in tongue, but in deed and in truth" (1 John 3:18).

Deep and fervent love involves actions. It is one thing to say, "I love you;" it is another to actually love in a biblical sense. Love that includes action is true Christian love. Again, this is why Paul commended the Thessalonians when he thanked God for their "labor of love" (1 Thess. 1:3).

THREE DIMENSIONS OF LOVE

The Scriptures present the concept of love as three dimensional. In its broadest meaning, it involves attitudes and actions that are right and proper, no matter how we feel. Generally speaking, the Greek word *agape* is used to describe this kind of love.

AGAPAO LOVE

Though *agape* love is a very comprehensive concept in the New Testament, it is frequently used to describe loving acts—that is, behaving in certain ways because it is the right thing to do. This kind of love is most profoundly illustrated by Jesus Christ when He loved us so much that He went to the cross, bearing the pain of that horrendous experience in order to bring us eternal life. This was and is the ultimate demonstration of *agape* love. And it is God's will that all Christians have as their goal in all relationships to "walk in love, as Christ also has loved us and given Himself for us, an offering and a sacrifice to God for a sweet-smelling aroma" (Eph. 5:2).

PHILEO LOVE

The Greek word *phileo* is often used interchangeably in the New Testament with *agapao*, but *phileo* is also used distinctively to refer to love that is emotionally positive in nature. Associated with true friendship, it involves delight and pleasure in doing something. Perhaps one of the best definitions of this kind of love is "a deep emotional feeling of trust generated from one person to another person."

This is the kind of love Paul was referring to in Romans 12:10 when he wrote: "Be kindly affectionate to one another with brotherly love, in honor giving preference to one another" (Rom. 12:10).

The Greek word translated "brotherly love" is *philadelphia*. It involves the idea of *phileo* love toward family members. In this context, Paul used loving relationships among parents and childrens and brothers and sisters to illustrate the kind of relationships that should also exist among members of God's family—the church. We are indeed brothers and sisters in Jesus Christ.

ERAO LOVE

The Greek word *erao* was another word that was used for love in the Greek speaking world. Normally, it referred to sexual love. Interestingly, this word is never used by New Testament authors. This does not mean that sexual love is wrong or improper or is never referred to in the New Testament. However, biblical writers seemed to avoid this word because it was so frequently used in their culture to describe illicit sexual activity. In God's scheme of things, erotic love is to be restricted to marital love and manifested in the context of Christlike behavior.

These three dimensions of love can best be illustrated with the circle of biblical love (see figure 5.1). *Agape* love—which involves proper actions— is doing what is right and best for someone, even if it involves negative

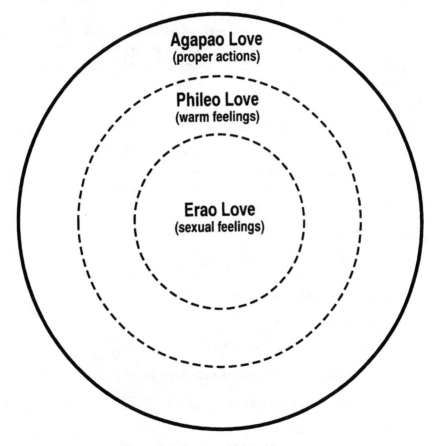

Agapao Love
(proper actions)

Phileo Love
(warm feelings)

Erao Love
(sexual feelings)

Figure 5.1: Circles of Biblical Love

feelings. What is "right and best" must be determined by the direct teachings of the Word of God (see figure 5.1).

Phileo love—which often includes warm feelings—is responding to someone's needs affectionately and with positive emotions, but always within the guidelines of *agape* love. It is *agape* love that keeps feelings of affections from becoming selfish and demanding. Many friendships have been destroyed by people who try to keep a relationship entirely to themselves. Again, the guidelines for *phileo* love are spelled out clearly in Scripture. In other words, *phileo* love must always operate within the context of *agapao* love (see figure 5.1).

Erao love—sexual feelings—is becoming both emotionally and physically involved with another person sexually. Again, this kind of love must always operate within the guidelines of *agapao* and *phileo* love.

Agapao love in Scripture dictates that *erao* love is to be a loving act between a man and a woman who are committed to each other in marriage. Furthermore, *erao* love should always reflect the qualities of *agapao* love—patience, unselfishness, sensitivity—that is, doing what is right and best for the other person. And when this happens, sexual love will also be warm, rewarding and a *phileo* experience (see figure 5.1) [1]

A DEFINITION OF *AGAPE* LOVE

As we have already seen in a previous chapter, love is best defined by Paul in 1 Corinthians 13. Henry Drummond in his classic little book, The Greatest Thing in the World, identifies the qualities Paul outlined in this chapter as the "spectrum of love."

He breaks this "spectrum" into nine qualities:

1 CORINTHIANS 13:4–6

1. Patience ("love suffers long")

2. Kindness ("and is kind")

3. Generosity ("love does not envy")

4. Humility ("love does not parade itself, is not puffed up")

5. Courtesy ("does not behave rudely")

6. Unselfishness ("does not seek its own")

7. Good Temper ("is not provoked")

8. Guilelessness ("thinks no evil")

9. Sincerity ("does not rejoice in iniquity, but rejoices in the truth") [2]

Note that these qualities are actions and attitudes, not feelings per se.

- We have opportunity to demonstrate patience usually when we are frustrated and even angry.

- Kindness is an act of the will that may or may not be generated by positive feelings.

- Generosity may involve actions that make us uncomfortable, especially if it means responding to others needs in a sacrificial manner.

- Humility involves considering others better than ourselves, not just looking to our own interests (Phil. 2:3–4). Here Paul reminds us that this was the attitude that Jesus Christ demonstrated toward us and we are to have that same attitude.

- Being courteous may involve "turning the other cheek" when someone irritates us or even hurts us.

- Unselfishness may not come easy, especially when we feel someone else is actually responding selfishly to us—or to someone else.

- Facing "bad tempers" in others usually doesn't make it easy to maintain a good temper ourselves. Maintaining our emotional equilibrium and staying calm and cool when we're frustrated and irritated by insensitive people may call for intense prayers and self-discipline.

- To keep our motives pure and to be guileless is always difficult when we are forced into a situation where everyone resorts to "dirty tricks" in order to come out on top.

- The true test of love is to sincerely rejoice when good things happen to others when those same good things do not happen to us!

As we have seen in chapter 2, the Corinthians violated most of these qualities. Though they had received more spiritual gifts than any other church, they were impatient with one another. Divisions permeated the church. Furthermore, their impatience reflected itself in unkind acts. They violated the quality of generosity because of their envy. They certainly were not humble in that they were prideful and puffed up. Courtesy was a lost art. Even in their communion meals, they demonstrated selfishness, gluttony, and drunkenness.

Unselfishness and guile permeated their business life because they were actually going to law against each other before pagan courts. And, of course, lingering anger was a part of that process. They were deceptive and deceitful, attempting to take advantage of each other. And how could they be sincere when they were actually rejoicing in the immorality that existed in the church?

If Paul were trying to make himself look good as the founder and initial pastor of this church, he certainly would not have laid out in front of us the willful, spiritual immaturity of this group of Christians. Though definitely believers (Paul addressed them as "saints"—1 Cor. 1:2), they were infants in Christ. Paul identified them as carnal—in fact, so fleshly, that if it were not for God's obvious grace in their lives in giving them the gifts of the Spirit, he would not have been able to discern that they were believers. They were "behaving like mere men" (1 Cor. 3:3).

The Corinthians' imperfections stated positively become goals for every local church. Paul identified this "spectrum of love" as "the greatest of these." Though faith and hope are essential qualities in measuring up to the stature of the fullness of Christ, the ultimate quality is love. It is indeed—as Dr. Francis Schaeffer has stated—"the mark of a Christian!"

THE BRIDGE TO THE WORLD

When Paul exclaimed that "the greatest of these is love!" he was not only referring to a dynamic that helps build up the body of Jesus Christ. He was also describing what we might call "the bridge to the world." When Jesus charged His disciples to love one another (John 13:34), He had in mind the very purpose for which He came to earth. He followed His command to love each other as He had loved them with a dynamic expectation:

> By this all will know that you are My disciples, if you have love for one another. (John 13:35)

As we have seen from Scripture, love produces unity. And significantly, after charging His disciples to love one another, Jesus prayed the following prayer:

> I do not pray for these alone, but also for those who will believe in Me through their word; that they all may be one, as You, Father, are in Me, and I in You; that they also may be one in Us, that the world may believe that You sent Me. (John 17:20–21)

Dr. Francis Schaeffer has called this truth the "final apologetic." Love and unity is the ultimate and most significant defense for the Christian faith. It is a means God designed to prove to the non- Christian world that Jesus Christ is who He claimed to be! And God's will is that every local, loving, functioning, and unified body of believers become a powerful witness, demonstrating this kind of love and unity.

While interviewing Max Lucado about this concept, he shared this penetrating illustration: "Every week I visit with a young couple. They are thinking about becoming Christians. I asked them the other day: 'What is it that's making you think about giving your life to Christ?' I guess I hoped they would say 'my messages' but they didn't say that. I hoped they might say the music at the church, but they didn't say that either. They said there's something in this church about the way people love one another that we don't find anywhere else, and it's very hard for us to leave."

The incarnation surrounds, undergirds, and impregnates the Christian Gospel! If Christ were not God, the Christian religion would be no different from any other major world religion. All have their leaders, but none have the credentials of Jesus Christ! Because He was one with God, He could become the God-man! He was truly "the Lamb of God who takes away the sin of the world" (John 1:29).

In chapter 6, we will see how the concept of love demonstrated Christ's deity by being "fleshed out," particularly in the Jerusalem church. And we will look carefully at the way every local body of believers can reach people for Christ by becoming a loving, dynamic community.

MEASURING YOUR WALK

1. Reread the directive to love given in this chapter. Which one is most difficult for you and why? How might you put this directive into action in your life?

2. How does your church measure regarding love? What characteristic about love stands out?

A LETTER TO THE CHURCH IN EPHESUS

A Contemporary Paraphrase of Rev. 2:1–7

Dear Brothers and Sisters:

I'm aware of the way all of you have helped others in need and the way you've stood firm in the face of persecution. I'm also aware that you have been on guard against false teachers, as Paul warned so many years ago when he met with your elders at Miletus.

However, I have a major concern. You have left your first love. In all of your effort to serve others and to maintain doctrinal purity, you have stopped focusing your hearts on Me. I have loved you with an everlasting love and I desire your love in return. I remember how much you worshipped and praised Me when you first became Christians. It's not too late to reverse your actions. If you draw near to Me, I'll draw near to you. Please open your hearts to what I'm saying.

The One who gave His life for you,

Jesus Christ

Dr. Bruce Wilkinson

I FIRST MET DR. GENE GETZ WHEN I WAS a student at Dallas Theological Seminary. I was fresh out of Bible college, and before long, Gene became one of my favorite professors. And as the years went by, he became a friend, then a mentor, and also my thesis advisor. My topic was "Walk Thru the Bible." You see, God used Gene to help shape my life and future ministry.

Gene also encouraged me to think differently. In fact, I experienced some paradigm shifts in my thinking—particularly about God's design for the church. I came into seminary thinking that the Bible taught certain things and then, as the weeks went by in Gene's classes, he opened the Scriptures in a new and fresh way. Before long, I said to myself, "This is hard to believe. All these years I've misunderstood what the Bible really says about the local church." What you're going to read in this chapter is dynamic and life-changing. Like me, you may discover yourself saying, "My glasses were fogged up until this point. But now as I begin to see the Scriptures clearly, I can finally see what God really had in mind for the church." So read carefully as my good friend, Dr. Gene Getz, takes you to the Jerusalem model.

MEASURING OUR CHURCH BY GOD'S STANDARD

> For this reason we also, since the day we heard it, do not
> cease to pray for you, and to ask that you may be filled
> with the knowledge of His will in all wisdom and spiritual
> understanding; that you may *walk worthy* of the Lord,
> fully pleasing Him, being fruitful in every good work and
> increasing in the knowledge of God.
>
> — Colossians 1:9–10

O NE OF THE GREATEST CHALLENGES all of us face as spiritual leaders is how to move our churches from where they are in their spiritual journey to what God wants them to be. It is one thing to know how God measures our maturity—the degree of faith, hope and love that exists in our churches—but quite another to know how to produce this kind of maturity in order to measure up to "the stature of the fullness of Christ."

CHURCH PLANTING EXPERIENCE

As I stated in the preface to this book, I had the privilege of launching a number of churches over the last twenty years. This experience began in the late seventies when a small group of people had heard about the "New Testament church" studies I had been doing with my students at Dallas Theological Seminary. Consequently, they invited me to share the results of these studies one evening in one of their homes.

That night all of us—about twenty people in all—developed a keen sense of excitement about launching a new church. Though these people did not ask me to change vocations from professor to pastor, they made it very clear that they desired to launch a new church and they wanted my wife and me to take primary leadership.

Frankly, I was also excited about this opportunity. In subsequent meetings, we all asked ourselves some very penetrating and basic questions.

First, what kind of experiences do believers need to become a dynamic church? In discovering answers to this question, all of us were deeply committed to the fact that these experiences must grow out of the activities and functions outlined and described in the New Testament. Furthermore, these experiences must be normative and supracultural. In other words, these kinds of experiences are needed by believers everywhere, no matter what their basic environment, economic status, cultural background, and educational experiences.

Second, we asked ourselves what kind of forms and structures we should develop to provide our new body of believers with these experiences. Since we were launching a new church, we decided early on we would not do things the same way just because they had been done that way before. However, we also decided we would not be different just to be different. Rather, we wanted to develop patterns and use methods in our own "cultural moment" that would help us do the very best possible job we could in applying New Testment principles of church life. If we needed to develop "new wine skins," we would do it. If "old wine skins" would do the job, we were open to that approach as well. In other words, what we all wanted were the best forms and structures to help us to apply to our lives and the lives of others the absolute and never changing principles of the Word of God. We wanted to be thoroughly biblical and yet culturally relevant. Like Paul, we wanted to be "all things to all men, that I[we] might by all means save some" (1 Cor. 9:22).

Third, we wanted to be totally open to the divine leading of the Holy Spirit. After all, Jesus said that He would build His church (Matt. 16:18). Furthermore, Jesus said that He would answer if we would ask for His help (Luke 11:9). Consequently, prayer—both personal and corporate—became a very vital part of our planning.

At this point Luke's description of the activities and functions of the church in Jerusalem became for all of us a very basic and foundational passage of Scripture. In this dynamic account, Luke recorded that these new believers in Jerusalem engaged in at least three vital functions. In turn, we noted that these three experiences were repeated elsewhere in other New Testament letters.

These three New Testament functions became three powerful pillars in our thinking as we launched this new church. In fact, we became convinced that the degree to which any group of believers has these three experiences will determine the degree to which that group will grow in faith, hope, and love.

THREE VITAL EXPERIENCES

In describing the church in Jerusalem, Luke outlined step-by-step what took place in these early days. Though there are various ways to outline these activities, I have found it very helpful to organize them around the following three fundamental and vital experiences.

A VITAL LEARNING EXPERIENCE WITH THE WORD OF GOD

And they continued steadfastly in the apostles' doctrine. (Acts 2:42a)

After the Holy Spirit descended on the day of Pentecost, the apostle Peter stood up to preach. Interpreting what happened by referring to prophecies in the Old Testament, he demonstrated that Jesus Christ, whom His own people had rejected, was indeed their Messiah (Acts 2:36).

Great conviction came into the hearts of a great multitude of Peter's fellow Jews—both the residents of Jerusalem and Judea as well as the Greek-speaking and God-fearing Jews that had come from all over the New Testament world to celebrate the feast of Pentecost. On that particular day, Luke recorded that "about three thousand" people were converted to Jesus Christ. And on that very day, these people were publicly baptized—demonstrating their allegiance to Jesus Christ (Acts 2:41).

From that point forward, these new believers "continued steadfastly in the apostles' doctrine" (Acts 2:42a). What the apostles taught that day— and the days that followed—was what they had learned from Jesus Christ Himself. Furthermore, they were able to teach additional truths because of the revelational messages they received directly from the Holy Spirit.

In chapter 7, we will look more deeply at the importance of building a church on the foundation of Scripture. As the apostle Peter has stated, only as Christians "desire the pure milk of the word" will they grow in their Christian lives (1 Peter 2:2). And Paul elaborates: "So then faith comes by hearing, and hearing by the word of God" (Rom. 10:17).

It is impossible for Christians to mature in faith, hope, and love without a knowledge of the "apostles' doctrine" as it appears in Scripture. As we have just noted, the Word of God gives us something to "believe in"—our faith (Eph. 4:13). The Word of God keeps us from being "tossed to and fro and carried about with every wind of doctrine"—our steadfast hope (Eph.

4:14). And the Word of God demonstrates what true love really is (Eph. 4:16). Without the historical record of what Jesus Christ did for the whole world in giving His life, we would never know the true essence of sacrifical and self giving love (1 John 3:16).

VITAL RELATIONAL EXPERIENCES WITH ONE ANOTHER AND WITH GOD

And they continued steadfastly in the apostles' doctrine and fellowship. (Acts 2:42b)

Not only did these Jerusalem Christians devote themselves to "the apostles' doctrine" or, "teaching," but also to "fellowship." Luke used the Greek word *koinonia* which means to participate in one another's lives. However, as we will see, this "participation" involved not only fellowship with one another but also fellowship with God the Father, God the Son, and God the Holy Spirit.

In God's scheme of things, relational experiences at the human level are integrally interwoven with relational experiences at the divine level. This becomes increasingly clear as Luke described these *koinonia* functions. These new believers "ate together," "prayed together," "shared their material possessions with one another" and they "praised God" together.

They ate together. And they continued steadfastly in the apostles' doctrine and fellowship, in the breaking of bread. (Acts 2:42c)

A vital aspect of this New Testament fellowship involved "the breaking of bread" (Acts 2:42c). In most New Testament churches this was more than having communion periodically, using token elements—such as a morsel of bread and a sip of juice. Rather, these first century believers actually participated in one another's lives by having a meal together. On occasions, these meals were called "love feasts" (Jude 12; 2 Peter 2:13). In fact, Paul severely admonished the Corinthians for misusing and abusing this meal (1 Cor. 11:17–34).

These love feasts were patterned somewhat after the Passover meal—the final supper which Jesus shared with His disciples before He faced the cross. During that meal, using the very elements they were eating and drinking together in order to meet their physical needs, Jesus broke bread and passed the cup, admonishing the Twelve to thereafter remember His broken body and shed blood with these elements.

The New Testament believers in Jerusalem took these instructions very seriously. In fact, it appears that most every time they had a meal together, as they went from house to house, they remembered the Lord's broken body and shed blood. Thus, they no doubt celebrated the Lord's death several times a day.

The important factor, of course, is not how often we remember the Lord in this way, or what kind of specific elements we use. Rather, the essence of this experience was fellowship—eating and drinking together, and at the same time, remembering the death of the Lord Jesus Christ. Here we see a dramatic mix between human relationships and a relationship with God. As these first-century believers ate together (at the horizontal, human level), they also remembered the Lord together (at the vertical, divine level). They were having both fellowship with one another and fellowship with God simultaneously.

This observation has tremendous implications for every local church today. As Christians worshipped God in Jerusalem, this experience was never separated from their dynamic relationships with one another. In fact, it was their day-to-day loving relationships at the human level that made their relationships with God experientially meaningful. Having dynamic relational experiences with one another (with those they could see) enabled them to have dynamic, warm and rewarding experiences with God (the One they could not see). This is what the apostle John had in mind when he queried: "For he who does not love his brother whom he has seen, how can he love God whom he has not seen?" (1 John 4:20).

They prayed together. And they continued steadfastly in the apostles' doctrine and fellowship, in the breaking of bread, and in prayers. (Acts 2:42)

Corporate prayer in Jerusalem was also a unique part of this dynamic *koinonia.* As these believers prayed, they were participating in each others' lives—as they not only asked God to reveal His power and presence, but also to meet their human needs.

Throughout the New Testament, prayer was often in the context of human relationships. Rather than being private, it was public. Rather than being personal, it was corporate. As we will see in chapter 7, this is illustrated again and again among New Testament believers.

This is not to say that personal prayer is not important. Jesus certainly exemplified that need in his own life, and frequently Paul made reference to his own personal prayers, especially in the letters he wrote from prison. However, there is far more said in the Book of Acts and in the rest of the New Testament relative to prayer that involves a corporate experience. Furthermore, prayer is interwoven into a variety of experiences as believers met together to be edified. They included prayer in all they did. This seems to be what was taking place in Jerusalem when "they continued steadfastly in the apostles' doctrine and fellowship, in the breaking of bread, and in prayers" (Acts 2:42).[1]

They Shared Their Material Possessions

Now all who believed were together, and had all things in common, and sold their possessions and goods, and divided them among all, as anyone had need. (Acts 2:44–45)

To comprehend what was actually happening in Jerusalem, we need to understand the unique cultural setting related to their Jewish customs. Every year God-fearing Jews from all over the Roman world made a trek to Jerusalem to worship (see figure 6.1). It was a fifty day celebration often involving whole families and culminated on the fiftieth day, which they called the day of Pentecost.

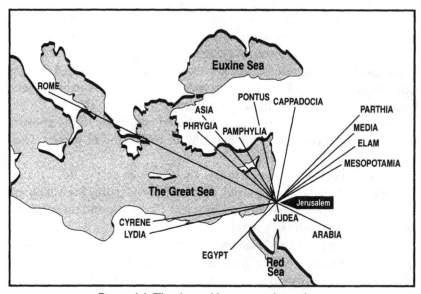

Figure 6.1: The Annual Journey to Jerusalem

It was on this final day that the Holy Spirit descended in Jerusalem and anointed and empowered the apostles—just as Jesus had promised (Acts 1:8). A "mighty rushing wind" filled Jerusalem. "Tongues of fire" appeared on the apostles' heads, which enabled these men to share the gospel message in a variety of languages (Acts 2:1–11). This unusual phenomena convinced thousands of Jews to respond to Peter's message and to put their faith in Jesus Christ, their Messiah. The Grecian Jews—those God-fearing men and women who had come from other parts of the Roman world—decided to stay on in Jerusalem, even though this was the final day of the feast of Pentecost.

This decision presented some unusual problems for the apostles. How could they care for the material needs of all of these people? However, the problem was solved when the believers who lived in Jerusalem and in the surrounding area shared their own material possessions with their brothers and sisters in Christ.

Though the cultural dynamics changed once these Christians understood that it was not God's plan to stay in Jerusalem indefinitely, many maintained their unselfish and generous spirit—a true mark of maturity among followers of Jesus Christ. Once believers understand how gracious God has been toward them in giving the gift of His Son, how can they do less than to respond by being generous in order to help others in need and to build the kingdom of God?

Note again that this kind of generosity was both a human and divine experience. It was human in that these believers were caring for each other's physical needs. It was divine in that anything that is given to meet the needs of a brother or sister in Christ is a divine gift to Jesus Christ. As Jesus once said:

> And whoever gives one of these little ones only a cup of cold water in the name of a disciple, assuredly, I say to you, he shall by no means lose his reward. (Matt. 10:42)[2]

They Praised God Together

> So continuing daily with one accord in the temple, and breaking bread from house to house, they ate their food with gladness and simplicity of heart, praising God (Acts 2:46–47a).

As these believers participated in these various kinds of fellowship experiences—eating together, praying for one another and sharing their material possessions—they were also "praising God." All of these activities became a means for praise and worship. This too was a part of their dynamic *koinonia*.

We can safely assume that singing was an intricate part of this praise experience. Jesus modeled this experience when He concluded the passover meal with His disciples. Mark recorded that "when they had sung a hymn, they went out to the Mount of Olives" (Mark 14:26).

The apostle Paul echoed the importance of this experience in his letters to the Colossians and the Ephesians:

Let the word of Christ dwell in you richly in all wisdom, teaching and admonishing one another in psalms and hymns and spiritual songs, singing with grace in your hearts to the Lord. (Col. 3:16; see also Eph. 5:18–19)

Note again that praising God with song is so interrelated with human relationships that it cannot be functionally separated. As they used the medium of music to speak the Word of God to one another, they also lifted their voices and hearts in praise and thanksgiving to God. Again, the warm dynamic feelings that were involved in intimate human relationships gave meaning to their relationships with God.

It is clear that these New Testament Christians in Jerusalem had four vital relationships with one another and with God. Furthermore, these human and divine relationships were significantly interrelated and intertwined:

- As they ate together, they remembered the Lord with holy communion.

- As they prayed for one another, they fellowshipped with God.

- As they shared their material possessions to meet each other's needs, they were worshipping the One who gave His life for them.

- As they taught one another with psalms and hymns and spiritual songs, they were lifting their voices in praise and thanksgiving to God.

VITAL WITNESSING EXPERIENCES WITH THE UNSAVED WORLD

And the Lord added to the church daily those who were being saved. (Acts 2:47)

Luke's final statement in the paragraph describing the various activities that were taking place in the Jerusalem church demonstrates the impact these believers were having on the unconverted Jews in Jerusalem, as well as in the lives of the God-fearing Greeks who had not yet accepted Jesus Christ as the Messiah. They were "having favor with all the people. And the Lord added to the church daily those who were being saved" (Acts 2:47).

Luke made it clear that many of the non-Christians in Jerusalem were very impressed with this new corporate lifestyle, this new faith in Christ, this new and vibrant community of love. Consequently, many of them listened to the apostles' message and put their faith in Jesus Christ and joined this growing body of believers.

The community of love became the most important ingredient that impressed these unbelievers. It communicated the reality of Christ to those who did not know Him. As the unconverted saw these Christians in Jerusalem eating together, praying for one another, sharing their possessions with each other, and praising God—they were deeply impressed. The Jerusalem believers' Christ-like lifestyle and mutual love became the bridge that enabled them to share the Gospel with people who had open and "listening ears."

The rapid growth of the church—both numerically and spiritually— happened because Christ's followers were carrying out His new commandment which He gave to them in the Upper Room. Jesus said: "By this all will know that you are My disciples, if you have love for one another" (John 13:35). This phenomenal spiritual response was also a marvelous answer to Jesus' prayer, which He prayed in the presence of His disciples on the way to the Kendron valley:

> I do not pray for these alone [the apostles], but also for those who will believe in Me through their word [the thousands of believers in Jerusalem and throughout history]; that they all may be one, as You, Father, are in Me, and I in You; that they also may be one in Us, that the world may believe that You sent Me [those who have been added to the church daily]. (John 17:20–21)

TYPICAL CHURCH STRUCTURES

What kind of structures does it take to carry out these three biblical functions and to provide believers with these vital experiences? Interestingly—and significantly—the Bible doesn't specify organizational structures, patterns, and methodologies. In fact, virtually no structure is described by Luke in this passage where he outlined these activities in the Jerusalem church. This is true throughout the New Testament. We can only speculate regarding the way first century Christians did things—or reconstruct from early church history the specific forms and methods they used.

This is by divine design. If the Holy Spirit had detailed divine and absolute structure and methodology regarding the way New Testament churches functioned, it would have locked us into their culture. And even if it were clear that structures were cultural, our intense desire for a sense of security would cause us to want to imitate structures—rather than dynamic biblical functions. This is why the content of Scripture focuses on directives, exhortations, activities and functions—the supracultural dimensions of Christianity. These can be duplicated any place in the world, whereas forms, structures and methods are definitely culturally and time oriented.

It is also interesting to note how Christians over the years have used this very "freedom in form" to design a variety of structures for the particular vital experience they believe is most important. We then tend to fixate on those very structures, making them absolute and normative. Though every church has its particular strengths, this kind of imbalance and rigidity leads to serious problems in becoming churches that measure up to "the stature of the fullness of Christ."

Though admittedly an oversimplification and sometimes overstated, the following observations will help us evaluate what kind of structures we have developed in our own churches to emphasize a particular vital experience.

BIBLE TEACHING CHURCHES

Some churches choose the first vital experience—continuing "steadfastly in the apostles' doctrine" (Acts 2:42a). They are often called "Bible teaching" churches—simply because their emphasis is on teaching the Scriptures. Their structures reflect the patterns of the Bible teaching institutions (Bible colleges and seminaries) where people are prepared for ministry. For example, pastors tend to function as "teachers" and "professors" and the people in the church often function more as "students" (see figure 6.2).

The strength in these churches relates to their theological stability, not being "tossed to and fro and carried about with every wind of doctrine" (Eph. 4:14). Their weaknesses, however, lie in their emphasis on "head knowledge" that frequently is not translated into their relationships with others, both Christians and non-Christians. Furthermore, as Paul states, "Knowledge puffs up" (1 Cor. 8:1). Learning biblical truths per se can easily lead to spiritual pride.

These churches also tend to be nonproductive in reaching people for Jesus Christ. They neglect outreach and evangelism and consequently become ingrown, which eventually leads to internal problems. There is no fresh flow of new life—as in the Jerusalem church—which is such an important factor in maintaining spiritual vitality.

Another weakness relates to body participation. Since the focus is on the "pastor-*teacher*," members of the church tend to be uninvolved in ministry. And since the people focus on their own personal learning process, they also become preoccupied with themselves rather than reaching out to others.

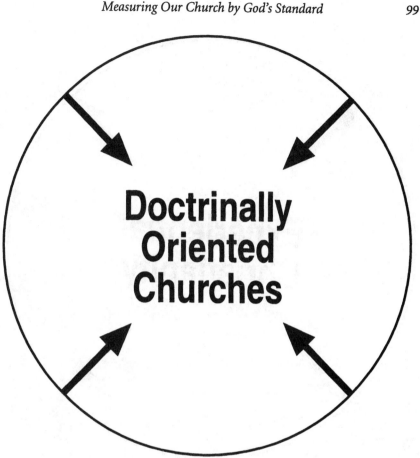

Figure 6.2: Bible Teaching Churches

RELATIONAL CHURCHES

Some churches emphasize the second vital experience—"fellowship with one another and with God." Their strength is in their warm, accepting environment and body participation. There is usually a strong sense of community and love. They are usually very generous people and reach out to all segments of the society (see figure 6.3).

There is a strong emphasis on worship and praise. And their music focuses on their love relationship with Jesus Christ. They also tend to have a strong faith in God and what He can do for them and others. Whatever they think the Bible says, they believe. This is a major reason some of these churches are the fastest growing churches around the world.

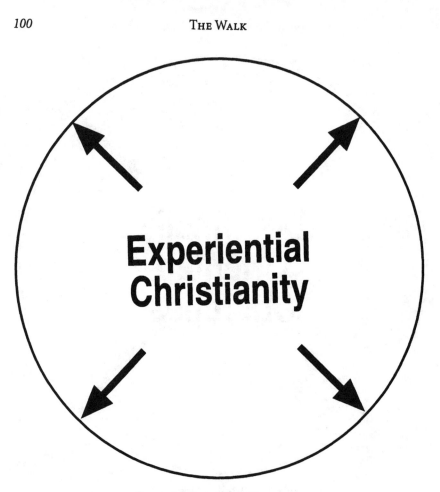

Figure 6.3: Relational Churches

Their weaknesses, however, lie in their doctrinal and emotional insta-bility. Since they are often experience oriented, rather than scripturally oriented, they often allow "feelings" rather than Bible doctrine to take precedence in their decision making. Frequently, experience dictates what they actually believe rather than a careful study of the Scriptures. Further-more, they often sincerely equate "emotional experiences" with the min-istry of the Holy Spirit, believing "ideas" and "thoughts" come from God, whereas they may actually come from their own inner selves. And since they are often weak in the study of the Scriptures, they sometimes follow "experiential" teachings and beliefs that are actually in contradiction to what is taught in the Bible.

Their emotional and spiritual life is also in direct proportion to their relational experiences. They often depend on corporate worship and praise experiences to maintain their "spiritual and emotional" equilibrium. They find it difficult to "feel good" about their Christian experience unless they are fellowshipping with other Christians.

Some of these churches often over-emphasize the miraculous. People come to depend on "signs and wonders" which leads to an inappropriate focus on human needs and concerns rather than on God's sovereignty and character. Furthermore, it can lead to self-deception, manipulation, and a false simulation of biblical realities. The end result is often disappointment and disillusionment in the lives of these people.

EVANGELISM CHURCHES

These churches are often identified as "soul winning" churches. Their main strength lies in their passion to reach people for Christ through public preaching and personal witnessing (see figure 6.4).

A major weakness lies in their strength—to get people to make decisions for Christ but then to allow them to lie dormant in their Christian lives. The pulpit ministry in these churches is frequently characterized by a diet of evangelistically oriented messages that make the gospel clear but which do not edify believers. Regular attenders are often starved for the Word of God, but many do not understand their problem.

These churches also tend to be operated in an authoritarian manner. The "preacher" is often in control and even board members serve only in a "rubber stamp" position. The leadership frequently lacks accountability, and the members are often highly motivated by guilt. Some of these groups tend to be highly legalistic in what they believe is spiritual behavior. These people are "busy beavers," engaging in lots of activity and attending numerous church meetings each week. However, they have little knowledge of the Bible since many sermons are topical and repetitive and their relationships are very superficial, both within and outside the church.

Within recent years, another movement has emerged — often called the "seeker" model for church structures. Many of these churches have rapidly become megachurches. Sunday morning services particularly, are designed for unbelievers. There is a strong emphasis on contemporary music, drama, need-oriented messages and other creative forms. Though unique expressions of the "freedom in form" the Bible allows and encourages, this approach — if not implemented carefully — produce the "mile wide" and "inch thick" church. Though energized with contemporary approaches, there is often a woeful lack of commitment and spiritual depth. Though

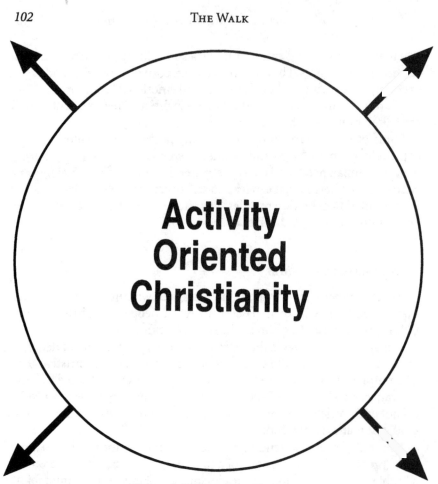

Figure 6.4: Evangelism Churches

characterized by rapid numerical growth, the spiritual life in some of these churches seems to reflect the superficiality and self-oriented lifestyle that permeates the American culture.

GOD'S IDEAL PLAN

As stated earlier, these three categories just described are oversimplified and, in some instances, overstated. Though some churches fit these extreme descriptions, most have a tendency in one direction or another with an imbalanced mixture of all three vital experiences. The fact is that God's ideal plan for every local church is to have structures that provide a balance in all three experiences—just as in the Jerusalem church. When we do, we

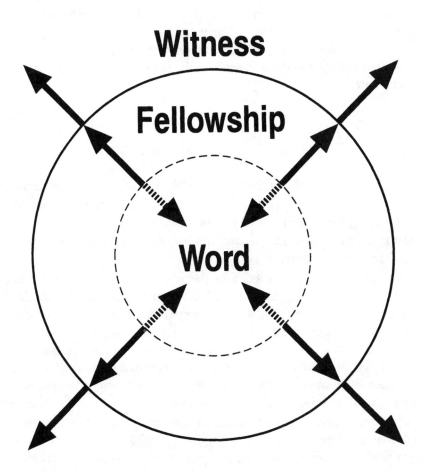

will have a church that is growing substantially in faith, hope and love—and especially love (1 Cor. 13:13). When this happens, believers will begin measuring up to "the stature of the fullness of Christ" (Eph. 4:15). We will truly begin to "have a walk worthy of the Lord, fully pleasing Him" (Col. 1:10).

God's ideal plan also is for churches to understand the difference between function and form. Normative functions that yield supracultural principles from the Bible are absolute and should never change (see figure 6.5). On the other hand, we must understand that forms and structures and methods are cultural patterns that are nonabsolutes. This is what enables a church to function in every culture of the world at any moment in history. This is the uniqueness of Christianity. This is definitely what

Paul had in mind when he said—"I have become all things to all men, that I might by all *means* save some" (1 Cor. 9:22, emphasis added). The apostle Paul never compromised on the absolutes of Scripture. However, he was always free and open to the leadership of the Holy Spirit in the area of the nonabsolutes.

CROSSCULTURAL EXPERIENCES

I have had the wonderful opportunity over the years to minister to Christians in a number of different cultural situations. Even at this very moment as I am doing the final edits on this manuscript, I have just returned from Poland where I ministered to a large number of pastors from all over that post-Communist country.

No matter where I have gone in the world, I have discovered that believers everywhere can identify with these three vital experiences described in the Jerusalem model. At the same time, they can discover and create ways to apply these principles in their particular cultures. Conversely, they often cannot identify with the *way* we do things in America. In fact, our methods may not work at all in their particular social situations. The reasons are obvious: These three vital functions and principles are supracultural whereas forms and patterns are cultural.

I remember particularly a wonderful experience ministering to pastors in Romania before the "walls" between East and West came down. We met for a week in a private and secret setting from morning until evening discussing New Testament principles of church life. Though these pastors could not utilize the forms and structures we developed in Dallas, they discovered ways to apply these three vital experiences in their own culture. For example, the law prohibited more than several people to meet in homes for any reason, since Ceausescu was fearful of a conspiracy against him and his ruling party. These believers had to meet in church buildings where everything that was said and done could be monitored by a Communist informant. In this sense, these believers could not even meet from house to house like the Jerusalem church.

However, in our discussions together, these men thought of unique and creative ways to provide their people with the vital experiences in the Jerusalem model, thus demonstrating that these experiences are supracultural and forms are cultural. Again, this is the genius of Christianity.

A Supernatural Process

Building and developing a mature church is both a natural and supernatural process. The very principles that build large organizations in the secular world can also build large churches. However, unless the process is guided, surrounded, and motivated by supernatural principles; unless our efforts are "built on the foundation of the apostles and prophets" with "Jesus Christ Himself being the chief cornerstone;" and unless our work is empowered by the Person and presence of the Holy Spirit, we will never produce a church that "measures up to the stature of the fullness of Christ." We will not build a church that reflects faith, hope, and love—and especially love (1 Cor. 13:13). As a result, we will not "walk worthy of our calling" as we should. Our next chapters will develop more fully these supernatural dimensions.

Measuring Our Walk

1. If you were to identify your church, which emphasis best characterizes your overall approach to ministry?

   • Is our church primarily a Bible teaching church?

   • Is our church primarily a relational church?

   • Is our church primarily an evangelistic church?

   Reread the list of strengths and weaknesses in each church. Which ones apply to your church?

2. Use your creativity and depend on the Holy Spirit to lead you in this question. What freedom does the Bible give you in the area of forms and structures? Are you able to differentiate between those things that are absolute (the truths that should never change) and the non-absolutes (the forms and structures that should change when necessary)?

Mrs. Vonette Bright

I T IS NO SECRET THAT WE ARE LIVING in a world that has changed dramatically in terms of what gives us guidance and direction. In our American culture, it used to be the basic principles of Scripture and our founding fathers' commitment to seek help from God through prayer. However, all of this has changed dramatically—and unfortunately, this trend has affected our churches as well. We have lost sight of these biblical priorities, to build our lives and ministry upon the Word of God and prayer.

In this chapter Dr. Gene Getz calls us back to these priorities in our churches, in our families, and in our personal lives. When culture generally teaches us that there are no absolutes and that we do not need to seek God's help, how much more we need to reinforce these priorities in our Christian lives.

As you read this chapter on God's plan for making disciples and building those disciples, I trust you will be challenged to evaluate your own life and your ministry in light of these very important biblical principles and priorities. Is learning the Word of God and devoting yourself to prayer priorities in your own life and in the life of your church?

Please read this chapter carefully and prayerfully. Allow the Holy Spirit to help you evaluate your personal life as well as the corporate life in your church. Is the Word of God and prayer indeed a priority?

SEVEN

MEASURING OUR COMMITMENT TO THE WORD OF GOD AND PRAYER

For I rejoiced greatly when brethren came and testified of the truth that is in you, just as *you walk in the truth.* I have no greater joy than to hear that my children *walk in truth.*

— 3 John 3–4

BEING DEVOTED AND COMMITTED to the Word of God and prayer were established early in the history of the church as spiritual priorities. This came into very clear focus on one particular occasion as the apostles faced an unusual challenge. Not surprising, their problem related to the rapid growth of the church in Jerusalem, but was also intricately related to the unique cultural dynamics that existed at that time.

Among the thousands of Grecian Jewish families who had come from various parts of the Roman Empire to worship during the Feast of Pentecost were a number of Grecian widows. They were the first to be neglected in the daily distribution of food. Since their resources were limited, they were the first to deplete their money supply which they had saved to make this annual trip. However, they—like all of the other Grecian Jewish families—decided to stay in Jerusalem to become a part of this great and wonderful happening.

When the problem surfaced and came to the attention of the apostles, they called a large group of people together—no doubt those who were converted Grecian Jews—and proposed a solution.

Therefore, brethren, seek out from among you seven men of good reputation, full of the Holy Spirit and wisdom, whom we may appoint over this business; but we will give ourselves continually *to prayer* and *to the ministry of the word.* (Acts 6:3–4)

The apostles' two priorities stand out clearly in these verses. They were in no way negating the importance of meeting people's physical needs. However, they knew that in order to be true to the Great Commission and to produce a mature church that would reproduce itself, they could not get sidetracked from their primary calling—*to pray* and *to teach the Word of God.* With this decision, these spiritual leaders—equipped and trained by Jesus Christ Himself—established divine guidelines for all church leaders thereafter.

THE APOSTLE'S DOCTRINE (TEACHING)

Of all the experiences listed by Luke in Acts 2:41–47 in which he describes the activities that were taking place in the church in Jerusalem, it is not accidental that these believers were, first of all, continuing "steadfastly in the apostles' doctrine" or "teaching" (Acts 2:42a). The ordering of names, events, and experiences are usually very important in Scripture. And Luke's sequential description of what was happening in the first church is very significant!

It was the "apostles' doctrine" that gave direction to everything else that happened in the church in Jerusalem. Christian experience, both at the horizontal, human level (such as fellowship and sharing with one another) and at the vertical, divine level (such as prayer and praise) must have divine guidelines. Without these guidelines, Christians can get sidetracked onto peripheral issues and even depart from the will of God. For example, a "Christ-centered community of love" can quickly digress into a "self-centered community." Therefore, all Christian experience must be rooted in and evaluated by Scripture. In this sense, continuing in the "apostles' doctrine" is foundational to all that we do in the church—and in life. This is why it appears first in Luke's list of activities. This sequence in Acts 2:42–47 was designed and orchestrated by the Holy Spirit Himself.

What was the "apostles' doctrine"? Where did it come from? And why is this experience so vital for all Christians today?

What the apostles were teaching that day was what they had learned from Jesus Christ Himself. Furthermore, they were able to teach additional truths because of the messages they received directly from the Holy Spirit.

This unusual process was a direct fulfillment of what Jesus had promised the apostles when He was with them in the Upper Room prior to His crucifixion. Note the following words of Jesus:

> These things I have spoken to you while being present with you. But the Helper, the Holy Spirit, whom the Father will send in My name, He will teach you all things, and bring to your remembrance all things that I said to you. (John 14:25–26)

Here Jesus promised two things to the apostles. First, the Holy Spirit would actually remind them of the things that Jesus Christ had taught them during the three and a half years He ministered with them. Obviously, Jesus taught many things they had forgotten—or did not understand. But once Jesus Christ had died and rose again, their whole frame of reference changed. They then began to understand why Jesus Christ had really come in the first place. (Luke 24:44–45)

Second, there were many things that Jesus had not taught them while He was with them. Jesus promised that the Holy Spirit would continue the process of teaching what He had begun. This can be seen from the following words of Jesus as He continued to teach them in the Upper Room:

> I still have many things to say to you, but you cannot bear them now. However, when He, the Spirit of truth, has come, He will guide you into all truth; for He will not speak on His own authority, but whatever He hears He will speak; and He will tell you things to come. (John 16:12–13)

On the day of Pentecost, these promises began to be fulfilled in the lives of the apostles. The Holy Spirit's teaching ministry initially enabled the Apostles to begin to carry out the Great Commission—to "make disciples" and to teach "them to observe all things" that Jesus had commanded them (Matt.28:19–20). Put another way, the Holy Spirit gave the apostles not only an evangelistic charge (to make disciples), but a body of truth to teach to these new believers so that they could begin the process of spiritual growth—learning how to "walk in newness of life" (Rom. 6:4). Furthermore, the apostles were able to begin to duplicate this process through every member of the body of Jesus Christ, just as Paul did with Timothy:

> And the things you have heard from me among many witnesses, commit these to faithful men who will be able to teach others also. (2 Tim. 2:2)

MAKING DISCIPLES

When Jesus met with the eleven apostles on a mountain in Galilee, He told them to first of all, "Go" and "make disciples of all the nations" (Matt. 28:19). Here Jesus was simply referring to bringing people to saving faith in Christ.

The term "disciples" is used in a variety of ways in the New Testament. There were "deceptive disciples"—like Judas. There were "disciples in name only"—people who followed Jesus when it was convenient, but when His words became too difficult for them to accept and apply, they forsook Him (John 6:60–66). And in the Gospels, we meet many "immature disciples" which certainly includes the apostles until after the Holy Spirit came on them at Pentecost.

As we move into the Book of Acts, the term "disciples" is normally used to simply refer to "believers" or "Christians," such as those who responded to the gospel in Derby. Luke recorded that "when they [Paul and Barnabas] preached the gospel to that city and *had made many disciples* [that is "converts to Christ"], they returned to Lystra, Iconium and Antioch, *strengthening the souls of the disciples*" [that is, these "new Christians"] (Acts 14:21–22). In actuality, Luke is describing the way Paul and Barnabas were carrying out the Great Commission—going and making disciples, baptizing them, and then "teaching them to observe all things that" Jesus had commanded (Matt. 28:20).

THE PLACE OF SCRIPTURE IN CONVERSION

The three thousand Jews who were converted to Christ and added to the church in Jerusalem on the day of Pentecost did so after they heard Peter preach. We are told they "gladly received his word" and "were baptized" (Acts 2:41).

What was this "word"? Clearly, it was the "Word of God" as proclaimed and explained by Peter. He quoted both the Old Testament prophet Joel (Acts 2:16–21) and David, the king of Israel (Acts 2:25–28,34). He also bore witness to what he and the other apostles had heard Jesus say and what they had seen Jesus do to verify that His message was from God.

We must never forget that it was the inspired Word of God used by the Holy Spirit that penetrated people's lives in these early days and brought them under conviction of sin, resulting in their conversion to Jesus Christ. This is illustrated again and again throughout the Book of Acts.

The Ethiopian Eunich. When Philip lead the Ethiopian Eunuch to put his faith in Christ, this God-fearing Greek "was reading Isaiah the prophet" (Acts 8:28). Philip began with that very passage in the Old Testament Scriptures that prophesied Christ's death as a sacrificial lamb (Acts 8:32–33) and "preached Jesus to him" (Acts 8:35). The man responded in faith and was baptized (Acts 8:36–38).

Antioch in Pasidia. When Paul arrived in Antioch in Pisidia on the first missionary journey, he and Barnabas immediately went into the synagogue. After one of the leaders in the synagogue stood and read a section from the "Law and the Prophets," Paul was invited to speak. He responded by expounding on these Old Testament Scriptures and demonstrated that Jesus was indeed the Messiah (Acts 13:16–41). Paul's Gentile listeners were so impressed that they literally "begged that these words might be preached to them the next Sabbath" (Acts 13:42). And a week later, Luke records that "almost the whole city came together to hear the *word of God*" (Acts 13:44). Many believed "and the *word of the Lord*" was being spread throughout all the region (Acts 13:49).

Berea. This was Paul's normal approach throughout his missionary career. He exposed unbelievers to the Scriptures. And when people had questions as to whether his message was indeed from God, he spent time helping them to explore the Scriptures—such as in Berea—where they "searched the Scriptures daily to find out whether these things were so" (Acts 17:11).

Athens. Interestingly, one of Paul's most ineffective ministries took place in Athens where he departed from his usual approach and discussed God in the context of philosophy and apart from a direct exposition of the Old Testament Scriptures. Though he created a great deal of interest, the spiritual results were minimal. Some believe that is why, when he arrived in Corinth—his next stop after Athens (Acts 18:1)—he went back to a more simple approach to preaching Jesus Christ from the Scriptures. This may explain why he wrote to the Corinthians: "And I, brethren, when I came to you, did not come with excellence of speech or of wisdom [as Paul did in Athens] declaring to you the testimony of God. For I determined not to know anything among you except Jesus Christ and Him crucified" (1 Cor. 2:1–2).

Of course, we certainly can and should use a person's "knowledge base" and perceived "psychological and sociological needs" to build bridges to people who need Jesus Christ. However, if we do not ultimately confront them with the Word of God, the response may be superficial and non-productive.

A CONTEMPORARY ILLUSTRATION

I have a very close friend, Jim Petersen, who has ministered with the Navigators for twenty-five years in Brazil. He and his wife, Marge, worked primarily with secular people, many of whom were Marxist and agnostics. Jim's approach again and again was to get these people to study the Scriptures, simply to see what the Bible says. Though it took time to bring people to faith in Christ, once decisions were made, they resulted from a comprehensive knowledge of God's truth. Furthermore, it was the Holy Spirit, the divine author of Scripture, who enabled these people to believe (1 Cor. 12:3).

One of these individuals was Mario Nitche who classified himself as an aethiest.When Jim met Mario he was attending a meeting where a Christian psychologist from the United States was speaking. Jim—who was relatively new on the field—was interpreting in Portugese for the guest speaker, and after the lecture, Mario approached Jim with some questions. Sensing Mario's inquisitive mind as well as his agnostic position, Jim asked him if he would like to study the Bible just to see what it says. Mario agreed.

They began to meet on a regular basis to study the Book of Romans. As they started reading in chapter 1, they came to the name "Jesus Christ." At that point, Mario informed Jim that he did not believe in Jesus Christ, even as an historical person. "That's alright," Jim replied. "Let's just call Him 'X'. Let's just see what Paul says."

Mario agreed to this arrangement and they read on. Next they came to the word "God." Again, Mario objected: He did not believe in God. And again, they agreed to just substitute the letter "X" for God. And so they continued meeting together weekly—off and on—for a period of four years. Finally, Mario became a believer.

The Process of Multiplication. During the years following Mario's conversion to Christ, he continued to study the Word of God, both with individuals and in small groups. Not only did he grow in his own faith, hope, and love, but he also helped lead many of his friends and colleagues to Christ.

Jim also continued the same process. He led many people to the Lord—simply by exposing them to the Word of God. As he did, the Holy Spirit opened their hearts to believe and receive God's revelation. Through the written word, they came to know the living Word—Jesus Christ.

Lasting Fruit. Interestingly, a study of those conversions over a twenty-five-year period reveals that almost 100 percent of these people continued in their faith and became strong Christians. In view of what we read in Scripture, it should not surprise us that one of the keys to both "making disciples" and "teaching those disciples" is helping people to understand the Word of God sufficiently so that their faith is activated by the Holy Spirit and based on a commitment to divine truth.

Do not misunderstand! This does not mean that people are unable to sincerely respond to a brief gospel presentation which is also based upon the Scriptures. There are many people—particularly in our culture—who have a general knowledge of the Scriptures but who do not understand the simple gospel. And once the message is made clear, they are able to respond by faith because of the foundations that have already been laid in their lives.

THE NEW TESTAMENT MODEL

In a sense, this is what happened among the God-fearing Jews and Greeks in Jerusalem. They had a significant background in the Old Testament Scriptures. It did not take a lengthy explanation to demonstrate to them that Jesus Christ was indeed the Messiah. However, it's also clear from the Pauline journeys, that the more New Testament missionaries moved into pagan areas, the more time it took to lay a foundation in the Scriptures. Notice that Luke began recording time factors in the book of Acts in areas where people knew very little about the Old Testament and who had never heard of Jesus of Nazareth. For example, Paul stayed on in Corinth for a year and a half (Acts 18:11) and in Ephesus for two years (Acts 19:10).

Taking into consideration the mentality of these people, their cultural backgrounds, their total ignorance regarding Christianity as well as the method of communication they were used to, the implication is obvious. Paul adopted an evangelistic methodology to enable him to more effectively reach these people. Furthermore, he knew he had no foundation on which to build. Consequently, he settled into these strategic communities, got to know the thinking of these people, and taught the Scriptures in-depth on their mental and emotional levels.

BUILDING DISCIPLES

A commitment to teach the Word of God is foundational in an evangelistic outreach that is biblical. But it is even more important in helping new believers grow in their Christian lives. As stated earlier, after Paul and Barnabas had "made many disciples" in Derby, Luke reports that "they returned to Lystra, Iconium and Antioch, strengthening the souls of the disciples" (Acts 14:21–22).

THE JERUSALEM MODEL

This process was first illustrated in the church in Jerusalem. Once people responded to an explanation of the Scriptures regarding who Jesus Christ was, they "continued steadfastly in the apostles' doctrine" (Acts 2:42a).

This process was also carefully followed by the Apostle Paul and his fellow missionaries in their church planting ministry. This is why Paul spent an entire year in Antioch teaching the disciples; a year and six months in Corinth; and at least six months in Thessalonica; and a total of three years in Ephesus. This is why he even went beyond a personal ministry among new converts and often sent Timothy and others back to the churches to continue teaching these believers the basic doctrines of Christianity (1 Thess. 3:2; 1 Cor. 4:17; Titus 3:12). And as illustrated in "The Pauline Strategy" (see Introduction), this is why Paul on subsequent missionary journeys returned to the churches that he had established. He wanted to strengthen these churches in the faith (Acts 15:36,41; 18:23). And this is why he eventually wrote thirteen letters, either to churches or to individuals in these churches.

All of this biblical evidence leads us to a very specific conclusion: *No church* can develop maturity—reflecting faith, hope, and love—without vital learning experiences with the Word of God.

THE INSPIRED SCRIPTURES

I personally believe that the Holy Spirit endowed the apostles with a special "gift of teaching" to enable them to author most of the reports and letters included in the New Testament. Consequently, God has made it possible for all of us—those of us living in the twentieth century—to still devote ourselves to "the apostles' doctrine" and "teaching." Though we cannot hear Peter preach as he did on the day of Pentecost, we can read the letters he wrote by the inspiration of the Holy Spirit. We cannot hear the apostle John teach as he stood by Peter's side in those early days. However, we can read the Gospel he wrote, as well as his three epistles—and that wonderful culminating document, the Book of Revelation.

The apostle Paul, of course, was not converted for at least five years after Pentecost. However, he was later called to be an apostle and the Holy Spirit enabled him to author more letters than any other New Testament author.

In essence, the New Testament Scriptures contain those very doctrines—plus much more—that Jerusalem believers were listening to in those early days of the church. However, for us they are beautifully and realistically woven into a variety of letters and written reports, many of which were penned directly to New Testament churches to help them "walk in the Spirit" rather than to "fulfill the lusts of the flesh" (Gal. 5:16).

What a creative way to relate doctrine to life and to help us grow in faith, hope and love. Rather than giving us a volume of systematic doctrine and theology, all neatly outlined and arranged, God has given us a plan where we can see biblical truth in relationship to real life experiences—and particularly in relationship to the problems we face as we live our Christian lives day by day.

OUR COMMITMENT TO PRAYER

A commitment to the Word of God and prayer are inseparable priorities in helping a church measure up to "the stature of the fullness of Christ." Even prior to the coming of the Holy Spirit, the apostles accompanied by a number of other disciples, "all continued with one accord in prayer and supplication" (Acts 1:14). And when the Holy Spirit came on the day of Pentecost and the church was born, all of those who responded to Peter's message "continued steadfastly in the apostles' doctrine and fellowship, in the breaking of bread, and in prayers" (Acts 2:42).

We must also remember that we do not even know how to pray without access to the Word of God. If we do not pray "in the will of God" as it is revealed in the "word of God," we will not experience answers to our prayers. Only as we "pray according to his will" does God "hear us" and respond (1 John 5:14–15; see also James 5:13–18).

THE BIBLICAL EMPHASIS ON CORPORATE PRAYER

When I began to research the subject of prayer several years ago, particularly as it relates to the church, I discovered a lot of books on the subject of personal prayer. However, at the time, I couldn't find a single volume on corporate prayer. I found this very surprising in view of the fact that most prominent illustrations in the Book of Acts and in the New Testament epistles are centered on the "church gathered" to pray.

It is understandable why so much has been written and presented on personal prayer. First, the Bible has a lot to say about this kind of praying. It should be a very important part of every Christian's life. It is modeled by Old Testament greats—men like Daniel, who knelt and prayed in his home three times a day (Dan. 6:10). And Nehemiah's prolonged period of prayer and fasting over the distressful situation in Jerusalem gives us another unique example (Neh. 1:4–11). And we know more about David's prayer life than any other Old Testament character since he wrote numerous psalms which in themselves are prayers. In the New Testament, Jesus Christ modeled personal and private prayer and the apostle Paul also made numerous references to his prayer life in his letters to the churches—particularly when he wrote from prison.

But why have we neglected the subject of corporate prayer when there is such a strong emphasis on this kind of praying in the Book of Acts and the epistles? The answer, I believe, relates to our culture and how it has influenced biblical interpretation. The hallmark of western civilization has been rugged individualism. Because of our philosophy of life, we are used to the personal pronouns *I* and *my* and *me*. We have not been taught to think in terms of *we* and *our* and *us*. Consequently, we tend to "individualize" many references to corporate experience in the New Testament, thus often emphasizing a *personal walk with Christ*—"personal prayer," "personal Bible study," "personal evangelism" and "personal Christian maturity." The facts are that more is said in the Book of Acts and the epistles about our *corporate walk with Christ*—"corporate prayer," "corporate learning of biblical truth," "corporate evangelism" and "corporate Christian maturity" than about the personal dimensions of these Christian disciplines.

Yes, both are intricately related—but the personal dimensions of Christianity are difficult to maintain and practice consistently unless they grow out of proper corporate experiences on a regular basis. This is why the emphasis in the scriptural record is clearly on corporate prayer serving as a context in which personal prayer becomes meaningful.

Note the relational and corporate context of prayer in the following passages in the Epistles:

> Be kindly affectionate to one another with brotherly love, in honor giving preference to one another . . . continuing steadfastly in prayer. (Rom. 12:10,12)

> Rejoice always, pray without ceasing, in everything give thanks; for this is the will of God in Christ Jesus for you. (1 Thess. 5:16–18)

Confess your trespasses to one another, and pray for one another, that you may be healed. (James 5:16)

But the end of all things is at hand; therefore be serious and watchful in your prayers. And above all things have fervent love for one another, for "love will cover a multitude of sins." (1 Peter 4:7–8)

In all of these passages of Scripture, the writer's intent was that prayer not only be a personal experience with God but a relational experience with other believers. These Christians were deeply involved in one anothers' lives—praying for one another[1]

PAUL'S PERSONAL PRAYERS IN THE EPHESIAN LETTER

Though we have a very strong emphasis on corporate prayer in the Book of Acts and in the Epistles, Paul's prayers for the various churches certainly demonstrate the importance of personal prayer, particularly as it relates to becoming mature in Jesus Christ, both as individual Christians and as a corporate body. For example, note Paul's prayer request for the Ephesians. For wisdom and understanding to know God better.

Therefore I also, after I heard of your faith in the Lord Jesus and your love for all the saints, do not cease to give thanks for you, making mention of you in my prayers: that the God of our Lord Jesus Christ, the Father of glory, may give to you the spirit of wisdom and revelation in the knowledge of Him. (Eph. 1:15–17)

Here Paul prayed that God would give these believers spiritual understanding and wisdom so that they might get to know God better. For in getting to know God better, we will grow into His likeness. Prayer is a very important key causing this to happen. Thus, Paul's prayer for the Ephesians should become our prayer request for ourselves and for one another.

Note also the correlation between Paul's prayer request for "the spirit of wisdom and revelation" and the Word of God itself. The Scriptures represent our major source of wisdom regarding who God is; it is indeed His written revelation to us. Though He is visible in His creation, what He is really like in terms of His love for the world can only be learned through the biblical record. Jesus Christ, who has revealed God the Father, no longer walks among us. But thank God, through the Scriptures we can still look up on "the Lamb of God who takes away the sin of the world!" (John 1:29). For understanding to know their glorious position in Christ.

[I pray that] the eyes of your understanding [be] enlightened; that you may know what is the hope of His calling, what are the riches of the glory of His

Here Paul prayed that these believers might understand in their hearts and minds what Christ had actually done for them in providing eternal life. The same power that raised Jesus Christ from the dead had raised them up with Christ and seated them with Christ "in the heavenly places" (Eph. 2:4–6).

Paul's prayer for these believers was the key for unlocking this wonderful and glorious truth in their hearts and minds. Thus, as Christians, we should also pray this prayer request for ourselves and for one another. And as we come to understand how great our position is in Christ, it will motivate us to turn our backs on "ungodliness and worldly lust" and to live "soberly, righteously and godly" as we look "for the blessed hope and glorious appearing of our great God and Savior Jesus Christ" (Titus 2:11–13).

For power to comprehend God's love and to reflect it through others.

For this reason I bow my knees to the Father of our Lord Jesus Christ, from whom the whole family in heaven and earth is named, that He would grant you, according to the riches of His glory, to be strengthened with might through His Spirit in the inner man, that Christ may dwell in your hearts through faith; that you, being rooted and grounded in love, may be able to comprehend with all the saints what is the width and length and depth and height—to know the love of Christ which passes knowledge; that you may be filled with all the fullness of God. (Eph. 3:14–19)

This is one of Paul's most powerful prayers for Christians everywhere. Here he prayed that these believers might experience the power of the Holy Spirit in their hearts to such a degree that Christ would become a living reality; that in this process, they would get to know Christ's unfathomable love so deeply that they could not help but reflect His holiness, His righteousness and His character. This is what Paul meant when he prayed that they would "be filled with all the fullness of God."

Paul summarizes his own prayer process for the Ephesians with a wonderful doxology—one that has become a theme promise for all churches.

Now to Him who is able to do exceedingly abundantly above all that we ask or think, according to the power that works in us, to Him be glory in the church by Christ Jesus throughout all ages, world without end. Amen. (Eph. 3:20–21)

ADDITIONAL PRAYERS BY PAUL

Note Paul's prayers for the Philippians and the Colossians. Though worded differently, they focus on the same request as Paul prayed for the Ephesians.

Paul's prayer for the Philippians:

And this I pray, that your love may abound still more and more in knowledge and all discernment, that you may approve the things that are excellent, that you may be sincere and without offense till the day of Christ, being filled with the fruits of righteousness which are by Jesus Christ, to the glory and praise of God. (Phil. 1:9–11)

Paul's prayer for the Colossians:

For this reason we also, since the day we heard it, do not cease to pray for you, and to ask that you may be filled with the knowledge of His will in all wisdom and spiritual understanding; that you may have a walk worthy of the Lord, fully pleasing Him, being fruitful in every good work and increasing in the knowledge of God; strengthened with all might, according to His glorious power, for all patience and longsuffering with joy; giving thanks to the Father who has qualified us to be partakers of the inheritance of the saints in the light. (Col. 1:9–12)

A CONTEMPORARY ILLUSTRATION

When we interviewed Vonette Bright about the content of this chapter, she gave a vibrant testimony regarding the meaningfulness of prayer in her own life personally. She stated:

"I've seen my own prayer life develop as I have made a commitment to become a pray-er," she stated. "And I've found that for prayer to be meaningful, it must be seen as a means to developing a relationship. It's the greatest privilege because it gives us access to the throne of God. And through prayer, I've learned how to develop a friendship with God—talking to Him like I would talk to my best friend. It has helped me to get to know the way that He works in my life and in the lives of others. And it helps me to get to know His character and His precepts. And by spending time with Him, He speaks to me. It's as though I'm developing a relationship with my very best friend."

Regarding corporate prayer, Vonette offered this observation:"The Scriptures confirm that when God's people come together in united and specific prayer—without exception—God hears, He delivers, He provides, empowers and does whatever is needed to answer their requests."

FREEDOM IN FORM

Teaching and learning the Word of God and being devoted to prayer can and should happen in a variety of ways. Again, the Scriptures do not dictate absolute forms and patterns. The functions of teaching, preaching and praying are frequently described in Scripture, but very seldom are we given specific detail as to *how* all of this took place.

Again, this is by divine design since God the Holy Spirit wants us to engage in these functions in every culture of the world—which will call for unique approaches. This is why the priorities of being devoted to the Word of God and prayer has circled the globe. Causing it to happen is not dependent on specific forms and structures.

Today, we need to first of all establish these experiences as biblical priorities. We then need to evaluate our present church structures and approaches to the ministry. Do our present forms allow us to teach the Word of God effectively and to motivate people to make prayer a priority?

As we evaluate our present patterns for ministry in the light of these biblical principles, we may need to design new methods, new approaches, new structures. Our old forms may not work as they used to, especially since cultural needs and societal structures have changed. In fact, we may have to conclude that our methods have never been the best forms. Perhaps we borrowed them from someone else—from some other time and place. Perhaps this is why they are not working as they should. We must not try to generate interest in these biblical priorities by promoting old approaches that were designed for a previous era. To do so is to make what God designed to be a "means to an end" the "end" in itself. When this happens, Christianity becomes institutionalized and loses its spiritual dynamic and power.

We can learn freedom in form from the Scriptures themselves. God the Father, God the Son, and God the Holy Spirit are the most creative personalities in the universe. Being three and yet one is perhaps one of the most creative aspects of deity there is!

Furthermore, notice the creativity in the composition of biblical litera-ture. For example, compare John's style in writing his Gospel with the style of Matthew, Mark, and Luke in writing their Gospel records. Compare Paul's writing style with John's style in writing their epistles. And notice the creativity Paul used in the way he composed his thirteen letters. All of this points to the fact that the Holy Spirit's divine creativity combined with man's human creativity has given us one of the most unique books every written.

Let us, therefore, not allow ourselves to lock into rigid forms and refuse to change these forms when they are no longer relevant. One thing is certain—and absolute: In order to produce maturity in our churches, we must devote ourselves to the Word of God and prayer. How we do that will vary from country to country, city to city, and town to town—and even within the subcultures of our particular sphere of influence.

MEASURING OUR WALK

1. How effective are you—in your church—in teaching the word of God? In motivating people to make prayer a priority?

2. What old forms in teaching the Word and praying are you promoting that may be ineffective in your particular cultural situation?

3. How can you make the truths of this chapter come alive in your church?

Dr. Charles Stanley

D R. GENE GETZ IS A FELLOW PASTOR and a real practitioner. What he writes is not just theory in his own life. He's applied these truths in several churches he has started and pastored.

I first heard Gene share the "One Another" concepts when I invited him to speak to my own congregation. And many of you are familiar with his excellent "One Another" books written to help Christians function as contributing members of the body of Christ.

The "One Another" exhortations in the New Testament, particularly in Paul's letters to various churches, are powerful and practical instructions that describe how members of Christ's body are to participate in building up the church. In this chapter, Gene will focus on a number of these one another exhortations and how they can be applied in churches everywhere. These universal ideas cross all cultural and ethnic barriers, just as they did in the first century world. I can promise you that if you obey these biblical injunctions as God intended, your church will never be the same.

EIGHT

MEASURING OUR COMMITMENT TO FELLOWSHIP AND WORSHIP

If we say that we have fellowship with Him, and walk in darkness, *we lie and do not practice the truth. But if we* walk in the light *as He is in the light, we have fellowship with one another, and the blood of Jesus Christ His Son cleanses us from all sin.*

— 1 John 1:6–7

THE VERY DAY I BEGAN WORKING on this chapter, I received a very encouraging letter from a young pastor named Michael Thuku, in Kenya, East Africa. At the time, he had started four churches in his area, walking long distances each day to minister to his people.

Michael's purpose in writing me was to thank me for a book I wrote several years ago entitled "Building Up One Another." He had read a copy when he was in Bible college—taking a lot of notes—and then secured his own copy once he got involved in ministry.

Michael was impressed with the concepts in the book, which outlines a number of "one another" injunctions issued by the apostle Paul in several of his letters. He told me he teaches these concepts every day—to his elders, to his youth groups, to his students in a Christian high school—and when he can, to his total congregation. Perhaps one of the most encouraging statements in his letter was that God had used the concepts to also build him up as a young pastor. I was deeply touched when he told me he carries my book—along with his Bible—as he travels from church to church ministering to his people.

Receiving this letter on the very day I was preparing to share these concepts was providential—and an affirmation from the Lord that what I was about to share in this chapter are very basic principles in bringing people to maturity in Jesus Christ. It confirmed to me that these directives given by the apostle Paul nearly two thousand years ago are just as relevant today. Furthermore, they are indeed supracultural. Not only do they work in a large metropolitan church in the United States or Canada or Korea or Argentina, but they also work in little village churches in East Africa—or wherever God's people gather together. They are essential concepts in building up the body of Jesus Christ.

"Joined and Knit Together" (Eph. 4:16)

Let us return once again to our "anchor passage." When Paul wrote to the Ephesians (and no doubt to the churches throughout Asia), he described very specifically how God intended for the church to grow and mature in Jesus Christ. As we have seen, Jesus Christ has appointed leaders—apostles, prophets, evangelists, pastors and teachers (Eph. 4:11)—but for a very specific purpose—"for the equipping of the saints for the work of ministry" (Eph. 4:12). God never intended for church leaders to do God's work all by themselves. Rather, Jesus Christ appointed these leaders to prepare all members of Christ's body to be involved in this dynamic process of conforming our lives to the image of Jesus Christ. In fact, only as this happens will the body of Christ mature and grow in "the knowledge of the Son of God" and become a "perfect man" that measures up to "the stature of the fullness of Christ" (Eph. 4:13).

Thus, Paul wrote:

> But, speaking the truth in love, [we] may grow up in all things into Him who is the head—Christ—from whom the whole body, joined and knit together by what *every joint supplies*, according to the effective working by which *every part does its share*, causes growth of the body for the edifying of itself in love. (Eph. 4:15–16)

How does a local church actually grow and mature in love—which Paul says is the ultimate mark of maturity? It happens when "every part does its share"—when "every joint supplies." Then, Paul states, the "whole body" will be "joined and knit together," (Eph. 4:16). The church will become what God wants it to become until she stands before her Bridegroom, Jesus Christ, "not having spot or wrinkle or any such thing, but . . . holy and without blemish" (Eph. 5:27 see also Rev. 19:6–8).

"Speaking the Truth in Love" (Eph. 4:15)

Before looking at some of the specific ways Paul exhorts all members of the church to build up one another, we must remind ourselves that once again this process must be rooted and grounded in God's revealed Truth— God's eternal Word. This is what we see in the Jerusalem model. Those who responded to Peter's message, first of all, "continued steadfastly in the apostles' doctrine" (Acts 2:42a). Their decision to follow Christ was based on the Word of God and their resolution to grow in Christ was built upon the same foundation.

Closely aligned with their vital learning experience with the Word of God was *koinonia*. These Jerusalem believers "continued steadfastly," not only in the "apostles' doctrine," but also in "fellowship" (Acts 2:42).

True Christianity, by God's own design, is to be deeply relational. John, often identified as the "apostle Jesus loved," underscored this truth when he wrote:

That which we have seen and heard we declare to you, that you also may have *fellowship with us;* and truly our fellowship is with the Father and with His Son Jesus Christ. (1 John 1:3)

However, as alluded to in chapter 6, relational experiences that are not grounded in and guided by scriptural truth can lead to all kinds of experiential deviations from God's will. Though extreme examples, the mass suicides under the leadership of Jim Jones and the tragic fire at the Davidic compound in Waco, Texas, illustrate this reality. Alongside these bizarre groups, however, are many other cults and -isms that claim to be Christian, but which have departed from a careful study of the Scriptures to follow their own relational and experiential theologies. Unfortunately, some of these communal-type systems include and justify various kinds of immorality, both heterosexual and homosexual. Sadly, it sometimes also includes the sexual abuse of children.

Having issued these warnings, however, we must proceed to underscore and illustrate that "Christianity" that is not relational and experiential is not vital *New Testament* Christianity. This truth is certainly illustrated in the church in Jerusalem and is taught throughout the New Testament letters to the churches. No concept demonstrates this more dramatically than the dozens of "one another" injunctions and exhortations.

OUR COMMITMENT TO ONE ANOTHER (ROM. 12, 15–16)

Beginning in chapter 12 of Romans, Paul, in some respects, builds his thoughts around these "one another" concepts. The first is foundational and correlates with Paul's body analogy that he used in our anchor passage in Ephesians chapter 4.

Paul used a number of metaphors to illustrate how the church should grow and function in this world. This in itself demonstrates what a wonderful creation the church really is. No single analogy can do it justice.

Paul often used the architectural metaphor. Writing to the Corinthians, he said, "You are God's building" (1 Cor. 3:9). Elaborating on this analogy in his letter to the Ephesians, he wrote that we are

> Built on the foundation of the apostles and prophets, Jesus Christ Himself being the chief cornerstone, in whom the whole building, being joined together, grows into a holy temple in the Lord, in whom you also are being built together for a habitation of God in the Spirit. (Eph. 2:20-22)

In his Corinthian letter, Paul also used an agricultural metaphor to illustrate the church. In the very same verse he identified the Corinthians as "God's building," he also wrote, "You are God's field" (1 Cor. 3:9). Paul, of course, had a great precedent for this analogy in Christ's parable of the sower and the four kinds of soil (Mark 4:1–20).

WE ARE "MEMBERS OF ONE ANOTHER" (ROM. 12:4–5)

Here, Paul used one of his favorite metaphors—an anatomical metaphor—the human body. Exclusively his own analogy in Scripture, he referred to this metaphor in verse 4:

> For as we have many members in one body, but all the members do not have the same function.

Paul elaborated on this analogy very extensively in his letter to the Corinthians (1 Cor. 12:14–26). He took great pains to spell out the various members of the human body and how they function as a unit. In his Roman letter, however, he simply summarized the concept and assumed that these Roman Christians would understand what he meant. Perhaps this difference is because the Corinthians were a very carnal and immature church characterized by divisions and disunity, whereas the Romans were much further along in their spiritual walk with Christ.

After simply stating the analogy—that "we have many members in one body, but all the members do not have the same function"—Paul went on immediately to apply the meaning of the metaphor to believers in the body of Christ:

> So we [as believers], being many, are one body in Christ, and individually members of one another. (Rom. 12:5)

This is a wonderful and marvelous truth. And it correlates significantly with Paul's statement in our anchor passage. As a church, we are "joined and held together by what every joint supplies," and when "every part does its share," the body will build itself up in love (Eph. 4:16).

This should also be one of the most encouraging truths in all of Scripture. It simply means that every Christian is important in every local church—wherever that church is located in the world. Every Christian has *something* to contribute. We are all needed for the body of Christ to function as it should.

This is indeed one of the most foundational "one another" concepts. Unless we take it seriously, we will not be following the Jerusalem model. Neither will we be responding to the numerous scriptural exhortations that spell out for us how all of this is to happen. And this naturally leads to Paul's next "one another" reference in his letter to the Romans.

"BE KINDLY AFFECTIONATE TO ONE ANOTHER WITH BROTHERLY LOVE" (ROMANS 12:10A)

Here Paul used another metaphor—the familial metaphor. Though more subtle, it is inherent in the Greek word, *philadelphia*, which is translated "brotherly love." The New Testament uses the term "brothers"—a generic word that often includes "sisters"—hundreds of times to indicate the church is a "family." We are brothers and sisters in Jesus Christ.

The family metaphor introduces us to a whole new experiential dimension for the church. The body metaphor help us understand what Paul meant when he said that "every joint supplies" and "every part does its share." The physiological aspects of this metaphor helps us to comprehend the concept of being "knit together by joints and ligaments" (Col. 2:19). The family metaphor, however, adds a dimension of reality, emotion and warmth. Whereas the body metaphor is physiological in nature, the family metaphor is psychologically oriented. Thus, Paul exhorts us to "be kindly affectionate to one another."

There is a great truth inherent in this illustration. One of the great tragedies throughout history is that sin has created imperfect family units. How quickly it happened in Adam's family when Cain became jealous of his brother Abel and took his life. From that moment forward, the world has been filled with dysfunctional family units. What is happening in our present societies is nothing new in human history. It is true, however, that in our own American culture, we have seen an escalated deterioration in family life, particularly since the beginning of the sixties. With our incredible changes in values, perpetuated by the United States Supreme Court decisions, the divorce rate has increased enormously, creating a unique set of problems for children growing up in one-parent families.

However, since the first century, God has put in place a means whereby healing can take place in the lives of people who have not experienced the warmth and love God designed for a human family. That means is the family of God—the church of Jesus Christ. When the body of Christ functions as it should, it becomes a reparenting organism. People who have never learned to love experientially in a human family can learn to receive and give love in the family of God.

If this is to happen, however, the church must function as God intended. We must "be kindly affectionate to one another with brotherly love." A dysfunctional church will never bring healing to people from dysfunctional families. It will only perpetuate their problems and cause the church to become more and more dysfunctional itself.

"In Honor Giving Preference to One Another" (Romans 12:10b)

In actuality, this "one another" injunction is an extension of the one preceding—that is, to "be kindly affectionate to one another with brotherly love." Ideally, this is the way brothers and sisters in a human family should function, but especially within the "household of God" (Eph. 2:19).

Paul elaborated on this concept in his letter to the Philippians when he said:

> Let nothing be done through selfish ambition or conceit, but in lowliness of mind let each esteem others better than himself. Let each of you look out not only for his own interests, but also for the interests of others.(Phil. 2:3–4)

Note that Paul did not say that we are forbidden to give attention to our own interests. However, as we think about ourselves and our own needs, we are to put others first. What a contrast to our human nature!

I often like to illustrate what it means to honor others above ourselves with a metaphor of my own. I think in terms of a piano accompanist—someone who makes a soloist look and sound good. An accompanist should never compete with or overshadow a soloist. Rather, a good accompanist, no matter what that person's skill, should always be in a support role.

And so it is in the family of God. Every Christian is to be an "accompanist" to every other Christian. We are to make each other "look and sound good." Imagine what would happen in local churches all around the world if all Christians took this exhortation seriously. What if every believer would have the mind of Christ and take "the form of a servant" as Jesus did (Phil. 2:5–8)? The results would be phenomenal, and like the Jerusalem church, we would be "having favor with all the people" in our communities. And I am confident the Lord would be adding people regularly to the church as they "were being saved" (Acts 2:47).

"Be Like-minded Toward One Another" (Rom. 15:5–6)

Paul's next "one another" injunction in this letter to the Romans is in the form of a prayer:

> Now may the God of patience and comfort grant you to *be like-minded toward one another*, according to Christ Jesus, that you may with one mind and one mouth glorify the God and Father of our Lord Jesus Christ. (Rom. 15:5–6)

In a sense, Paul's prayer culminates his earlier "one another" injunctions. Unity and one-mindedness result when believers truly function as one body, truly demonstrating that they are "members of one another." And when Christians are "kindly affectionate to one another with brotherly love" and are "in honor, giving preference to one another," the result will be the very thing Paul prayed for unity.

What happens when the members of our human body do not function properly? I saw this demonstrated dramatically one day after a great day of snow skiing. I came off the mountain and got on a shuttle bus to head back to the ski lodge. As I sat there, I noticed an older man getting on the bus carrying a young woman. She was a teenager and probably this man's daughter. Initially, I thought she had injured herself skiing.

But then I noticed that was not the case. She had a brain injury, probably at birth. Though she was obviously very intelligent and a very beautiful person inside, the "members of her body" would not respond properly to the signals from her brain. Even her smile was contorted and if her father had not held her in the seat, she would have fallen to the floor of the bus.

As I sat there and thought about the great day of skiing I had had and how my own body members had responded to my brain—enabling me to enjoy this wonderful sport—I reflected on this young woman's human tragedy. But then I thought of an even greater tragedy—members of the body of Christ who do not respond as they should to Jesus Christ, the head of the church.

It is no accident that Paul's prayer for unity correlates with Jesus' prayer for His disciples—and all of us who have come to know Jesus Christ because of the "apostles' doctrine" and "teachings." Following His Upper Room discourse with these men, preparing them for His death and resurrection and their future ministry, He "lifted up His eyes to heaven" and prayed that His apostles and all who would believe in Christ as a result of their preaching and teaching would be one as He was one with the Father (John 17:1,20–21).

As we will see in chapter 10, both Jesus' prayer and Paul's prayer represent two of the greatest and most meaningful evangelistic prayers in the New Testament. In fact, the believers in Jerusalem demonstrate what happens when Christians reflect this kind of unity and oneness. They were "having favor with all the people. And the Lord added to the church daily those who were being saved" (Acts 2:47). These new converts believed that God had sent Jesus Christ to be the Savior of the world (John 17:21).

"THEREFORE, RECEIVE ONE ANOTHER" (ROM. 15:7)

Paul's prayer for unity is both culminating and transitional. When he used "therefore" in Romans 15:7, he moved on to a point inherent in the previous "one another" exhortations. Body unity can only happen when we "accept" and "welcome" one another into the body of Jesus Christ.

Again, this is a powerful injunction. Unfortunately, New Testament churches experienced the same prejudicial attitudes that many churches face today in various parts of the world. Their tensions existed basically because of two major groups—Jews and Gentiles. This was a problem Paul addressed in most of his letters to first century churches. He wanted them to know that in Christ—

> There is neither Greek nor Jew, circumcised nor uncircumcised, barbarian, Scythian, slave nor free, but Christ is all and in all. (Col. 3:11; see Gal. 3:26–28; Eph. 2:11–18)

Today, various ethnic, social, and language groups have multiplied—at least in terms of those who have come to know Christ. But the same truth still stands. We are "all one in Christ Jesus." There is neither black or white, Hispanic or Asian, German or Scandinavian, American or African, Korean or Chinese, rich or poor, lower class or upper class, educated or uneducated. In Jesus Christ, we are all sinners saved by God's grace and we are all "members of one another" and we all belong to the same family. Therefore, as Paul wrote to the Galatians—"Let us not become conceited, provoking one another, envying one another" (Gal. 5:26).

It may surprise some of you that I grew up in a church community where some of the older people in the congregation actually believed that Jesus spoke German. They believed that Luther's translation of the Bible was indeed the original manuscripts given by God and that German would be the "language of heaven." Today, we smile at this mentality and ignorance. But, as strange as it may seem, there are Christians today who have a similar mentality about their own ethnic backgrounds. There is a subtle pride that makes them feel they are better than other people.

Let us never forget the words of James who spoke to this issue even more pointedly:

> My brethren, do not hold the faith of our Lord Jesus Christ, the Lord of glory, with partiality. If you really fulfill the royal law according to the Scripture, "you shall love your neighbor as yourself," you do well; but if you show partiality, you commit sin, and are convicted by the law as transgressors. (James 2:1,8–9)

In conjunction with James' exhortation to avoid prejudice in the body of Christ, Dr. Stephen Olford shared a rather challenging, but sobering story. When he came from Britain to pastor Calvary Baptist Church in New York City, he discovered that the church was racially segregated. Right there he made a commitment to the Lord that somehow the situation would have to change or he could not continue in that ministry. And in hope, he began to preach on the will of God in this matter and to cry out to God in prayer for help.

He reports that he will never forget the day when a church meeting took place where the majority of the people were opposed to integration. But he came to that meeting and delivered a message from the Word of God about maintaining the unity of the Spirit in the bond of peace. When the vote was taken, only eleven people were against integrating the church. Later, seven of those eleven said:"Pastor, we'll stand with you even though we don't see eye to eye." However, the other four were totally opposed. Within one month, every one of those four people had been taken home to heaven. Dr. Olford reports that great fear came upon the church, just as in Jerusalem when Ananias and Sapphira lied to the Holy Spirit. Destroying unity in the church is a serious offense against God (see 1 Cor. 3:16–17).

"ADMONISH ONE ANOTHER" (ROM.15:14)

The Bible is a marvelously balanced book. We see this in Paul's next "one another" statement. After exhorting these believers to "receive" and "accept one another" unconditionally, he moves to another dimension of love—one that some call "tough love." He wrote:

> Now I myself am confident concerning you, my brethren, that you also are full of goodness, filled with all knowledge, able also to *admonish one another.* (Rom. 15:14)

Personally, I find it relatively easy to accept people—no matter what their backgrounds. Though I grew up in a religious environment where prejudice was ingrained, the Lord taught me some very painful lessons that revealed how deeply prejudiced I really was. I have never forgotten that "wilderness experience" emotionally or spiritually—and I trust I never will. My struggle now lies on the "other side" of love—in "admonishing" those who are walking out of the will of God.

I believe I know why this is difficult for me. First, I am a sensitive person and I do not relish hurting people's feelings. Second, being emotionally sensitive, I do not like risking rejection. And we can be very sure this will happen when we follow Paul's injunction to "admonish one another." But when we do take that risk, it is a mark of true love.

Note, however, that Paul makes it clear that there are certain personal requirements that qualify us for this task. First, we are to be "full of goodness." This simply means we have our own life in order sufficiently to help someone else get his or her life in order.

This is what Jesus had in mind when He was delivering His Sermon on the Mount:

> And why do you look at the speck in your brother's eye, but do not consider the plank in your eye? Or how can you say to your brother, "Let me remove the speck out of your eye"; and look, a plank is in your own eye? Hypocrite! First remove the plank from your own eye, and then you will see clearly to remove the speck out of your brother's eye. (Matt. 7:3–5)

Jesus did not teach that we should ignore the "speck"—or little sins—in our fellow Christian's life. Rather, He simply taught that we should remove the larger sins from our own lives so we can help a fellow pilgrim in his walk with Jesus Christ.

Neither did Paul—or Jesus—teach that we must be perfect in our own walk with Christ in order to help someone else who is walking out of the will of God. However, they taught us that we must have reached a certain level of Christian maturity to earn the right to help someone else. This, of course, has tremendous implications for Christian parents who are trying to nurture and discipline their own children. Certainly, we do not want them to rise up and call us "hypocrites."

Second, to qualify to admonish another Christian, Paul states that we must be "filled with all knowledge." This means that we, indeed, know what God's will is regarding the issues we are confronting. Normally, even people who are "out of the will of God" in their attitudes and actions respect the Word of God—not necessarily our "opinions" regarding what we "think" God's will is! This is why it is so important to have a good knowledge of the "apostles' doctrine"—what God has revealed in the Scriptures. This is also why it is important to focus on direct biblical teachings and principles rather than on traditions or legalistic, man-made rules.

At this point, Paul's classic injunction in our anchor passage in Ephesians is vitally important. To "admonish one another" successfully, we must always be "speaking the truth in love" (Eph. 4:15). The way we approach others who are living out of the will of God often dictates acceptance or rejection of our efforts. Paul elaborated on this process in his letter to the Galatians when he gave us a similar "one another" exhortation:

> Brethren, if a man is overtaken in any trespass, you who are spiritual restore such a one in a spirit of gentleness, considering yourself lest you also be tempted. *Bear one another's burdens,* and so fulfill the law of Christ. For if anyone thinks himself to be something, when he is nothing, he deceives himself. (Gal. 6:1–3)

In this Galatian passage, Paul gave us more guidelines for admonishing others. First, he underscored the same point he made in Romans. Only "spiritual" people—those who are walking in the Spirit and reflecting the fruit of the Spirit (Gal. 5:16,22–23)—should attempt to deal with other people's sins. Christians who are "carnal"—those who are reflecting "the works of the flesh" (Gal. 5:16,19–21)—are in danger of getting trapped in the same sins.

Second, more than one "spiritual Christian" should be involved when attempting to restore a Christian who is trapped in some sin. Thus Paul wrote, "You [plural] who are spiritual" should be involved in this process.

There are many practical reasons, which are beyond the scope of this chapter, as to why this is such an important spiritual guideline. However, as a pastor, I have been involved in enough of these situations to understand why I should never attempt this kind of task alone.

It should be noted that what Paul described in Romans and Galatians is not the same process that Jesus talked about in Matthew chapter 18. In that instance, Jesus was dealing with a brother or sister who had sinned against another brother or sister personally. In Galatians, however, Paul was talking about sins that are committed against the "body" of Jesus Christ. And those who are involved in this kind of confrontation are not the "offended parties." First and foremost, Jesus Christ is the offended One. Therefore, Paul bypassed the "one-on-one" approach described by Jesus. It is important to note this difference because people who are trapped in sin—and who know the Scriptures—often use these verses out of context to defend their actions (Matt. 18:15–17).

Though this kind of confrontation is always difficult for me, it has brought some of the most rewarding results in the ministry. I remember one young man who told me with tears streaming down his cheeks, "You're the first person who has loved me enough to tell me what's wrong with me." Another man—a close friend—who had left his wife and family for another woman, many months later threw his arms around me and said, also with tears, "Thank God you didn't let go of me when I was rejecting you and all of your efforts at restoration."

I wish I could report that all results were this positive. They are not. But let us remember that even Jesus' closest disciples, at one point in time, turned their back on Him and walked away. Though the Scriptures do not guarantee results—even when we are obedient to these injunctions–the important thing is that we are obedient! And if only one person is restored, it is worth the effort (Luke 15:1–7).

"GREET ONE ANOTHER WITH A HOLY KISS" (ROM. 16:16)

This was a very important exhortation in the mind of Paul. In fact, he repeated this exhortation in three other letters (1 Cor. 16:20; 2 Cor. 13:12; 1 Thess. 5:26). Peter also emphasized the same kind of greeting (1 Peter 5:14).

Obviously, there is a cultural dimension to this exhortation. Forms of physical greeting differ from culture to culture and even the nature of a "kiss of greeting" varies.

But there is also a supernatural dimension to this greeting. Physical touch is an integral and important part of family relationships. This can even be part of the healing process in the life of an individual who has come from a dysfunctional and unloving family.

On the other hand, we must be sensitive in expressing these greetings. They must always be pure, righteous and holy. Furthermore, we must also recognize the need that some people have for "space"—particularly because of their cultural backgrounds or especially if there has been some kind of physical or sexual abuse in a person's life. For example, a woman who has been sexually abused by a father or an uncle or some other male often is extremely fearful to receive any kind of physical affection from another man—no matter how sensitive that Christian may be! In these cases, it is the part of wisdom to allow that other person to initiate the degree of physical touch with which they feel comfortable and if this problem exists in a marital relationship, it is a case for serious and in-depth counseling.

But there is another supracultural principle that goes beyond physical touch which is the emotional and spiritual sincerity with which we express our greetings to one another. How easy it is to meet someone and say, "How are you?" And how easy it is to respond, "I'm fine. How are you?" The facts are, however, that our questions and responses may be meaningless and pure protocol.

I once learned a great lesson in this regard. One evening I walked into the church and asked a young teenager how he was doing. A few moments later, one of our spiritual leaders tapped me on the shoulder and said, "Gene, I must admonish you about something." At first, I thought he was joking. But then I noticed that he was very serious. He had overheard the question that I had asked this young man. He also noticed that I moved quickly by this individual and did not hear his response. What I did not hear was that this teenager—responding to my question—was not doing very well because his brother was in a motorcycle accident that day.

Incidentally, this experience illustrates why we need others in the body of Christ to help us. I have never ceased to be grateful that this fellow pastor had the courage to confront me with this oversight and insensitivity. It gave me the opportunity to go back and apologize to the young man, which I did immediately. And I also thanked the pastor for noticing and caring enough for both the young man and myself to communicate what he had overheard.

I must point out as well that when this spiritual leader approached me, he did so with great sensitivity and love. In fact, before telling me what he had overheard, he said, "Gene, I must admonish you regarding something you just did that I often do myself." I sensed a humble spirit, as well as concern. I did not feel put down, embarrassed, humiliated, or any sense of rejection. This man was "speaking the truth in love."

To "greet one another" then involves more than physical touch. It calls for emotional and spiritual sincerity and sensitivity. It involves our concentration on what others are saying. It means caring enough to ask questions and then caring enough to listen and to become involved in that person's experience. As Paul states: "And if one member suffers, all the members suffer with it; or if one member is honored, all the members rejoice with it" (1 Cor. 12:26).[1]

OUR COMMITMENT TO WORSHIP

As you read through Luke's account of the dynamic church in Jerusalem, you will notice that these Christians' relationships with God (worship) are highly integrated and interrelated with their relationships with one another. This simply indicates that some of the most dynamic and exciting experiences we have with God result when we see God actively involved in people's lives—including our own. It should always be a worship experience in itself to learn God's Word and then to apply it to our lives. Worship involves not only engaging in prayer but also experiencing answers to prayer. Worship takes place when we remember the death of Jesus Christ as we participate in Holy Communion. Worship involves sharing our material possessions with one another and seeing others actually sacrifice to meet the needs of fellow believers. Worship involves music, lifting our voices in praise and thanksgiving to God. And one of the greatest worship experiences of all is to see other people come to know Jesus Christ as their personal Savior.

Worship, then, cannot be separated from any of these vital experiences engaged in by the believers in Jerusalem (Acts 2:42–47). However, perhaps the most significant aspect of worship involves our relationships with one another as spelled out with the "one another" concepts. In practicing these injunctions we experience love relationships with one another that provide a spiritual and emotional foundation and basis for truly experiencing what it means to have a love relationship with God the Father, God the Son, and God the Holy Spirit. Our dynamic relational experiences with those we can see enable us to relate to the eternal God whom we cannot see (1 John 4:20). This is why relational Christianity is so vital and important. Without it, God—who is Spirit and invisible—often remains a person who seems distant, untouchable, and unreachable.

Of course we should not avoid carefully structured worship. But as we do, we should keep in mind that worship should not be something that is compartmentalized and separated from all of the other experiences described by Luke in the Jerusalem church. Neither should it be traditionalized to the point that we are not flexible and free under the leadership of the Holy Spirit. And let us never forget to practice the "one another" concepts which form the basis for experiencing warm, loving and intimate fellowship with God.

FREEDOM IN FORM

Again it must be emphasized that the Bible does not dictate specific forms and patterns for applying these "one another" exhortations in a local church or in structuring for worship. However, if these functions are to take place, our approach must allow people to get to know one another and to be involved in each other's lives.

This is why the church in Jerusalem was so dynamic. Not only were they "continuing daily with one accord in the temple"—obviously involving thousands of people in one place—but they were also "breaking bread from house to house" as "they ate their food with gladness and simplicity of heart" (Acts 2:46).

In its early days, the New Testament church had no choice but to meet in homes. Very early in their history, Christians were forbidden to meet in the temple courts or in synagogues. Furthermore, they were not able to secure property to build church buildings as we do today in many places in the world.

This does not mean that God dictates that meeting in homes is required in terms of form. In fact, in some places in the world Christians are forbidden to meet this way. As illustrated in previous chapters, in Romania any political or religious group—other than family members—were forbidden to meet in a private dwelling. Christians were forced to meet in church buildings where everything that happened could be monitored by the Communist government.

In Hong Kong it is virtually impossible for the average person to own a home, instead living in small apartments located in huge skyscrapers. Millions of people are centralized in a very small section of the world. Because of limited space, they find it very difficult to utilize their own personal facilities.

The facts are, however, that to practice the "one another" injunctions, the church must be structured in such a way so as to provide an opportunity for intimacy. This is why in Korea and other places in the world, where some churches number in the hundreds of thousands, small groups do meet in homes and other locations in order to supplement their large corporate meetings. This, of course, is also a wonderful option in the places where many people can own their own houses and have sufficient space to demonstrate this kind of hospitality to other members of their Christian family.

"ONE ANOTHER"

In closing, Dr. Charles Stanley offered this perspective on who "one another" involves: "The apostle Paul said we're to bear one another's burdens. And you know, as a pastor, many times in all of these years I have served the Lord, I have helped to bear many people's burdens. I've helped carry their load, shared with them, listened to them and wept with them."

"On the other hand, in a number of occasions in my own life I desperately needed someone to help bear my burdens, to share my load, and to help lift the heaviness that I had in my heart. I'm privileged to have four very special friends with whom I have fellowshipped over the years. And each time they have seen me experience a crisis, I have been blessed to see how sensitive they've been and how they have literally borne my burden. They said things such as, 'Pastor, we know you're hurting. We're right here. We're going through this with you. We want to encourage you. Whatever load you're carrying, we're going to help you carry it.' Remember that we all need each other—pastor and people. This is what loving one another is all about! This is what Paul had in mind when he wrote to the Ephesians and told them that 'every joint should supply' and 'every part should do its work' (Eph. 4:16). When that happens, the body of Christ builds itself up in love."

MEASURING OUR WALK

1. Examine each "one another" injunction described in this chapter. What ones are your family—and your church—following well? Which ones need to be better understood so that they could be practiced?

2. Join with another person—family member, church member, fellow believer—in practicing these "one another" concepts. Pray that God will expand your participation to include your larger family, your church, and the body of Christ as a whole.

Dr. Joseph Stowell

MY FRIEND, DR. GENE GETZ, TAKES US back two thousand years to study two groups of people. First, he describes a group of believers in Jerusalem who were abundantly generous in advancing the cause of Christ. By contrast, he describes another group of believers in Corinth who, while well intended, never quite got their moneybags out.

In the foreword I wrote to Gene Getz's *A Biblical Theology of Material Possessions*. I mentioned that true generosity is not a matter of habit or head. Rather, it's a matter of our hearts. Did you know that you can tell a lot about where people's hearts are by watching them read the newspaper? If their hearts are in sports, they go right to the sports section. If their hearts are in current events, they go right to the front page. If their hearts are in politics, they go right to the editorial page. Or if life's insane, they go right to the comic page.

Jesus Christ says that He can tell a lot about where our hearts are by what we do with our money. He said, "Where your treasure is, there your heart will be also" (Matt. 6:21). If our heart is focused on advancing the kingdom of God by spreading the gospel, it will not be difficult for us to be generous. My friend, Haddon Robinson says that you can tell a lot about a Christian's spirituality by reading the ledger of their checkbooks.

In this chapter, Gene Getz outlines God's plan for being generous. Read carefully and with an open heart. If you apply these truths, you will never lack what you need—and you will experience the joy of being a generous Christian.

MEASURING OUR COMMITMENT TO GENEROSITY

See then that you *walk circumspectly*, not as fools but as wise, redeeming the time, because the days are evil. Therefore do not be unwise, but understand what the will of the Lord is.

— Ephesians 5:15–17

M Y WIFE AND I ATTENDED A SEMINAR advertised locally as an opportunity to learn how to be successful, particularly in business. Though I was a full-time seminary professor at the time and had no interest in going into business, we were intrigued to hear what the featured speaker had to say.

Interestingly, the gentleman conducting the seminar had a strong religious tone in his presentation. At least, he believed in a "higher power" or a "divine mind" and did not hesitate to point out that to be successful in any venture, we had to be in harmony with "whoever" this ultimate power and personality is. This man was a New Ager before the term was being used.

During the presentation, the speaker made a statement that I have never forgotten. He underscored very dramatically that in order to be successful in business, you must be generous—that as people are blessed financially, they must share those material blessings with others. Then, and only then, will people continue to be successful.

What made this experience so profound for me is that I was a Christian, and this man was not—nor did he claim to be. But the fact still remains that this speaker made a point that changed my attitudes and actions.

As a Christian, even though I had developed a habit of giving very regularly to my church, I saw in my heart elements of selfishness that I had not seen before. From that point forward, I determined to become more generous—not so I would become more successful, but that I might become *more grateful* as a Christian. And it took a non-Christian business entrepreneur to get that point across to a seminary professor! Listening to this man made me more aware that Christians, of all people, should be generous. A non-Christian taught me something I should have been more committed to myself.

Interestingly, one of the areas in my own life where I was convicted was not so much in the area of giving to my church—though I certainly needed to improve in that area as well. However, I changed my attitude regarding the opportunities I had for others to make an honest living. I changed my attitude about taking my car to be serviced, calling a service man to fix my plumbing or my furnace, or having to hire someone to help me complete a personal project.

One area of conviction was about tipping in restaurants. Frankly, I did not like to tip. I did it—but I was a "letter of the law" tipper. When 10 percent was customary in the United States, I never went over 10 percent—and if I was not totally satisfied with the service, I penalized the server. And when suggested "tips" went up to 15 percent, I had a really tough time making the transition. For quite a while, I left 10 percent until I was eventually shamed by my wife into raising the amount. She began checking the amount I left and adding to it before we left the table!

And then my heart changed—after I heard this non-Christian man speak on generosity. I began to see tipping as another opportunity for demonstrating generosity. I realized that if Christians eat out, they should be the most generous tippers. In fact, I now believe that if Christians cannot afford to be generous tippers, they can't afford to eat out! To be perfectly frank, we ought to be ashamed to bow our heads in prayer in a restaurant where everyone sees us—including the waiter or waitress—and then not be a generous tipper. Stated positively, being a generous tipper adds to our testimony and affirms our thankful hearts—which we demonstrate as we bow our heads for prayer. (Tipping is not a universal expectation. However, it definitely is in America.)

THE JERUSALEM MODEL

The Jerusalem church, probably more than any church in history, stands out as a model and example in terms of generosity. Not only did these believers continue "steadfastly in the apostles' doctrine and fellowship, in the breaking of bread, and in prayers," but they "were together, and had all things in common." Luke recorded that they "sold their possessions and goods, and divided them among all, as anyone had need" (Acts 2:42–45).

THE CULTURAL SETTING

As described in chapter 6, cultural dynamics and Jewish customs were involved in this unusual demonstration of mutual love and caring. God-fearing Jews and some proselytes to Judaism had come from all over the Roman Empire to celebrate the "Feast of Weeks," also called "Pentecost."

The precedent for this annual event is rooted in Jewish history and God's commandments to Israel. During each year they were to set aside a second tithe (10 percent of their annual material blessings) to make this trip to their holy city—Jerusalem—in order to worship God. Whole families ascended to Jerusalem during this period of time, increasing the population enormously. Jeremias has recorded that the normal number of residents in Jerusalem at this time numbered approximately 55,000. During this festive occasion, another 125,000 visited Jerusalem for this time of worship and celebration.[1]

As this fifty-day period came to a close, something very unexpected happened to the great majority of the people in Jerusalem. On the final day—the day of Pentecost (Acts 2:1)—the Holy Spirit came upon those gathered in an Upper Room, probably a group numbering "about a hundred and twenty" (Acts 1:15).[2]

Several months earlier, when the apostles were terribly confused and emotionally distraught with Jesus' statements that He was going to leave them (John 14:1), the Lord reassured them by telling them on a number of occasions and in several different ways that He was going to send the Holy Spirit to enable them to carry on His work once He was gone (John 14:16–17,25–26; 15:26–27; 16:7–15). And just before He ascended to the Father, He had told these eleven men not to return to their homes in Galilee, but rather they were to wait in Jerusalem until the Holy Spirit came upon them and "endued" them "with power from on high" (Luke 24:49; Acts 1:4–5).

What Jesus promised, happened! Luke recorded:

And suddenly there came a sound from heaven, as of a rushing mighty wind, and it filled the whole house where they were sitting. Then there appeared to them divided tongues, as of fire, and one sat upon each of them. And they were all filled with the Holy Spirit and began to speak with other tongues, as the Spirit gave them utterance. (Acts 2:2–4)

Evidently, the wind was heard all over Jerusalem (Acts 2:6), and a great multitude gathered to investigate what was happening. Amazingly, those who had come from a variety of countries from all over the Roman Empire, heard the apostles speaking in their own languages (Acts 2:5–11).

At this point Peter stood up and began to expound the Scriptures. And at this point "those who gladly received his word were baptized; and that day about three thousand souls were added" to their number (Acts 2:41). The church in Jerusalem was born!

AN ECONOMIC DILEMMA AND A REMARKABLE RESOLUTION

What happened next is predictable! Since this was the final day of the Feast of Pentecost, those who were visitors in Jerusalem had to make a choice. Were they going to return home or wait for the next chapter in this exciting story to unfold? They did what most of us would do—they stayed!

This, of course, created the unusual cultural dynamics described in the early chapters of the Book of Acts. Many who had saved their money for this trip had depleted their financial reserves. However, those who were residents in Jerusalem, with generous hearts, opened their homes and shared their material possessions with these people. Some even "sold their possessions and goods, and divided them among all, as anyone had need" (Acts 2:45).

Luke described this incredible demonstration of unselfishness and love in more detail in chapter 4:

> Now the multitude of those who believed were of one heart and one soul; neither did anyone say that any of the things he possessed was his own, but they had all things in common. And with great power the apostles gave witness to the resurrection of the Lord Jesus. And great grace was upon them all. Nor was there anyone among them who lacked; for all who were possessors of lands or houses sold them, and brought the proceeds of the things that were sold, and laid them at the apostles' feet; and they distributed to each as anyone had need. (Acts 4:32–35)

As you read Luke's account of this incredible outpouring of love, you cannot miss the total involvement of these Christians. Not one claimed that what they had belonged to themselves. Furthermore, all of those who owned property were involved in liquidating their assets to help their fellow believers who were in need. This, of course, is what made this church such a dynamic model.

At this point the Holy Spirit chose to record for us a beautiful personal example of generosity. Barnabas, a Grecian Jew evidently from Cyprus and a real estate developer in Jerusalem, sold a piece of land that he owned and brought the total proceeds "and laid it at the apostles' feet." The apostles were so encouraged with this man's unselfish attitude and actions that they actually changed his name from Joses to Barnabas—which means "son of encouragement" (Acts 4:36).

What was happening in Jerusalem was certainly not designed by the Holy Spirit to be a pattern for Christians of all times. God did not dictate a "communal" type society where Christians must "have all things in common." In fact, once these believers understood more fully the Great Commission—that they were not to stay in Jerusalem—but to carry the gospel back to their own towns and cities (Acts 1:8), they returned to their homes. And eventually, persecution temporarily drove even the residents of Jerusalem out of their city (Acts 8:1). When this happened, they went back to a more normal way of earning a living and caring for their own personal needs. In fact, Paul had to correct some improper attitudes regarding a biblical work ethic when he wrote to the Thessalonian Christians and issued some very strong directives:

> If anyone will not work, neither shall he eat. For we hear that there are some who walk among you in a disorderly manner, not working at all, but are busybodies. (2 Thess. 3:10b–11)

However, a supracultural principle emerges from this dynamic event and is applicable to Christians of all times and in all places in the world— no matter what our cultural and economic conditions. *Christians are to be generous people, sharing their material possessions in proportion to the way God blesses them.*

ADDITIONAL SUPRACULTURAL PRINCIPLES

Several years ago, I had the privilege of spending nearly a year with my own lay leaders in the church I pastor. Along with a special task force, we researched everything the Bible says about material possessions and how Christians should use them. Beginning with the church in Jerusalem, we worked through the whole New Testament, noting correlations with the Old Testament as well. At the conclusion of our study, we had found what we believe are 126 supracultural principles for guiding Christians in the way they use their material possessions.[3]

Obviously, we cannot look at all of these principles in this presentation. However, I would like to share eight from Paul's letters to the Corinthians. In fact, there are more supracultural principles to guide Christians in using their material possessions in the Corinthian letters than in any other of the New Testament epistles (we discovered at least twenty).

Perhaps Paul devoted so much effort to communicating these truths to the Corinthians since they were without doubt the most carnal and selfish church we know about in the New Testament world. As Jesus said, "For where your treasure is, there your heart will be also" (Matt. 6:21). And, as we have seen, the Corinthians' hearts were certainly not focused on eternal values. Though they, probably had good intentions when it came to being generous, they—as so many Christians today—failed to follow through. This is clearly evident from what Paul wrote to them in his letters.

Following are a number of divine directives given by Paul to the Corinthians—which in turn yield at least eight clear-cut supracultural principles for Christians of all times.

1. CHRISTIANS SHOULD BE REGULAR AND PROPORTIONAL GIVERS

Now concerning the collection for the saints, as I have given orders to the churches of Galatia, so you must do also: On the first day of the week let each one of you lay something aside, storing up as he may prosper, that there be no collections when I come. (1 Cor. 16:1–2)

Paul's instruction regarding giving to the Corinthians involved a special project for meeting the needs of Christians in Jerusalem. Interestingly, the church that had demonstrated more generosity than any other church in the New Testament eventually became a church in deep need financially. Because of a serious famine that hit the Roman world—and especially Judea—Christians particularly were in trouble (Acts 11:27–30). History tells us that there was plenty of food products made available to people in this area from other parts of the Roman Empire. However, since Jews who became Christians were alienated and isolated from the channels for welfare in Judaism, Christians did not have access to this system. Furthermore, those who had food products available inflated the prices, making it impossible for Christians to buy food. This explains why the Christians in Antioch evidently sent money rather than "products."

Paul encouraged the Corinthians to be involved in meeting this human need in Jerusalem. In turn, this biblical illustration gives us a principle that applies to every situation:

> *Principle 1: Christians should set aside a certain percentage of their income on just as a regular basis as they are paid, in order to be able to systematically and proportionately give to God's work.*

Ron Blue, president of Central American Missions, once said: "Most Christians are tipping, not tithing, with their income to the church. In fact, most Christians tip waitresses more than they tip God at church. At least waitresses get 15 percent."

2. CHRISTIANS SHOULD BE A MODEL TO OTHERS

Moreover, brethren, we make known to you the grace of God bestowed on the churches of Macedonia: that in great trial of affliction the abundance of their joy and their deep poverty abounded in the riches of their liberality. (2 Cor. 8:1–2)

Here Paul used the Macedonian Christians—probably the Philippians, the Bereans and the Thessalonians—as models. Rather than giving out of a comfortable lifestyle, these Christians gave out of rock-bottom poverty. Paul taught us here that as a local church:

> *Principle 2: We need to be a real-life example of modeling generosity. In view of the fact that the Macedonians gave out of poverty, should we not be a model in giving out of plenty?*

3. CHRISTIANS SHOULD BE ACCOUNTABLE

So we urged Titus, that as he had begun, so he would also complete this grace in you as well. (2 Cor. 8:6)

The apostle Paul held the Corinthians accountable for their promise to contribute to this special project.

First, he sent Titus to help them complete the project (2 Cor. 8:6). Second, he wrote the Corinthians a personal letter, encouraging them to "finish the work" (2 Cor. 8:10–11). Third, he sent a group of "brothers" ahead of time to make sure they had collected the money before he himself had arrived in Corinth (2 Cor. 9:3). Fourth, he alerted the Corinthians regarding his personal plans to arrive with some Macedonian Christians so that they would be prepared and not be embarrassed (2 Cor. 9:4).

The principle is clear:

> **Principle 3:** *Christians need to make themselves accountable regarding the way in which they use—or do not use—their finances to support God's work.*

What Paul did with the Corinthians certainly demonstrates how easily we can forget what we may want to do, especially when our own "desires" overshadow the "needs" of others.

4. CHRISTIANS SHOULD BE RESPONSIVE IMMEDIATELY

When Paul wrote to the Corinthians, they had already failed to do what he had asked them to do. They had not been systematic and regular in their giving. Therefore, Paul encouraged them to begin immediately with what they had. Thus, he wrote:

For if there is first a willing mind, it is accepted according to what one has, and not according to what he does not have. (2 Cor. 8:12)

Again, the principle is clear.

> **Principle 4:** *God accepts and honors believer's gifts once they begin to give regularly and systematically, even though they may not give proportionately as much as they will eventually once they have their economic lives in order.*

This means that we should begin to give regularly—and immediately. But you say: "But I can't give 10 percent." God understands that. But how much can you give—1 percent? 2 percent? 3 percent? Don't wait until you can tithe 10 percent before you give regularly. Begin today! And see what God will do to enable you to give even more.

5. Christians Should Be "Faith Promise" Givers

The Corinthians had made a "faith promise" based on projected future earnings. Thus, Paul wrote:

> Therefore I thought it necessary to exhort the brethren to go to you ahead of time, and prepare your bountiful gift beforehand, *which you had previously promised.* (2 Cor. 9:5)

This faith promise was not presuming on God's grace. Most of us today use this practical guideline regularly in terms of making purchases, planning business ventures, and working out our budgets to cover many areas of our personal and vocational lives.

Paul's teaching here is:

Principle 5: He wants us to trust God for future income and for the proportion that we can give to God's work.

Obviously, He is not going to send us a bill if we do not make it—as the bank would where you have your mortgage on your house or your car or on other things. The fact is that when we trust God to be able to give specific amounts of money, more often than not, He makes it possible—even beyond what we have imagined! What a thrill that is!

6. Christians Should Be Joyful, Willing Givers By Planning Ahead

> Therefore I thought it necessary to exhort the brethren to go to you ahead of time, and prepare your bountiful gift beforehand, which you had previously promised, that it may be ready as a matter of generosity and not as a grudging obligation. (2 Cor. 9:5)

Paul teaches:

Principle 6: When money is available because we have planned our giving, it becomes a joyful experience to share that money.

Conversely, when we do not plan our giving, many of us do not have the money to give. Consequently, if we give under these conditions, we respond grudgingly.

One of the lay leaders in our church who is in the banking business has worked with many Christians who have requested loans. As usual, he asks them for their personal budgets. Invariably very few Christians who presented their budgets had God in their financial plan. They had everything else—but not the Lord's work.

But we are commanded to honor God with our firstfruits (Prov. 3:9). He should be on the top line of our budgets. Everything else should be secondary.

7. CHRISTIANS SHOULD BE GENEROUS IN THEIR GIVING

Paul reminded the Corinthians that "God loves a cheerful giver." More specifically, he wrote:

> But this I say: He who sows sparingly will also reap sparingly, and he who sows bountifully will also reap bountifully. (2 Cor. 9:6)

Earlier, Paul had exhorted the Corinthians to be regular and systematic givers. But that does not necessarily mean that Christians who do give regularly are being generous.

Principle 7: We only become generous when we are proportional in our giving.

My wife and I believe in tithing—giving a minimum of 10 percent to our church. However, we do not believe that is always proportional giving on our part. As God blesses us, we go beyond 10 percent.

One member of our body told me just recently that he and his wife have a goal—and that is to increase their giving beyond ten percent by five percent a year—as God makes it possible. Their hope is that by the year 2000, they will be giving at least 50 percent of their income to the Lord's work. That, my friends, is proportional giving—and generosity. And what an encouragement it was for me to hear this person share this goal. May his tribe increase!

8. CHRISTIANS SHOULD BE TRUSTING GIVERS

Paul reminded the Corinthians that if they were faithful in their giving, God would meet their needs. Thus he wrote:

And God is able to make all grace abound toward you, that you, always having all sufficiency in all things, have an abundance for every good work. (2 Cor. 9:8)

Later, he also observed: "While you are enriched in everything for all liberality" (2 Cor. 9:11a).

Here Paul did not teach prosperity theology. He did not say that the more they gave, the more they would get. Rather, he was teaching that God would take care of them if they were faithful. Again, the principle is clear:

Principle 8: God will meet your needs when you put Him first. He will not necessarily give you all you want, but He will take care of you.

Furthermore, when Paul said we will be made "rich in every way," he did not use the word "rich" to refer to material possessions. Rather, he referred to being rich in grace. The Macedonian believers illustrated that, for earlier Paul made it clear it was the grace that God had given the Macedonian churches that enabled them to give "out of a great trial" and "deep poverty." What they gave "abounded in the *riches of their liberality.*"

A DYNAMIC CHURCH MODEL

The principle of "local church modeling" is also clear in Scripture and deserves special attention. Many of us in affluent cultures have no concept of sacrificial giving. And yet groups of Christians in third world countries are "Macedonian" in nature. They are actually giving out of poverty, while most of us give out of plenty. We need to know about these believers—since it will help activate many of us to greater commitment.

I was deeply impressed with a story of a small struggling church in northern Chile. Most of the believers were very poor with large families. It was not uncommon for parents to send a child to the store to buy one egg and two potatoes. Initially, the monthly offerings in the church totaled no more than six dollars.

A missionary involved in planting this church was concerned about the financial condition of this small body of Christians. How could he help them become self-supporting? He began to pray about the matter.

About six weeks later, the missionary stopped to visit a middle-aged couple who had recently become Christians. They had begun reading the Bible on their own and had discovered the concept of tithing. They began to ask questions. It did not occur to the missionary initially that this was an answer to his prayers. In fact, he tried to dodge the question. The man was a carpenter and had been without work for months. He and his wife had somehow managed to care for themselves and their twenty-five Rhode Island Red hens on the income from the eggs laid each day. He was certain it would be a waste of time to talk to them about tithing.

But this couple would not be denied. So the missionary showed them the classic passages regarding regular and systematic giving in 1 Corinthians 16 and 2 Corinthians 8–9. The rest of the story is remarkable, one that every American church needs to know about. Here is how the missionary described it:

> The following Sunday at the end of the meeting, Manuel handed me an envelope. When he saw the puzzled look on my face, he said with a note of pride, "That's our tithe!"
>
> I could scarcely believe it and stood for a long moment with the envelope in my hand. When he had gone, I opened the flap and saw two or three small bills equaling about 19 cents.
>
> The next Sunday afternoon I was passing their house on my bicycle when they waved me down. They had some exciting news. The Tuesday morning after they had given their tithe, there wasn't a crumb of bread in the house for breakfast, nor money to buy more.
>
> Their first impulse was to take the few pesos that had accumulated in the tithe box. But on second thought, Manuel said, "No, we won't. That's God's money. We will go without breakfast this morning."
>
> There wasn't anything to do but attend to the chickens. Much to their amazement, several of the hens had already laid eggs—at 6:30 in the morning! Never before had they laid before noon.
>
> They gathered up the eggs, and Manuel hurried to the corner store. Eggs brought a good price, so he came back with enough bread for the entire day.

That same afternoon, a little old man with a pushcart knocked on their door, asking if they might have any fertilizer to sell. They hadn't cleaned out the chicken house for some time, so they were able to gather twenty sackfuls.

That, too, brought a good price. They bought feed for the hens, staple groceries for themselves—and had money left over.

They decided the wife should buy a pair of shoes with the extra money. The next afternoon, she got on a bus and rode twelve kilometers around the bay to a bigger town.

As soon as she got off the bus, she bumped into a nephew she had not seen for five years. They greeted each other affectionately, and he asked what she might be doing in his town. When she explained, he said, "Well, I've got a shoe store right behind you. Come on in and see what you can find."

She soon found just what she needed, at the exact price she dared spend. The nephew wrapped up the package, and she handed him the money. "Oh no, Aunt, I can't take your money. These shoes are a gift from me."

"No, no, Nephew! That wouldn't be right. Please take the money."

When the argument ended, she found herself out in the street with both the shoes and the money.

The following week, Manuel got a job on a project that would last for two years. The workmen were paid every fifteen days. And sure enough, after each payday, this couple arrived at church with their tithe, which now amounted to more than the offering of the rest of the congregation.

Word got around the church, and others began to experiment in giving. I had been paying the rent on the old building, along with the light and water bills, but soon there was money in the treasury to cover all three.

The congregation continued to grow, and so did the income. Each month our books showed more surplus in the treasury. I knew that one of the mission's national pastors working among the Indians was not receiving the support he needed and deserved, so I suggested that we designate some money for him. The congregation agreed, and we sent him the equivalent of $20 each month.

Before long, the church was ready to have its own pastor, and an invitation went to that same man. When he arrived, my wife and I were free to move to a new location and start another church.

The next two years brought continued good news. As the congregation continued to grow, they bought the old building and lots I had rented for them. They began remodeling, and soon they had an attractive, modern structure with Sunday school rooms and an auditorium seating two hundred.

On our last visit, they had just completed a house for the pastor, solidly built of cement blocks, with a living room, kitchen, bath, and four bedrooms, and they had started a branch church in a housing area a mile away.

We had offered up a little bit of prayer and 19 cents, and God did the rest.[4]

Giving to the church has far deeper meaning than just carrying out His work in this world. As someone once said: "God doesn't want us to give because He needs the money. He wants us to give so He can change our lives."

MEASURING OUR WALK

1. Which of the following principles do you need to apply more diligently in your life?

   • Being a regular and proportional giver

   • Being a model to others

   • Being accountable in my giving

   • Being responsive immediately in my giving

   • Being a "faith promise" giver

   • Being a joyful willing giver by planning ahead

   • Being truly generous in my giving

   • Being a trusting giver

2. What kind of accountability system do you need to help you to be faithful in sharing your material possessions?

3. To what extent are you able to step out in faith and start giving regularly—believing that God will take care of you and meet your needs?

CHRIST'S LETTER TO THE CHURCH IN LAODICEA

A Contemporary Paraphrase of Rev. 3:14–22

Dear Brothers and Sisters:

I wish I could write to you the same words I wrote to your brothers and sisters in Philadelphia. But I can't! Yes, I know you're busy doing a lot of things, giving the impression you care for the poor. But I've seen your tax returns! I know how much money you made last year, and I also know how much you have given to carry on my work. Sadly, your walk doesn't match your talk!

I must be blunt with you! Hypocrisy and lukewarmness nauseate me. You claim to be one thing and you're something else. You claim to be rich in good deeds, but you're wretched, pitiful, poor, blind, and naked!

I know these straightforward words will make many of you angry. But I must only be true to who I am! Hopefully my tough love will awaken you. It is not too late to change. You can still lay up treasures in heaven. You can clothe yourself with righteousness. You can open your eyes and see clearly. And if you do, I'm here—standing at the door. Simply open it and I'll walk in and we can once again have intimate fellowship with one another. I'm waiting!

The One who is faithful and true,

Jesus Christ

Dr. Luis Palau

Before Jesus ascended to heaven, He left His followers with the Great Commission—to "make disciples of all the nations, baptizing them in the name of the Father and of the Son and of the Holy Spirit, teaching them to observe all things" that Jesus had commanded them (Matt. 28:19–20). You might be saying, "I'm not an apostle; I'm not an evangelist; I'm not a pastor; I'm not a preacher; I'm not a missionary. What part can I have in the Great Commission? What can I do?"

As you read this chapter written by my great friend Dr. Gene Getz, you will see there are two ways we are all involved in carrying out the Great Commission. Just before Jesus went to the cross, He said, "A new commandment I give to you, that you love one another; as I have loved you, that you also love one another. By this all will know that you are My disciples, if you have love for one another" (John 13:34–35).

Later Jesus prayed for His followers, "I do not pray for these alone, but also for those who will believe in Me through their word; that they all may be one, as You, Father, are in Me, and I in You; that they also may be one in Us, that the world may believe that You sent Me" (John 17:20–21).

In these verses, Jesus points to the two great marks the world is looking for—love and unity. These qualities are foundational to verbal communication of the Gospel of Jesus Christ and are God's plan for your marriage, for you family, and for your local church. God wants us, first and foremost, to live out the Christian life so that when we do speak out, what we say has credibility.

Before Jesus told His followers to go and make disciples, He wanted the world to know what disciples looked like when they love one another as He has loved them. And, of course, this kind of love produces unity of heart and mind.

This is what this chapter is all about. You may discover a whole new perspective on God's great missionary and evangelistic plan—and how you are a very important part of that plan.

TEN

MEASURING OUR COMMITMENT TO REACHING OTHERS

Walk in wisdom toward those who are outside, redeeming the time. Let your speech always be with grace, seasoned with salt, that you may know how you ought to answer each one.

— Colossians 4:5–6

O n one occasion I had an opportunity to minister to a group of missionaries in Quito, Ecuador. They had gathered for their annual conference for spiritual refreshment and encouragement.

Prior to the beginning of the conference, I spoke with one of the veteran couples that had ministered in that area of the world for many years, particularly to a large Ecuadoran Indian tribe. Without knowing the subject I was going to speak on, they shared with me how that at a particular point in time in their ministry, they experienced an unusual outpouring of the Holy Spirit when literally thousands of these Indians responded to the gospel and put their faith in Jesus Christ for salvation.

I was naturally intrigued with their encouraging story and I asked them if there was any particular thing they could point to that may have precipitated this unusual spiritual response. They both thought about that question for a moment—and then the missionary wife responded by saying, "Yes! There was something very significant that happened! And once that happened," she continued, "it was then that we saw this unusual response to the Gospel message."

Unknown to this couple, they shared an experience that was directly related to one of the messages I had planned for the whole group of missionaries gathered at this annual conference.

THE UPPER ROOM EXPERIENCE

My text for that message that day came from Jesus' exhortations to His disciples in the Upper Room prior to His crucifixion—

A new commandment I give to you, that you love one another; as I have loved you, that you also love one another. By this all will know that you are My disciples, if you have love for one another. (John 13:34–35)

Furthermore, the illustration I had planned to use was the dynamic demonstration of this kind of love by the church in Jerusalem.

CHRIST'S NEW COMMANDMENT

When Jesus told these eleven men (Judas had already left the room to carry out his evil deed) about this new commandment—to "love one another"—they, of course, were well aware of the "old commandment," or more accurately, the "old commandments" (plural). Jesus clearly contrasted the "new commandment" with the law of Moses as embodied in the Ten Commandments given directly by God at Mount Sinai.

On earlier occasions, Jesus had already summarized the law by referring to "love." For example, one day when Jesus was teaching in Jerusalem, a religious leader—a scribe—approached Him and asked, "Which was the most important commandment in the law?" Jesus responded:

The first of all the commandments is: "Hear, O Israel, the LORD our God, the LORD is one. And you shall love the LORD your God with all your heart, with all your soul, with all your mind, and with all your strength." This is the first commandment. And the second, like it, is this: "You shall love your neighbor as yourself." There is no other commandment greater than these. (Mark 12:29–31)

As Jesus prepared His disciples that day in the Upper Room for His death and resurrection, He also prepared them for their mission in the world. All along, Jesus had emphasized the need for these men to put God first in their lives. This was the premise of the prayer He taught these men when He said:

Our Father in heaven, hallowed be Your name. Your kingdom come, Your will be done On earth as it is in heaven. (Matt. 6:9–10)

Later, in the same sermon, Jesus added:

But seek first the kingdom of God and His righteousness, and all these things shall be added to you. (Matt 6:33)

However, in the Upper Room, Jesus focused on the horizontal, human, and relational dimension of love—to "love one another." Jesus said what Paul later explained in his letter to the Romans—that is, all of the commandments given at Mount Sinai that deal with human relationships are summarized with one commandment—the commandment to love others:

Owe no one anything except to love one another, for he who loves another has fulfilled the law. For the commandments "You shall not commit adultery," "You shall not murder," "You shall not steal," "You shall not bear false witness," "You shall not covet" and if there is any other commandment, are all summed up in this saying, namely, "You shall love your neighbor as yourself." Love does no harm to a neighbor; therefore love is a fulfillment of the law. (Rom. 13:8–10)

CHRIST'S UNUSUAL EXAMPLE

When Jesus gave His disciples this "new commandment" to "love one another," He did not ask them to do something He was not willing to do Himself. In fact, John began this chapter with the words, "Jesus knew that His hour had come that He should depart from this world to the Father." We then read that He, "having loved His own who were in the world, He loved them to the end" (John 13:1).

The "end" was Christ's willingness to die on the cross for the apostles' sins and for the sins of the whole world (John 3:16). However, these men in no way were prepared at this moment in their lives to understand that Christ was to die for them. Though He had told them it was going to happen, they could not understand it, believe it, or accept it. Therefore, Jesus prepared them step by step to understand what real love is all about.

Jesus Became the Servant. Jesus illustrated this love by washing their feet. When they arrived in that Upper Room, the meal was prepared. Everything was in place. In fact, there was a basin of water and a towel available. However, one important person was missing. There was no servant to wash their feet when they arrived.

To wash feet prior to a meal was very customary in these days. After all, they had been walking through the dirty, dusty, and contaminated streets of Jerusalem—either barefoot or with sandals.

Significantly, when they arrived in the room—with the servant missing—not one of these men volunteered to be the servant. They knew what was customary—and necessary. They were simply unwilling to serve one another.

I believe that Jesus purposely waited to give one of them an opportunity to become "the servant" before He made His move. He "rose from supper and laid aside His garments, took a towel and girded Himself." He next "poured water into a basin and began to wash the disciples' feet, and to wipe them with the towel with which He was girded" (John 13:4–5).

*Peter's Embarrasment.*When Simon Peter's turn came, Peter resisted Jesus. The reason, I believe, is that Peter was ashamed—which may explain his extreme reactions (13:8–9). He no doubt sensed Jesus' reason for his actions, since he—knowing he should—had not volunteered to be the servant. To his credit, he at least revealed his own embarrasment by initially not allowing Christ to wash his feet.

A Powerful Lesson. When Jesus completed this act of love, He made His point. He began with a question:

> Do you know what I have done to you? You call me Teacher and Lord, and you say well, for so I am. If I then, your Lord and Teacher, have washed your feet, you also ought to wash one another's feet. For I have given you an example, that you should do as I have done to you. (John 13:12b–15)

In many respects this was a shocking experience for the disciples. It threatened them, especially in view of their prideful arguments among themselves as to who was to be the greatest. It hit at the very heart of their self-centeredness, their desire to dominate and control one another. As Dr. Merrill Tenney comments, "They were ready to fight for a throne, but not for a towel!"[1]

CHRIST'S ULTIMATE PURPOSE

Jesus had a far greater purpose in washing the disciples' feet than simply teaching them to serve one another. "By this," He said, "all will know that you are My disciples, if you have love for one another" (John 13:35).

There were many disciples in Jesus' day—disciples of Moses, disciples of the Pharisees, and, of course, those who still called themselves disciples of John the Baptist. At this point in time, a disciple was a learner, a follower of some particular teacher or leader. Jesus wanted everyone to know that these men were His disciples, and the way this would be known would be by their "love for one another." Later, these same disciples were called Christians because they were followers of Christ (Acts 11:26). They exemplified His life.

THE VINEYARD EXPERIENCE

Eventually the disciples left the Upper Room and made their way to the outskirts of the city of Jerusalem (John 14:31). While they were walking along, Jesus again underscored the fact that He wanted them to make Him known to others. As they walked by a vineyard He said, "By this My Father is glorified, that you bear much fruit; so you will be My disciples" (John 15:8).

During the Passover meal, Jesus had used the foot washing incident to help the disciples understand the meaning of His love and how they should demonstrate that love to one another. This time Jesus used the story of the vine and the branches. He used this natural opportunity to make a spiritual point.

No doubt referring to an actual vineyard on the edge of Jerusalem, Jesus must have pointed to the freshly pruned branches and said as He passed by:

> I am the true vine, and My Father is the vinedresser. Every branch in Me that does not bear fruit He takes away; and every branch that bears fruit He prunes, that it may bear more fruit. (John 15:1–2)

Judas, though he had appeared to be a fruit bearing branch, had already left the group and was making final plans to betray Christ. His tragic destiny lay just ahead, but the eleven men who remained belonged to Christ.

In this illustration, Christ made it very clear that the vinedresser or gardener was His Father (John 15:1). He also made it very clear that He was the true vine. Obviously the freshly pruned branches represented the eleven disciples who had not forsaken Him (John 15:2–3). However, Christ did not initially and directly define the word *fruit* as He did the other aspects and elements in this allegory.

What did Christ actually mean? When we compare the statement Jesus made in the Upper Room with the statement He made as He was passing by the vineyard, the similarity is obvious:

- "By this all will know that you are My disciples, if you have love for one another" (John 13:35).

- "By this My Father is glorified, that you bear much fruit; so you will be My disciples" (John 15:8).

Since both of these statements were made by Christ as He was preparing His disciples for His death and resurrection, it is logical to conclude that the fruit referred to in John 15 also refers to their love for one another. This is verified as you proceed in the passage and look at the very next statements that Jesus made:

> As the Father loved Me, I also have loved you; abide in My love. If you keep My commandments, you will abide in My love, just as I have kept My Father's commandments and abide in His love . . . This is My commandment, that you love one another as I have loved you. Greater love has no one than this, than to lay down one's life for his friends . . . These things I command you, that you love one another (John 15:9–10,12–13,17).

A DEEPER DIMENSION OF LOVE

Frequently, when we read in Scripture that we are to "love one another," we think of ways in which we can demonstrate kindness, patience, unselfishness, etc., as defined in 1 Corinthians chapter 13. However, even in this classic love chapter, love has a deeper dimension. It includes the way we treat each other at a moral and ethical level. In this sense, it involves righteousness, holiness, and purity in our relationships with one another.

Paul developed this dimension of love in his letter to the Philippian Christians, particularly in his prayer for them.

> And this I pray, that your love may abound still more and more in knowledge and all discernment, that you may approve the things that are excellent, that you may be sincere and without offense till the day of Christ, being filled with the *fruits of righteousness* which are by Jesus Christ, to the glory and praise of God. (Phil. 1:9–11)

Paul's words to the Ephesians also emphasized this dimension of love. He wrote:

> For you were once darkness, but now you are light in the Lord. Walk as children of light (for the *fruit of the Spirit* is in all goodness, righteousness, and truth) (Eph. 5:8–9)

Jesus' Prayer For Unity

The next major event in this unique sequence of events involves Jesus' prayer as He and His eleven disciples were heading toward the Kedron Valley. Jesus "lifted up His eyes to heaven" and prayed:

> Father, the hour has come. Glorify Your Son, that Your Son also may glorify You, as You have given Him authority over all flesh, that He should give eternal life to as many as You have given Him. And this is eternal life, that they may know You, the only true God, and Jesus Christ whom You have sent. (John 17:1–3)

Later in Jesus' prayer, He specified very clearly His divine plan for convincing people that He had come from God. Note also that He not only prayed for His disciples—but for us as well, Christians all over the world who have come to know Christ down through the centuries. Thus, Christ prayed:

> I do not pray for these alone [His disciples], but also for those who will believe in Me through their word [all Christians]; that they all may be one, as You, Father, are in Me, and I in You; that they also may be one in Us, *that the world may believe that You sent Me.* And the glory which You gave Me I have given them, that they may be one just as We are one: I in them, and You in Me; that they may be made perfect in one, *and that the world may know that You have sent Me,* and have loved them as You have loved Me. (John 17:20–23)

Jesus' statement in the Upper Room, plus His comments as He referred to the vine and the branches, and then His words in His prayer—all of these statements combine together to form one of the greatest missionary and evangelistic statements of all time. It is clear from these passages that before Jesus told these men to go and make disciples (Matt. 28:19), He wanted the world to know what dedicated disciples of Jesus Christ really are like. In essence, they are to reflect this commitment to Christ through their love for one another and the unity and oneness this love produces.

The Jerusalem Model

This is why the Jerusalem model is such a powerful example. We see fleshed out in this church what Jesus was taught in this section of Scripture. As the unsaved people in Jerusalem observed these believers continuing "steadfastly in the apostles' doctrine and fellowship, in the breaking of bread, and in prayers;" as unbelievers saw those following Christ selling "their possessions and goods" and sharing the proceeds with all those in need; as they saw the disciples "continuing daily with one accord in the temple, and breaking bread from house to house," eating "their food with gladness and simplicity of heart, praising God;" as they observed this incredible display of love and unity—the very thing Jesus prayed for—these believers had "favor with all the people." The result was that "the Lord added to the church daily those who were being saved" (Acts 2:42–47).

There is no question that the dynamic love and oneness that was demonstrated among the Jerusalem Christians became the bridge to the unsaved world. It provided a basis for proving that Jesus Christ was indeed who He said He was—God in the flesh who had come with one basic purpose in mind, to seek and save those who are lost along with the apostles, these Christians carried out Jesus' new commandment given in the Upper Room. They were "bearing fruit" in all of their relationships, thus demonstrating their abiding relationship with Jesus Christ. Furthermore, what we see in Jerusalem is a dramatic answer to Jesus' prayer in John chapter 17. Those who were added to the church daily truly believed that Jesus Christ was the Messiah, the Son of God.

GOD'S PLAN IN PERSPECTIVE

To understand more fully God's unique evangelistic and mission strategy for building a bridge to the world through the local church, let's look at a series of questions and answers, particularly as they relate to why John wrote his Gospel in the first place.

QUESTION 1: WHY DID JESUS CHRIST COME INTO THIS WORLD?

Jesus answered that question clearly in His discourse regarding His being the good Shepherd.

> I have come that they may have life, and that they may have it more abundantly. I am the good shepherd. The good shepherd gives His life for the sheep. (John 10:10–11)

In His discourse on the bread of life, He said:

> I am the living bread which came down from heaven. If anyone eats of this bread, he will live forever; and the bread that I shall give is My flesh, which I shall give for the life of the world. (John 6:51)

Speaking to Martha, after her brother Lazarus had died, Jesus said:

I am the resurrection and the life. He who believes in Me, though he may die, he shall live. And whoever lives and believes in Me shall never die. Do you believe this? (John 11:24b–26)

Speaking to the doubters in Jerusalem, He said:

I have come as a light into the world, that whoever believes in Me should not abide in darkness. (John 12:46)

The answer to our first question is very clear. Jesus Christ came into this world for one purpose—to provide eternal life for all who believe that He came from God and died for the sins of the world and rose again so that we might live also.

QUESTION 2: WHY WAS JESUS CHRIST ABLE TO BE OUR SAVIOR FROM SIN?

To understand Christ's prayer in John chapter 17, we must understand His relationship to God. As He spoke to the Jewish leaders of His day, He left no questions in their minds regarding who He claimed to be:

"Your father Abraham rejoiced to see My day, and he saw it and was glad." Then the Jews said to Him, "You are not yet fifty years old, and have You seen Abraham?" Jesus said to them, "Most assuredly, I say to you, before Abraham was, I AM." (John 8:56–58)

At this point, the Pharisees knew exactly who Jesus was claiming to be. When Jesus claimed to be the "I AM," their minds would go immediately to the time when Moses was frightened and fearful to return to Egypt. God reassured him and told him to tell Pharaoh that "I AM" had sent him (Ex. 3:14). The Pharisees knew that Jesus Christ had claimed to be without beginning and without end; in essence, He was claiming to be God.

Later, Christ made His message to the Jews even clearer. When they asked Him to tell them plainly who He was, He said, "I and My Father are one" (John 10:30).

QUESTION 3: HOW DID CHRIST VERIFY HE WAS INDEED ONE WITH HIS FATHER?

Christ did not rely on words alone to convince people that He was the Son of God and the Savior of the world. He demonstrated His deity and verified His words with miraculous signs. In fact, one of the major purposes John had in mind in writing his Gospel was to demonstrate Christ's deity by selecting and recording some very unique miracles. John states his purpose toward the end of his treatise:

> And truly Jesus did many other signs in the presence of His disciples, which are not written in this book; but these are written that you may believe that Jesus is the Christ, the Son of God, and that believing you may have life in His name. (John 20:30–31)

John recorded and described seven miracles that were uniquely designed to cause people to believe that Jesus Christ was God in the flesh.

- Jesus changed water into wine at a wedding in Cana (John 2:1–11).

- Jesus healed a royal official's son while the boy was in one town and Jesus was in another (John 4:43–54).

- Jesus caused a man to walk who had been crippled for thirty eight years (John 5:1–14).

- Jesus fed over five thousand people with "five barley loaves and two small fish" (John 6:1–14).

- Jesus walked on the water in the midst of a boiling storm on the Sea of Galilee (John 6:16–21).

- Jesus healed a man who had been blind from his birth (John 9:1–38).

- Jesus brought Lazarus back from the dead after he had been in the tomb for four days (John 11:1–44).

Merrill Tenney points out that with each miracle, John was demonstrating a unique aspect of Christ's deity. [2]

- When Jesus changed the water into wine, it was the best wine, demonstrating that He was the master of *quality*.

- When Jesus healed the nobleman's son, while the boy was more than twenty miles away, He showed He was the master of *distance* or *space*.

- When Jesus instantaneously healed the impotent man who had been crippled for thirty-eight years, He demonstrated that He was the master of *time*.

- When Jesus miraculously fed the five thousand (besides women and children), He demonstrated He was the master of *quantity*.

- When Jesus walked on the water, He demonstrated He was the master of *natural law.*

- When Jesus healed the man who had been born blind, He demonstrated He was the master over *misfortune.*

- When Jesus raised Lazarus from the dead, He demonstrated He was master over *death.*

It is obvious why John selected these seven miracles. Each one points dramatically to the fact that Jesus Christ is who He claimed to be—God in the flesh. This is why John began his Gospel by coming right to the point:

> In the beginning was the Word, and the Word was with God, and the *Word was God.* He was in the beginning with God. All things were made through Him, and without Him nothing was made that was made. . . . And the Word became flesh and dwelt among us, and we beheld His glory, the glory as of the only begotten of the Father, full of grace and truth. (John 1:1–3,14)

QUESTION 4: WHAT IS GOD'S PLAN TODAY FOR DEMONSTRATING THAT JESUS CHRIST WAS GOD IN THE FLESH?

As we have observed, Jesus claimed to be God and demonstrated that fact with a variety of signs and miracles. But now, in His high priestly prayer, He asked for a new kind of sign to demonstrate to the world that He was from God—the miracle of oneness and unity among His followers. He would no longer be visibly present to demonstrate His deity, as He had for three and one half years. But He left behind a small group of men, who through their love and unity would demonstrate their relationship to Jesus Christ. Throughout the centuries, God's plan was that Christians everywhere emulate Christ—and His plan for His disciples.

Dr. Francis Schaeffer has called this unity "the final apologetic." [3]

No amount of intellectual argumentation to prove the deity of Christ will ever be able to replace the reality of Christianity flowing through Christians who are in a proper relationship with one another. Interestingly, Christians are to judge whether or not people are true Christians by what they believe—their doctrine (1 John 2:20–23). Anyone who denied that Jesus was the Christ and from God could not be classified as a true believer. But the world is to judge Christianity by the way Christians live—their love and their fruit—all of which reflects itself in unity and oneness. In this dynamic context, the Holy Spirit releases His miraculous power to convince unbelievers that Christ is one with God, and the Savior of the world.

QUESTION 5: WHAT HAS BEEN SATAN'S STRATEGIC PLAN FROM THE FIRST CENTURY UNTIL THE PRESENT TIME?

Satan has had—and continues to have—a two-pronged attack. On the one hand, he attempts to get people to simulate love and unity who deny the deity of Christ. On the other hand, he attempts to destroy love and unity in the churches that truly believe that Jesus Christ came from God.

Satan's Tactic To Simulate Love And Unity. The reality of this first tactic lodged deep in my heart one day when I talked to a missionary to the Mormons. He told of a young man who had graduated from a prominent evangelical Bible school with plans to go to the mission field under the auspices of a well-known mission. However, after graduating, and before he went to the mission field, he decided to visit a Mormon community. He wanted to see how they operated—how they did their work.

Surprisingly, after being exposed to Mormonism, this young man who believed that Jesus Christ was God—decided to become a Mormon and to join a religious community that openly denies that Jesus Christ came in the flesh and was one with God. When asked why he converted to Mormonism, his reply was quick and to the point. He felt he had seen and sensed more love and unity in the Mormon church than he had ever seen in an evangelical church that taught that Jesus Christ was God and that the only way to heaven was to accept Jesus Christ as personal Savior.

In another case, one young woman was attracted to Sung Myung Moon's Unification church. She, too, felt love, acceptance, and a sense of oneness of purpose among these people—something she evidently did not sense in her home or in the church she had attended from childhood. When she was in the movement, no amount of "sound doctrine" could convince her that these people were in violation of Scripture. Having her emotional needs met was far more important to her than intellectual arguments regarding the deity of Christ.

Both of these stories illustrate the power that Satan has in blinding people to the most basic truth in all of Christianity. If Christ were not God, He could never have been the perfect sacrifice on the cross. The incarnation is the essence of the gospel—as Paul stated—

Now all things are of God, who has reconciled us to Himself through Jesus Christ, and has given us the ministry of reconciliation, that is, that God was in Christ reconciling the world to Himself, not imputing their trespasses to them, and has committed to us the word of reconciliation. (2 Cor. 5:18–19)

Satan's Tactic To Destroy Love And Unity. Satan's second tactic is to destroy love and unity in churches that truly believe in the deity of Jesus Christ. It would be startling and very disturbing to know for sure how many people have left churches that teach right doctrine to join various cults and -isms—primarily because they were disillusioned with Christians who did not walk their talk.

Disunity among Christians is one of the worst forms of ugliness and repulsion, whereas true love and unity in Christ is attractive and beautiful. It provides the backdrop against which we can share the message of salvation. And strange as it may seem, this too is a miracle of God's power. In some respects, this convinces people that Jesus Christ was the Son of God—perhaps more so than the miracles Jesus Himself performed. Certainly God can work miracles anytime. But so-called "miracles" today can also be fake. But most people know it is impossible to fake true love and unity. How sad that some non-Christian groups demonstrate more love and unity than true Christians!

Thankfully, this need not happen. Satan does not have to be victorious. Christ *prayed* for us! Furthermore, we have His Word which exhorts us often to endeavor "to keep the unity of the Spirit in the bond of peace" (Eph. 4:3). And we have the Holy Spirit dwelling in each of us personally and in our churches corporately in order to release God's power to defeat Satan (Eph. 3:16–21; 6:10–18).

THE POWER OF LOVE AND UNITY (THE REST OF THE STORY)

As I began this chapter, I referenced a missionary couple's experience with a group of Ecuadorian Indians. After preaching the gospel to this large South American tribe for a number of years, they told me something had happened that brought thousands of conversions. When I asked if there was any one thing they could point to that had caused this unusual spiritual response, the missionary wife responded by giving me a very specific answer.

For a lengthy period of time there had been disunity in the rather large group of missionaries working among this tribe. And then God's Holy Spirit did a special work of grace in the hearts of these missionaries. They confessed their faults to one another and asked forgiveness. Unity was restored, and the love among these people was very obvious to the people to whom they were ministering. Then the Holy Spirit worked in the lives of these people who had been resistant to the Gospel. Literally thousands put their faith in Jesus Christ for salvation.

This story illustrates graphically the reality of what Jesus taught His disciples; it is also an answer to Jesus' prayer. These Indians saw that these missionaries—like the apostles—were true disciples of Jesus Christ. It happened because they loved one another as Christ had loved them.

Furthermore, they saw that this kind of love results in unity—which demonstrated to these people that Jesus Christ indeed had come from the Father. God used this "miracle" to convince these unbelievers to respond to the Gospel of Jesus Christ.

THE TRUE MEASURE OF A CHURCH

What we have observed in this chapter also correlates with the true measure of a church. Paul wrote, "And now abide faith, hope, love, these three; but the greatest of these is love" (1 Cor. 13:13). All three concepts are important in modeling Christianity. But Jesus affirmed Paul's words and demonstrated with His own life that love is the greatest because it reveals who He is.

That day in the Upper Room when Jesus taught this dynamic lesson on love, the apostle John was listening. Though he did not understand everything then—since he was one of the men who was seeking to be the greatest in the kingdom of heaven—he later understood what Jesus really meant. Nearly forty years later, he gave a true definition of love in his first epistle. He wrote:

> By this we know love, because He laid down His life for us. And we also ought to lay down our lives for the brethren. (1 John 3:16)

Had John repeated the lesson he had heard from Jesus forty years before in the Upper Room, he may have written: "By this we know love, because Jesus washed our feet and we also ought to wash one another's feet."

But this, of course, was not what Jesus had in mind. He began where they were—with what they could understand. Before they could be motivated to love each other enough to die for each other, they would have to become humble enough to be willing to wash one another's feet.

When the Holy Spirit came on these men at Pentecost, they learned their lesson well. Ironically, tradition tells us that all of the apostles—except John—died a martyr's death. They gave their very lives for Christ and others. They "loved others" as "Jesus had loved them."

MAKING THE INVISIBLE GOD VISIBLE TODAY

With this great plan, God achieved another wonderful goal. Jesus came into this world to reveal the Father. He did so, not only by claiming to be God, but He demonstrated that He was God through His miracles. As we read in the Book of Hebrews, this great salvation was first spoken by the Lord Jesus Christ. Later it "was confirmed to us by those who heard Him"—obviously the apostles. But we also read that "God bore witness to this message"—both the message taught by Jesus and the apostles—"with signs and wonders, with various miracles, and gifts of the Holy Spirit, according to His own will" (Heb. 2:3–4).

How could this message be verified once Jesus Christ returned to heaven? How could this message be verified once the apostles passed off the scene—the primary recipients of these special gifts of power?

I believe John gives us the answer in his little epistle:

> Beloved, if God so loved us, we also ought to love one another. No one has seen God at any time. If we love one another, God abides in us, and His love has been perfected in us. (1 John 4:11–12)

Here John describes the miracle of love and unity. If a local body of believers love each other as Christ loved them, God in Christ is "fleshed out" in these people. When this happens, we demonstrate that Jesus Christ was indeed God in the flesh. The invisible God becomes visible when Christ is incarnate in a body of loving, unified believers. The very unity Jesus Christ had with the Father is seen and experienced. This is indeed miraculous.

This was what was happening in Jerusalem. This is why they had favor with all the people. And this is why people were added to the church daily as they put their faith in Jesus Christ. The true Source of the message of eternal life was sensed, felt, accepted, and believed!

MEASURING OUR CHURCH

As we've come to the end of this study, I want to ask you four questions.

1. To what extent are you contributing to the love and unity in your local church?

2. To what extent are you demonstrating the character of Christ?

3. Is your church penetrating your community with the message of love, unity and righteousness? How?

4. Are you verbally sharing the good news that brings eternal life?

CHRIST'S LETTER TO THE
CHURCH IN SARDIS

A Contemporary Paraphrase of Rev. 3:1–6

Dear Brothers and Sisters:

It saddens me deeply to have to call to your attention that of all the churches in your geographical area, you are the most worldly and sinful. It may surprise you that I feel this way about you since everyone is talking about the size of your church building, the number of people who attend your services, and your social work in the community. However, in your hearts and souls, you're not alive! You're dead! All of your works are purely external and for show. You remind me of those religious leaders whom I confronted when I walked the earth. They were like white-washed tombs—like dead men's bones.

You must awaken from your sleep, or I will come quietly like a burglar and judge you severely. This I do not wish to do, but those I love I must discipline.

In closing, I must reassure you that I know by name a few of you who truly love me. You are not living hypocritical lives. I will not forget you. You will be rewarded greatly for your faithfulness in spite of the overall conditions that exist in your church. But my word to most of you is, please listen carefully to my exhortations for I will do what I say.

The One who loves His church,

Jesus Christ

Dr. Norman Wright

D URING THIS NEW TESTAMENT study with Dr. Gene Getz, you have been looking at what the Word of God says about our Christian walk, not only as individuals but as a corporate body of believers. As you've seen, most of what we read in the New Testament epistles involves instructions addressed to local churches.

However, whether you realize it or not, what you have been studying about the church applies to individual households—Christian families. As Gene will demonstrate in this chapter, the family in Scripture really appears as the "church in miniature." What is written to the church is also written to the family. Conversely, the family serves as a basic model for effective church function.

Personally, I believe Gene Getz captures, in this chapter you are about to read, the essence of what might be called a "theology of the family" as it appears in the New Testament. He accomplishes this goal because he builds from the broader theological concepts outlined in the previous chapters of this book, demonstrating that God's plan for the church is intricately related to God's plan for the family.

I also believe Gene helps resolve some of the tensions that exist between those who have championed a more feminist approach to leadership positions and functions both in the church and the family. He holds firmly to the concept of male authority being designed by God for marriage, the family, and the church—but with the view that focuses on servant-leadership and which eliminates any justification for authoritarianism, domination, inappropriate control, and "one way" submission. His model is comprehensive and challenges the compartmentalization that often exists between the family and the church.

I would ask that you read this chapter with an open mind. Whatever your predetermined conclusions, Gene presents a fresh paradigm for "measuring our commitment to the family" and how this God-ordained institution relates to the local church.

ELEVEN

MEASURING OUR COMMITMENT TO THE FAMILY

> As you know how we exhorted, and comforted, and charged every one of you, as a father does his own children, that you would *walk worthy* of God who calls you into His own kingdom and glory.
>
> 1 Thessalonians 2:11–12

IN CHAPTER SEVEN I TOLD OF JIM PETERSEN'S ministry in Brazil and his relationship with an agnostic named Mario Nitche. As you will remember, Jim built a relationship with Mario and they met for four years—an average of once a week—to study the Bible. Though Mario was a Marxist and initially did not believe in God or Jesus Christ, eventually he became a strong believer—and a great Christian leader.

On one occasion, I had an opportunity to be in Mario's home. I asked him to share his story—how he met with Jim and studied the Bible—and how he eventually came to put his personal faith in Christ.

After he related the story, I asked Mario what caused him to continue to meet with Jim for four years to study a book that he did not believe contained the truth? He paused for a moment and then responded very quickly and without equivocation. He said, "It was definitely the love relationship I saw between Jim and his wife Marge. It was the way they treated their children. And it was the love and unity developed in that family. "That," he said, "is why I continued to study the Bible."

Mario went on to explain to me that he became convinced that there had to be a relationship between the Bible Jim and Marge believed in, and the way it impacted their lives. In his heart he wanted this kind of relationship with a woman and a family. Ironically, as I sat at Mario's breakfast table—being served by his wife and eating breakfast with his children—I saw the Petersen's model replicated in the Nitche family.

THE FAMILY—THE CHURCH IN MINIATURE

Several years ago I began to do an in-depth study of the family in Scripture, I was initially quite puzzled that there seemed to be so few direct instructions to family members in the New Testament.

A THEOLOGY OF THE CHURCH—A THEOLOGY OF THE FAMILY

As I reflected carefully on this observation in the light of the total message of the New Testament, I began to understand that in their thinking, scriptural writers often did not separate individual "family units" from the "larger family unit," the local church. In essence, what they wrote to churches was what they wrote to individual families. Though there are certainly uniquely designed relationships for the family that are not designed for the church (such as husband and wife intimacy), in general a "theology of the church" is also a "theology of the family." Furthermore, it is very important to develop a perspective on what God says the church should be before we attempt to understand God's will for the family. To reverse this order can lead to serious misinterpretations, if not outright false conclusions.

It is inappropriate then to attempt to develop a set of principles unique to the church and the family without carefully interrelating what the Scriptures teach about both. To do so will either lead to redundancy in basic spiritual guidelines, or more seriously, to an artificial dichotomy that is based on isogesis rather than exegesis. The facts are that those specific directives that are given to the family, such as in Paul's letters to the Ephesians and Colossians, must be carefully interpreted in the context of what Paul was writing to the churches. In other words, Paul assumed his readers understood his concerns for and instructions to the "larger family—the church," regarding submission to authority, loving as Christ loved, obedience to those who are charged with leadership responsibility and servant-leadership when interpreting what he teaches about these same areas to wives, husbands, children, and fathers.(Eph. 5:22—6:4; Col. 3:18–21).

The Danvers Statement

Unfortunately, evangelical Christians often seem to be influenced by the trends of the world rather than becoming a counter culture. When this happens it also affects their interpretation of Scripture. The Council on Biblical Manhood and Womanhood captured this concern when they stated their "rationale" for "the Danvers Statement;" namely,

> The increasing prevalence and acceptance of hermeneutical oddities de-vised to reinterpret apparently plain meanings of biblical text . . . and behind all this the apparent accommodation of some within the church to the spirit of the age at the expense of winsome, radical biblical authenticity which in the power of the Holy Spirit may reform rather than reflect our ailing culture.[1]

Thus, since most exhortations in the New Testament are directed at the church, and since the family unit is assumed by biblical writers to be an integral part of the church, we must never separate our thinking from this larger social unit, particularly as we seek God's will in Scripture. In many respects, the family *is* the church in miniature. In fact, as we will see, many New Testament churches began as individual households and then multi-plied into multi-family units, particularly when these original family units were large, extended families.

The Household Metaphor

As stated earlier, the scriptural writers use a variety of metaphors to describe the church, simply because it is such a marvelous creation with so many dimensions. No one analogy can communicate all of its wonderful and glorious aspects. However, no metaphor is used more frequently than that of the "family." That is why the church is frequently called the "house" or "household" of God (Gal. 6:10; Eph. 2:19; 1 Tim. 3:15; 1 Peter 4:17). Again and again in Scripture, members of God's family are called brothers (and sisters) in Christ, and God is identified as our "heavenly Father."

The family metaphor is wonderful to illustrate the church, since the church itself is in many respects an extension of the family model. It is God's original creation, designed to be a perfect reflection of the Lord Himself (Gen. 1:26–27; 2:18–23). But when Adam and Eve disobeyed God—distorting what God had in mind—they plunged the whole world into sin and affected us all. Their failure gave birth to marital stress, family strife, and in general, human deterioration in all relationships in life (Gen.

3:15–16). The history of families, tribes, nations and cultures verifies this reality.

But God had a marvelous plan for restoration. He initiated this plan by choosing Abraham *and his family*, who eventually gave birth to a whole nation—*many families*—God's people Israel. And from this nation came the ultimate seed—Jesus Christ (Gen. 3:15; 12:1–3). Jesus, in turn, gave birth to His own unique family—His church—which is made up of people from "all families" of the earth regardless of their nationality, ethnic background, color or language. Mixing metaphors—as the scriptural writers often do—we are all called Christ's "brothers," His "sisters," His "mother" (Matt. 12:50) and His "bride" or "wife" (Rev. 19:7; Eph. 5:25–26).

Human history, then, began with the family, which became the foundational institution for all societies. This is why whole nations and cultures rise and fall based on the spiritual and psychological health of this unique social unit. The facts are that many nations today are in danger of disintegration—particularly in the Western culture—because of the deterioration of the family unit. It is a well-known fact that this was one of the key factors that eventually led to the demise of the Roman Empire. This is how important the family is in God's scheme of things. Furthermore, what is happening to the family in our present culture is also affecting the spiritual vitality of our churches.

THE FAMILY UNIT IN THE NEW TESTAMENT WORLD

One of the positive advantages for New Testament missionaries was the general commitment to the importance of the family unit that existed, particularly in the Jewish culture. In fact, this was one of the primary reasons the church in Jerusalem grew so phenomenally in its early days. Whole families were converted to Jesus Christ. In fact, the very day Peter and John were taken into custody because of their healing and preaching ministry, Luke recorded that the "number of men" who believed after hearing Peter's sermon "came to be about 5,000" (Acts 4:4).

HOUSEHOLD CONVERSIONS

Most Bible interpreters agree that this reference is to approximately five thousand fathers who would obviously represent five thousand households. This interpretation, of course, is in harmony with the fact that God-fearing Jewish families as a whole made this annual trip to Jerusalem during the Feast of Pentecost to worship in the temple. And since the "extended family" was a strong unit in Israel—including fathers, mothers, grown children and their mates and their own children—the number five thousand could be multiplied many times in terms of the number of people who decided to follow Jesus Christ that day.

We have another illustration of this approach to reporting numbers in the ministry of Jesus. One day a great multitude of people followed Him to the other side of the Sea of Galilee. Jesus had these people sit down so He could miraculously feed them with the five barley loaves and two small fish. John recorded that "the men sat down, in number about five thousand" (John 6:10).

Matthew clarified that the actual number of people present was far greater than the original number mentioned. He reports that "those who had eaten were about five thousand men, besides women and children" (Matt. 14:21). This reference certainly correlates with Luke's report in Acts regarding the five thousand men who were converted to Jesus Christ. We could safely conclude that there were "five thousand men besides thousands of women and children" who became a part of the church in Jerusalem. And for the most part, these extended families often included servants.

This phenomena also took place as the gospel was carried beyond Jerusalem. Though the numbers were not as great, simply because of the different cultural setting, the concept of "household" response to the gospel is illustrated frequently. Furthermore, this happened not only in Jewish families but among God-fearing Gentiles as well. This indicates that the family structure at this point in time was still a strong entity in the Roman Empire.

Specific Examples

Cornelius, a God-fearing Gentile, was converted to Jesus Christ with his *whole household*, including his relatives and close friends as a result of Peter's ministry (Acts 10:1–48). It appears that his household was the original church in Caesarea and what began as one "household church" eventually included many households. When Paul returned from his second missionary journey and "landed at Caesarea," he went "up and greeted the church" (Acts 18:22)—obviously a church that had grown and multiplied since Cornelius' conversion.

Lydia is an example of a well-to-do single mother who came to Christ and started the church in her home. She was "a seller of purple from the city of Thyatira" and was converted to Christ when she heard Paul preach by a riverside in Philippi. She and her *whole household* were baptized (Acts

16:15) and evidently, she opened her home as a meeting place for the church. In fact, Paul and his missionary team made her home their base of operations (Acts 16:15).

The Philippian jailer was also from Philippi. After a rather traumatic experience, he and his whole family responded to the gospel just like Lydia. Following the earthquake that opened the doors of the prison and loosened the chains on the prisoners, this man came running in and "fell down trembling before Paul and Silas." His question was specific and to the point: "Sirs, what must I do to be saved?"

Paul responded, "Believe on the Lord Jesus Christ, and you will be saved, you and *your household.*" And once his whole family believed, Luke recorded that "immediately he and all his family were baptized" (Acts 16:29–33).

There are other examples in the New Testament. "Crispus, the ruler of the synagogue" in Corinth "believed on the Lord with *all his household*" (Acts 18:8). Later in his first letter to the Corinthians, Paul also made reference to the fact that he had "baptized the *household* of Stephanas" (1 Cor. 1:16). And Philemon also stands out as a great example of a whole household that had come to Christ. In this instance, it is clear that his "extended family" not only included his children and their children, but his servants as well. Onesimus, the reason for Paul's letter to Philemon, was one of these servants.

Commenting on these biblical illustrations, the late Dr. George Peters made this comment:

> Household evangelism and household salvation are the biblical ideal and norm in evangelism and salvation. God wills that the family be one, that it remain a solid and peaceful unit, that the family be evangelized and that the family be saved.[2]

There is no question that the family structure was a very important unit in the New Testament world. These strong family structures were an important key in helping churches mature in Jesus Christ. Though cultures vary today in terms of family structures—particularly in the Western World—the fact still remains that "strong families" build "strong churches." Conversely, the weaker the family unit, the more difficulties we face in helping a church to measure up to the stature of the fullness of Christ.

The Family Model In Ministry

Nurturing Christians In The Faith

In many respects, the family as God designed it to function also establishes a model for ministry in God's larger family—the church. We see this influence particularly in Paul's approach to bringing people to the measure of the stature of the fullness of Christ.

For example, he used the "mother-child" and "father-children" illustrations to describe the nature of his own ministry when he wrote to the Thessalonians. Following the natural growth process in a newborn, he first identified with a mother:

> But we were gentle among you, just as a *nursing mother* cherishes her own children. (1 Thess. 2:7)

This is a beautiful illustration. It communicates unconditional love, patience, tenderness, and all the other qualities that can be described when a mother nurses her child at her breast. It is noteworthy that a single man like Paul—and a man's man at that—would use such an intimate illustration to communicate the way new babes in Jesus Christ should be treated.

Later in the same passage, Paul identified his ministry with that of a father as he becomes involved in the nurturing process as his children grow older. Thus he wrote:

> You know how we exhorted, and comforted, and charged every one of you, as a *father does his own children,* that you would have a walk worthy of God who calls you into His own kingdom and glory. (1 Thess. 2:11–12)

This word picture gives us tremendous insights into how Paul viewed the fathering process. He was obviously influenced by his Old Testament background and knowledge of the law of Moses. The father was central in the nurturing process, Moses' directives to the fathers of Israel probably rung in Paul's own ears as he carried out his own church planting ministry. These instructions are clearly outlined in Deuteronomy chapter 6:

> And these words which I command you today shall be in your heart; you shall teach them diligently to your children, and shall talk of them when you sit in your house, when you walk by the way, when you lie down, and when you rise up. You shall bind them as a sign on your hand, and they shall be as frontlets between your eyes. You shall write them on the doorposts of your house and on your gates. (Deut. 6:6–9)

The picture is clear. God's plan for mother-father nurture in the Old Testament served as a model to Paul in winning people to Christ and then helping them to grow in their faith. Initially, he tenderly "nursed" them as "newborn babes" with the "pure milk of the word" (1 Peter 2:2). As they grew in their faith, he nurtured and brought "them up in the training and admonition of the Lord"—just as Paul had instructed fathers to do with their own children when he wrote his letter to the Ephesians and Colossians (Eph. 6:4; Col. 3:21). And when his spiritual children did not respond as they should, Paul emotionally went through the birthing process all over again. Thus, he wrote to the Galatian Christians: "My little children, for whom I labor in birth again until Christ is formed in you" (Gal. 4:19).

SELECTING LEADERS FOR THE CHURCH

The Old Testament family model also influenced Paul and other New Testament writers in selecting pastoral leaders for the church. When Paul wrote to Timothy—whom he had left in Ephesus to establish and organize the church—he directed him to select elders or bishops who were exemplary fathers.[3] Thus, he wrote: "A bishop then must be . . . one who rules [or manages] his own house well, having his children in submission with all reverence." Paul then applied this requirement to the larger family—the church—("For if a man does not know how to rule [or manage] his own house, how will he take care of the church of God?") (1 Tim. 3:2,4–5).

Later, when Paul wrote to Titus, whom he had left in Crete to also establish the churches in various cities (Titus 1:5), he wrote a similar letter. In outlining the qualifications for spiritual leaders in the church, he wrote that an elder must have "faithful children not accused of dissipation or insubordination" (Titus 1:6).

These requirements as outlined by Paul certainly do not mean that these spiritual leaders had to be perfect fathers. If that were true, there would be no one qualified to lead the church. However, a close evaluation of these texts in context will reveal that a true mark of maturity in a father is the extent to which he has the respect of his children and that they—particularly as older children—are committed to their father's same spiritual values and lifestyle.[4]

Note that Paul is in no way teaching that a father should demand respect through an authoritarian approach to parenting. This illustrates why Paul's statements regarding a father's role must be interpreted in the light of the overall teachings in Scripture regarding a Christian's leadership style. A father, like all Christian leaders, must win respect by exemplifying a servant leadership role as demonstrated by Jesus Christ. Though God's ordained and appointed leader of his household, he must become this family's servant. In this respect, he models what Jesus modeled among His disciples when He washed their feet. Though their Lord and Master, He became their servant.

Furthermore, a father who is qualified to lead the church has effectively applied what Paul instructed fathers to do in his letters to the Ephesians and Colossians. He has not provoked his "children to wrath" but he has brought "them up in the training and admonition of the Lord" (Eph. 6:4). He has not discouraged them by making them angry (Col. 3:21). Rather, he has "exhorted, and comforted, and charged" each one of them—just as Paul said a father should do when he, Paul, modeled his own ministry after this fathering process (1 Thess. 3:11).

Here Paul's instructions to fathers correlates with what he and other New Testament writers wrote to elders. For example, note Peter's exhortations to these spiritual leaders:

> Shepherd the flock of God which is among you, serving as overseers, not by constraint but willing, not for dishonest gain but eagerly; nor as being lords over those entrusted to you, but being examples to the flock. (1 Peter 5:2–3)

When writing to Timothy regarding what should characterize a pastor's leadership style, Paul stated:

> But avoid foolish and ignorant disputes, knowing that they generate strife. And a servant of the Lord must not quarrel but be gentle to all, able to teach, patient, in humility correcting those who are in opposition, if God perhaps will grant them repentance, so that they may know the truth. (2 Tim. 2:23–25)

The Church, The Family And Individuals

At this juncture, we need to clarify more specifically how all of God's ordained social units interrelate with each other. Figure 11.1 will help make these correlations.

The Local Church

Let's begin with the larger circle, which represents a local church. As we have seen, the New Testament is in essence the story of the church. As Jesus told Peter, "I will build My church, and the gates of Hades shall not prevail against it" (Matt. 16:18b). Jesus Christ Himself is the "foundation," the "chief cornerstone" and the grand architect of God's eternal "household." The church will be victorious and triumphant.

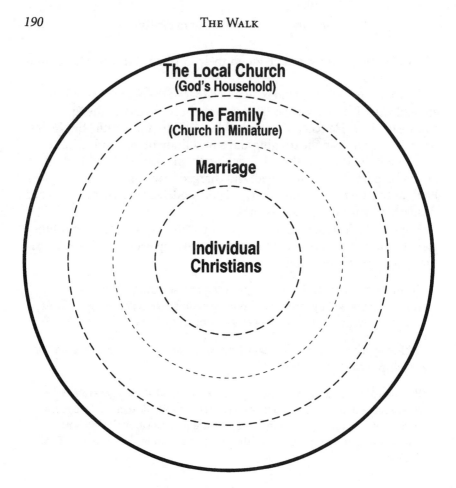

Figure 11.1: God's Ordained Social Units

Jesus Christ laid the ground work for this great "mystery" now revealed (Eph. 3:1–11) by selecting and equipping twelve men to continue His work once He ascended to the Father. As we have already seen, Peter and the other apostles—including Paul, Barnabas, Silas—and co-workers like Timothy and Titus were to be key players in this great unfolding plan. Today, the "household of God" is—as Jesus said it would be—in process of being "built on the foundation of the apostles and prophets" with "Jesus Christ Himself being the chief cornerstone" (Eph. 2:19–20).

Local churches, then, are the major social units described by scriptural writers. Nearly all of the letters in the New Testament were written either to local churches or to leaders like Timothy and Titus who were involved in establishing these local churches.

THE FAMILY UNIT

The next circle, within the larger circle, represents the family—the "church in miniature." Note that I have used a dotted line to distinguish the family *from the church*, but to also relate this social unit *to the church*. This simply means that the family, in terms of function, should not be separated from the church. Though there are unique relationships, particularly between the husband and the wife, the family is an integral part of the church. And as we have seen, the family becomes a biblical model for the way the church should function as a larger family unit—as fathers and mothers and as brothers and sisters in Jesus Christ.

THE MARITAL RELATIONSHIP

The next circle, moving toward the center, represents the marital relationship—a subunit within the family. This relationship, of course, is also a part of the larger circle, the church. In fact, the husband-wife relationship is so unique in God's scheme of things that Paul used this relationship to illustrate the way we, as Christ's body, relate to our head, Jesus Christ. The husband is to be the loving head of his wife, just as Christ is our loving head. And as the church is to be dedicated to Jesus Christ, so the wife is to be dedicated to her husband (Eph. 5:23–28).

THE INDIVIDUAL CHRISTIAN

The inner circle illustrates that all of God's uniquely designed social units—the church, the family and the marriage—are composed of individuals, both young and old. In marriage, these two individuals become one and form a new social unit. In the family, God's ideal plan is that what began as two becoming one, multiplies into a larger unit where God's love is modeled and children are nurtured into a mature family unit, reflecting the stature of Jesus Christ. And as these families mature and reflect the fullness of Christ, they become the strong building blocks of the church. In this sense, mature families automatically create mature churches.

However, the fact still remains that an individual may never marry and choose to remain single. In fact, Paul honored singleness as an opportunity to serve Jesus Christ in a single-minded way (1 Cor. 7).

Nevertheless, every single person comes from a human family. When these individuals are young, they are still a part of that family functionally. As they get older, however, God's plan is that they continue to have a warm relationship with their human family, but that they eventually establish themselves apart from being dependent on that family for emotional and financial support.

However, according to God's wonderful "extended family" plan, every Christian single who never marries and who does not establish his own family, should have a "larger household"—the church—where he receives emotional and spiritual support. Furthermore, within this larger family, each single person should function and contribute his part to the building up of the body of Christ. In fact, singles (non-married), if qualified, may function at the highest levels of leadership. Paul and Timothy certainly illustrate this in their own lives since they were no doubt single men. And as a relatively young man, Timothy was responsible to appoint older men to be elders and to even correct them when they were operating out of the will of God (1 Tim. 3:1–7; 5:1). That's why Paul wrote to Timothy and said:

> Let no one despise your youth, but be an example to the believers in word, in conduct, in love, in spirit, in faith, in purity. (1 Tim. 4:12)

God has even made provision for the church to take care of older singles who cannot care for themselves financially and physically. Paul devoted a whole chapter in his letter to Timothy to instruct the church in Ephesus regarding how to take care of widows who have no support system on this earth. Though the family unit is always to take care of their own, there are instances when that is not possible. Therefore, Paul outlines a plan for the larger family—the church—to become involved (1 Tim. 5:3–16).

GOD-ORDAINED LEADERSHIP ROLES

One of God's important principles, for both individual families as well as the church (the family of God), relates to role definitions. These role definitions and relationships are very consistent throughout the New Testament, both within the family and the church. When these roles are confused or abused—as they are in our particular culture, even among Christians—it will lead to all kinds of problems. The consistency and interrelationship of these roles can also be illustrated with the same basic graphic used earlier (in figure 11.1).

In terms of leadership roles, God intended spiritual leaders (elders, bishops, pastors, deacons, etc.) to relate to the church family in the same basic way as fathers relate to their families and as husbands relate to their wives (see figure 11.2). In other words, God has one set of leadership principles that flow throughout these interrelated social units; God does not have one set of principles for leadership roles in marriage, another set for leadership roles in the family, and yet another set of principles for leadership roles in the church.

Misunderstanding these interrelated concepts has led to unusual confusion among many Christians today, particularly because of the feminist movement. For example, I believe that Christians have often reinterpreted Scripture in order to teach "equal partnership" and "egalitarian relationships" in marriage. In so doing, some teach that God never intended for a husband to have any authority over his wife. The term "headship" is redefined as meaning "source" rather than having a responsibility to be the leader of the wife.

On one particular occasion, I had a very stimulating dialogue with a leadership couple who were committed to "equal partnership" in marriage. Both, however, were committed to a high view of Scripture. They, like some evangelicals, did not teach that Paul was chauvinistic and was a product of his Rabbinical background. However, they redefined Paul's teachings, particularly in Ephesians and Colossians on the subject of headship and submission. They also cited the omissions in Jesus' teachings regarding these subjects. Therefore, they believed that since all people are "one in Jesus Christ" in terms of our relationships with Jesus Christ and one another—as Paul taught in Galatians (Gal. 3:28)—there then can be no distinctions in leadership roles between a husband and wife. Consequently, both husband and wife have equal authority. They believed that Paul's later teaching in Ephesians and Colossians on "headship" and "submission" could be explained by understanding the cultural dynamics that existed at that time.

After listening to their explanations, I asked them if this same interpretation applied to leadership in a church. "No," they responded. "That's different." When I asked them if the same lack of authority applied to a father, they were somewhat more hesitant to be that direct. However, they still were determined that marriage was an entirely different social relationship and God had different guidelines for a husband and wife when properly interpreted.

At this juncture, I tried to explain what I believed from Scripture and how we attempt to work this biblical perspective out practically in our church. (See figure 11.2).

We believe that the husband should relate to his wife, as a father relates to his maternal partner and their children, and as elders (bishops, pastors, etc.) and their wives (if married) relate to the overall church family. The husband is the head of his wife, the father is the primary leader of the family (if the family is still intact), and the elders are the primary leaders of the

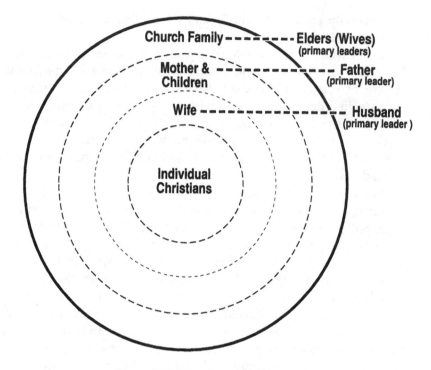

Figure 11.2: Church and Family

church. If the father is absent from the family either through divorce, desertion, or death, the mother obviously becomes the primary leader.

However, a husband, a father, and elders/pastors (in essence, multiple fathers of the church family) are to be servant leaders. They are to love others as Christ loved them and to be willing to "lay down their lives" for those they are called to serve. They are never to "lord it over" those in their charge. They are to practice the principles of mutual submission as husband and wife, as father and mother, and as elders/pastors and congregation. But at the same time they are God-ordained leaders who have delegated authority from Jesus Christ to lead others as He led the apostles when He was on earth—and as He leads His church today.

Following this model, we also believe that a husband and wife are a unique team (a "brother and sister" in Christ as well as a married couple), and if they both follow the principles of love and servanthood outlined in Scripture for all Christians, they will experience all of the supposed benefits of "equal partnership" and "egalitarianism" in their marriage without eliminating the husband's headship and his position of authority in the marriage. This, we believe, is God's ideal. And since this social unit includes only two people, consensus can be the norm in decision making—especially if both spouses are committed to Jesus Christ and want the best for each other. Aquila and Priscilla serve as a beautiful example of this kind of relationship (Acts 18:1–4, 18–26; 1 Cor. 15:19; Rom. 16:3–5).

In the family, we believe the "father and mother" are also a team. And if they follow the same biblical principles outlined for husbands and wives (and the whole body of Christ), they will lead the family as a team arriving at consensus in decision making, and at the same time, not eliminating the father's leadership role in the family. In fact, this kind of balance provides a beautiful model for their children who will, in the most part, someday "leave father and mother" and establish their own family units.

In the church, to be consistent with what we believe is a biblical model, elders (bishops, pastors, etc.) and their wives can and should lead the church as teams. Wives are not elders, just as they are not "husbands" in their homes. Neither are mothers elders, just as they are not "fathers" in the home. However, together, a man and woman in the church become a father-mother team along with other father-mother teams who lead the church family the same way they lead their own families. In this way, men lead the church, the family and the marriage—as we believe God designed—but mothers and wives and single women as well are called alongside to help, assist, give input, and to help make strategic decisions. In fact, as pastors and elders at Fellowship Bible Church North, we have discovered that consulting our wives as well as mature single women before we make certain decisions gives us wisdom that we would not otherwise have. At times, this wisdom has changed our perspectives, our conclusions, and our decisions. This same dynamic should be taking place in families and marriages.

This is why it is important to appoint leaders in the church who reflect a high level of maturity. Both husband and wife, mother and father, elder (bishop, pastor, etc.) and wife, as well as single men and women, must reflect Jesus Christ in their lifestyles, or they cannot lead effectively as God intended either in their families or in the church.

MODELING JESUS CHRIST TO THE UNSAVED WORLD

If the family is "the church in miniature"—which I believe it is—then all of the principles that we've looked at thus far in terms of "corporate evangelism" apply to each individual Christian family unit. In fact, individual families have a greater opportunity to model Jesus Christ to the world than the church family at large. After all, most families live in various places throughout a geographical area. Surrounding each home are unbe-lievers who need to see love and unity fleshed out in Christian families. In this sense, each church in miniature becomes a bridge to the world—as illustrated earlier with the Petersen example.

This, I believe, was what happened in Jerusalem. As Christians "contin-ued steadfastly in the apostles' doctrine and fellowship, in the breaking of bread and in prayers," they went "from house to house." Everywhere, throughout the city of Jerusalem, non-believing people saw the church in miniature and the church at large multiplied a thousand times. In the context of love and unity and sharing, eating together and praising God, these "family units" had "favor with all the people." In this context "the Lord added to the church daily those who were being saved." This won-derful Christian dynamic fleshed out who Jesus Christ really was and it became the foundation for belief. This in no way became a substitute for the message of salvation; however, as Jesus prayed it would, it verified the message that was being shared and preached and made that message believable.

MEASURING OUR WALK

1. How does your church—and you—view the family? Is it seen as the church in miniature?

2. What areas of commitment are necessary for you to exhibit God's design for families?

CHRIST'S LETTER TO THE CHURCH IN THYATIRA

A Contemporary Paraphrase of Rev. 2:18–29

Dear Brothers and Sisters:

It grieves me deeply to have to write to you and warn you against a very serious problem in your church. On the one hand, I'm aware of how much effort you've expended to obey me. You've demonstrated love and faith, and you've worked hard to serve others. You've also stood firm against false teachers. However, you have not taken a strong stand against those in your congregation who are sexually immoral. Unmarried singles are living together as if they were married and even some of your leaders are having adulterous affairs. And I'm terribly grieved that some of your women—both married and single—are having abortions. And what can I say about the fact that you're even considering ordaining elders in your church who are practicing homosexuals. As my servant Paul wrote nearly two thousand years ago to the Romans: "These people will receive in themselves the due penalty for their perversion."

I have been very patient about this, giving all of you time to repent and to turn from your sins. However, if there is not a change in your lifestyle, I will discipline you severely. Even your children will suffer because of your sins.

I do not wish to make your church an example of what happens when sin is tolerated. But I must be true to my own character. Please listen to what I'm saying.

The One who is holy and pure,

Jesus Christ

Dr. Tony Evans

I HAVE KNOWN DR. GENE GETZ FOR A number of years and he has greatly influenced my own life and ministry as one of my key professors at Dallas Theological Seminary. I was privileged to serve as the first fully supported missionary from the original Fellowship Bible Church—the church Gene founded in 1972. Because of this relationship I was able to launch Oak Cliff Bible Fellowship and later, the organization we call Urban Alternative.

This book is focused primarily on corporate maturity and the way we, as Christians, should walk together as a corporate body, loving one another and reflecting the righteousness of Jesus Christ. But when all is said and done, Christianity is intensely personal. God is very concerned about our personal walk with Christ.

A lot of times, people talk about the church as though it is simply an entity. But the church is more than an entity. It is people—personal lives that need to be built up in Jesus Christ. My prayer as you read this final chapter is that you will make a decision to grow in Jesus Christ and to become a spiritually mature Christian—so that all the rights, privileges and benefits that come from knowing Him will be yours. You not only can benefit from these benefits, but transfer them to others as well.

TWELVE

MEASURING OUR COMMITMENT TO PERSONAL MATURITY

> For you were once darkness, but now you are light in the
> Lord. *Walk as children of light* (for the fruit of the Spirit
> is in all goodness, righteousness, and truth).
> — Ephesians 5:8–9

M Y FRIEND, MIKE CORNWALL, HAS served with me as a lay
pastor at Fellowship Bible Church North for a number of years.
Mike and his wife, Sharon, are wonderful, dedicated Christians
and have always challenged me with their own walk with God.

Mike is a banker. One Saturday morning, he and Sharon were eating breakfast. As they looked out their kitchen window, a bus pulled up in front of their home. A number of people got off the bus, picked up placards and began to picket in front of their house.

In a few minutes, a man knocked at the door with a document in his hands. He wanted Mike to sign a statement that his bank—a large savings and loan conglomerate throughout Texas—demonstrated prejudicial decisions against minorities when making loans. Standing beside this man was another individual with a camera, ready to take a picture of Mike's reactions—assuming they would be negative, which would probably be displayed the next day in the Dallas Morning News.

In reality, what had happened was that the United States government had passed legislation that had been interpreted by minorities as prejudicial treatment. Since Mike was the C.E.O. of this large savings and loan association, the minorities targeted him as a means to make their point.

As a Christian, what would you have done in this situation? Frankly, my own reactions may have been less than mature. I do not like to be used in this way. Later, I will give the rest of the story—Mike's reaction that illustrates in an incredible way what the Scriptures teach should be a proper response for a Christian whose personal Christian walk reflects the life of Jesus Christ.

THE WALK—BOTH CORPORATE AND PERSONAL

This study has focused on what the New Testament says about the local church in terms of our Christian walk and commitment to spiritual maturity. Unfortunately, the "one heart and one mind" experiences so prevalent in the early days of Christianity (Acts 4:32) are often woefully lacking in our religious communities today, particularly in cultures where individualistic thinking has dominated and controlled our thoughts and our lifestyles. Personally, I do not believe we can really understand God's plan for His people unless we think "ecclesiologically" as we read the New Testament. The church is a predominant entity in God's divine plan.

On the other hand, Christianity is also intensely personal. It begins with a personal relationship with the Lord Jesus Christ. Conversion, to be valid, must involve an individual decision to accept Jesus Christ as personal Lord and Savior. Furthermore— as we've seen in our anchor passage — for the body of Christ to function properly, it must be "joined and knit together by what every joint supplies." It's when "every part does it's share" the body is edified and built up in love (Eph. 4:16). Here Paul illustrated in an emphatic way the importance of personal involvement in the body of Christ.

In this sense, Christianity is both personal and corporate. The plan God designed and describes in the New Testament letters is an interactive process. As the body in general grows in faith, hope and love, it provides a wonderful womb for newborn Christians to be nurtured and to grow in their personal lives. To see authentic Christianity lived and modeled is God's foundational plan for spiritual growth to take place. Paul, Silas and Timothy demonstrated this principle in Thessalonica among the new believers. So consequently, Paul could write to them:

> You are witnesses, and God also, how devoutly and justly and blamelessly we behaved ourselves among you who believe. (1 Thess. 2:10)

It naturally follows that as individual believers grow and mature in faith, hope, and love, their personal growth in Christ folds into the "body at large" and contributes to the "growth of the body" and corporate manifestation of these spiritual qualities.

However, when all is said and done, the process of spiritual growth *is* personal. It must happen to each of us as individuals, whether we are husbands or fathers, or wives or mothers, or children or young people living at home, or singles (which includes divorcees, separated people, widows, widowers—or people who have never been married at all).

Unfortunately, as the Corinthians illustrate, we can choose to remain carnal Christians (Christians who manifest the "works of the flesh"), or we can also choose to become spiritual Christians (those who manifest the "fruit of the Spirit"). However, if we choose to remain carnal and if we are true children of God, we will be disciplined by a loving heavenly Father in order to encourage us to live a holy and righteous life. And if I am not eventually disciplined when I deliberately walk out of the will of God, I must look carefully at my heart and life to see whether or not I am indeed a true believer.

This point is made very clear and precise in the letter to the Hebrews:

> If you endure chastening, God deals with you as with sons; for what son is there whom a father does not chasten? But if you are without chastening, of which all have become partakers, then you are illegitimate and not sons . . . Now no chastening seems to be joyful for the present, but grievous; nevertheless, afterwards it yields the peaceable fruit of righteousness to those who have been trained by it. (Heb. 12:7–8,11)

PAUL'S PROFILES

When Paul wrote his pastoral epistles to Timothy and Titus, he outlined ten profiles for measuring our personal maturity in Christ. Timothy was in Ephesus assisting the church in its spiritual growth. Following Paul's evangelistic ministry in Crete, Titus remained behind to organize and establish churches in several cities and to appoint spiritual leaders in each church (Titus 1:5).

Paul's maturity profiles in his first letter to Timothy focus on leadership qualities, whereas his profiles in his letter to Titus include qualities for both spiritual leaders as well as all believers. As we'll see, however, the profiles for leaders are in the most part also profiles for all Christians. Paul informed Timothy and Titus that when they looked for spiritual leaders in the church, the people they choose should measure up to a certain level of maturity so they can model Christianity and lead others to the same level of maturity—with the goal of "measuring up to the stature of the fullness of Christ."

ELDERS OR BISHOPS (PASTORS) (1 TIMOTHY 3:1–13)

This is a faithful saying: If a man desires the position of a bishop,[1] he desires a good work. A bishop then must be blameless, the husband of one wife, temperate, soberminded, of good behavior, hospitable, able to teach; not given to wine, not violent, not greedy for money, but gentle, not quarrelsome, not covetous; one who rules his own house well, having his children in submission with all reverence (for if a man does not know how to rule his own house, how will he take care of the church of God?); not a novice, lest being puffed up with pride he fall into the same condemnation as the devil. Moreover he must have a good testimony among those who are outside, lest he fall into reproach and the snare of the devil. (1 Tim. 3:1–7)

DEACONS

Likewise deacons[2] must be reverent, not double-tongued, not given to much wine, not greedy for money, holding the mystery of the faith with a pure conscience. But let these also first be proved; then let them serve as deacons, being found blameless.(1 Tim. 3:8–10)

Let deacons be the husbands of one wife, ruling their children and their own houses well. For those who have served well as deacons obtain for themselves a good standing and great boldness in the faith which is in Christ Jesus. (1 Tim. 3:12–13)

DEACONESSES

Likewise their wives[3] must be reverent, not slanderers, temperate, faithful in all things. (1 Tim. 3:11)

ELDERS OR BISHOPS (PASTORS) (TITUS 1:5–9)

For this reason I left you in Crete, that you should set in order the things that are lacking, and appoint elders in every city as I commanded you—if a man is blameless, the husband of one wife, having faithful children not accused of dissipation or insubordination. For a bishop must be blameless, as a steward of God, not self-willed, not quick-tempered, not given to wine, not violent, not greedy for money, but hospitable, a lover of what is good, sober-minded, just, holy, self-controlled, holding fast the faithful word as he has been taught, that he may be able, by sound doctrine, both to exhort and convict those who contradict. (Titus 1:5–9).

OLDER MEN (TITUS 2:1–2)

But as for you, speak the things which are proper for sound doctrine: that the older men be sober, reverent, temperate, sound in faith, in love, in patience. (Titus 2:1–2)

OLDER WOMEN (TITUS 2:3)

The older women likewise, that they be reverent in behavior, not slanderers, not given to much wine, teachers of good things. (Titus 2:3)

YOUNGER WOMEN (TITUS 2:4–5)

That they admonish the young women to love their husbands, to love their children, to be discreet, chaste, homemakers, good, obedient to their own husbands, that the word of God may not be blasphemed. (Titus 2:4–5)

YOUNGER MEN (TITUS 2:6–8)

Likewise exhort the young men to be sober-minded, in all things showing yourself to be a pattern of good works; in doctrine showing integrity, reverence, incorruptibility, sound speech that cannot be condemned, that one who is an opponent may be ashamed, having nothing evil to say of you. (Titus 2:6–8)

SERVANTS (TITUS 2:9–10)

Exhort servants to be obedient to their own masters, to be well pleasing in all things, not answering back, not pilfering, but showing all good fidelity, that they may adorn the doctrine of God our Savior in all things. (Titus 2:9–10)

CHRISTIANS IN GENERAL (TITUS 3:1–2)

Remind them to be subject to rulers and authorities, to obey, to be ready for every good work, to speak evil of no one, to be peaceable, gentle, showing all humility to all men. (Titus 3:1–2)

A COMMON PROFILE FOR MEASURING SPIRITUAL MATURITY

When you analyze all of the characteristics that are listed in these ten profiles, certain qualities stand out through specific repetition. The ten characteristics that follow have been selected because Paul emphasized them approximately the same number of times and several of them appear in all ten profiles.[4]

1. HAVING A GOOD REPUTATION

In both of Paul's letters—the first one to Timothy and the letter to Titus—he began with the concept of being "blameless," or of "being above reproach." In essence, Paul referred to having a good reputation. To Timothy he wrote:

> If a man desires the position of a bishop,[5] he desires a good work. A bishop then must be blameless [be "above reproach" or have a "good reputation"]. (1 Tim. 3:1–2a; see also Titus 1:6–7; see also 1 Tim. 3:10 where Paul mentions this same qualification for deacons).

The Brothers in Lystra and Iconium. Timothy himself illustrates this quality. When Paul came to Lystra on his second missionary journey, he heard about this young man. Luke recorded that "he was well spoken of by the brethren who were at Lystra and Iconium" (Acts 16:2).

Note three things. First, people were saying positive things about Timothy. A good reputation generates this kind of feedback.

Second, more than one person said positive things about Timothy. A good way to test our reputation is the extent to which a number of people respect us.

Third, key people talked positively about Timothy in Lystra and Iconium. Timothy's reputation was outstanding both in his hometown and in the neighboring city.

When Paul heard these good things about Timothy, it was then that he encouraged him to become a fellow missionary (Acts 16:3).

Timothy's Mother and Grandmother. The Christian brothers in Lystra and Iconium were not Paul's only source of information regarding this young man's reputation. He also had positive reports from Timothy's family, both his mother, Eunice, and his grandmother, Lois (2 Tim. 1:5). Though it appears that Timothy's father was an unbeliever (Acts 16:1), Paul saw the influence of these two godly women in his life. Paul recognized Timothy's thorough knowledge of the Old Testament Scriptures that he had learned from childhood—which had provided the biblical foundation to bring this young man to a strong and dynamic faith in Jesus Christ (2 Tim. 3:15–17).

Each of us as Christians should have as our goal to develop a good reputation. Although we will never be like Christ totally until we see Him "face to face," as maturing Christians, we should acknowledge our mistakes. And when sin is involved, we should confess that sin—and move onward and upward on our spiritual journey to reflect Jesus Christ in all that we do. Furthermore, our spiritual goals can help us to build a good reputation—which, of course, is a lifetime process.

One final note before moving on to the next quality of life. Paul concluded his profile for pastoral leaders in his letter to Timothy in the same manner that he begins—having a "good reputation." However, his focus is on having "a good testimony among those who are outside" (1 Tim. 3:7)—being "above reproach" with unbelievers, those "outside the church." Not only should we be "well spoken of" by our fellow Christians, but also by those who do not know Christ personally. Even though unbelievers may not agree with our belief system, if we're living a Christ-like life, they will in the most part respect our moral, ethical, and gracious lifestyle. This is definitely what happened in Jerusalem when the believers had favor with all the people (Acts 2:47).

2. Being "worthy of Respect"

Closely aligned with the concept of "being blameless" (or having a good reputation) is the concept of "being worthy of respect." The basic Greek word is *semnos*, meaning "august, venerable, reverent, honorable, dignified." Paul used this concept to challenge both men and women who served in the church (1 Tim. 3:8,11). He also challenged Titus to be this kind of man in his own leadership role. Thus, he wrote:

> In all things showing yourself to be a pattern of good works; in doctrine showing integrity, reverence, incorruptibility, sound speech that cannot be condemned. (Titus 2:7–8a)

Actually, the word "grave" is frequently used as an English word to capture the meaning of *semnos*. In that sense, it means a person who has a serious and dignified quality of life or demeanor.

This does not mean that a Christian cannot laugh, express humor, and enjoy life. As we read in the Proverbs, "A merry heart does good, like medicine" (Prov. 17:22a). God is the author of laughter, happiness, and joy.

However, Christianity *is* serious business. We represent the God of the universe, who is a holy and righteous God. We are children of the King of kings, and we are joint heirs with His Son, Jesus Christ. Therefore, we should live in such a way as to be respected because of our high position and calling in Christ. This involves the way we relate to both God and our fellow human beings—both Christians and non-Christians—and the way we order our lives on this earth.

Adorning The Gospel Of Jesus Christ. Paul used another word that makes "being worthy of respect" very practical. The Greek word *kosmeo* is translated in the New King James as "good behavior" and in the New American Standard as "respectable" (1 Tim. 3:2).

The verb form, *kosmeo*, is variously translated. But perhaps the most unique and descriptive English phrase is "to adorn." Paul used this phrase when he was exhorting slaves:

> To be obedient to their own masters, to be well pleasing in all things, not answering back, not pilfering, but showing all good fidelity, that they may adorn [*kosmeo*] the doctrine of God our Savior in all things. (Titus 2:9–10)

Being "Cosmetics" to the Gospel. Kosmeos is also the word from which we get our English word "cosmetics." Paul used this word to describe the way a woman should adorn herself so that she reflects the beauty of Jesus Christ (1 Tim. 2:9).

Most of us can identify with this analogy. We use some kind of "cosmetics" to make ourselves attractive to others—perfumes, powders, sprays, etc. Applied to our Christian lives, the way we live should attract people to Jesus Christ for everything we say and do should be like "cosmetics" to the Gospel. This is what it means to be "worthy of respect," "reverent" and "respectable" in the way we live. This also correlates with the two metaphors that Jesus used to describe the way we should be perceived in the world—we are to be "light" and "salt" (Matt. 5:13–16).

3. BEING MORALLY PURE

In his profiles for spiritual leaders in his letters to both Timothy and Titus, Paul lists the qualification of being the "husband of one wife." What did Paul have in mind? What did he really mean?

Though there are various interpretations, I believe Paul simply referred to being a "man of one woman"—that is, having one woman and only one in your life—if, of course, you are married. In other words, this concerns marital fidelity and faithfulness—in short, "moral purity."

It was a very common practice in the New Testament world for a married man to have more than one woman in his life, particularly if he was wealthy. For example, he could visit a temple prostitute on a regular basis and often would have a slave girl who was available to him in his home.

These were not secret relationships. Wives knew all about their husband's extracurricular activities since it was culturally acceptable. Ironically, divorce and even polygamy were not acceptable in the Roman Empire. However, extramarital affairs were commonplace. Though wives particularly were certainly not fond of this cultural standard, they really didn't have much choice in the matter.

A Contemporary Illustration. I once met a relatively young husband with a family when I ministered in another country. When this young man had reached the age of puberty, his father selected a prostitute for him, put her on a financial retainer to teach his son about sexual activity and to care for his "sexual needs" on a regular basis. Consequently, this young man was very experienced sexually.

When he was old enough to marry, however, he found it very difficult to break off his relationship with the prostitute. Even when he became a Christian, he found himself so addicted to this immoral behavior that he would leave his workplace in the evening and before coming home to his wife and children, he would visit the prostitute. Yet, when I met this young man, he had been loyal to his wife for several months. Through a group of caring, loving and confronting Christians to whom he had made himself accountable, he was able to break away from this sinful pattern of the flesh and become a "one-woman man."

In some respects, this specific illustration describes the New Testament culture in general. Consequently, when Paul instructed Timothy and Titus to look for spiritual leaders in the church, he advised them to select men who had broken away from their old habits and were maintaining moral purity by being loyal to their wives—and to their wives only.

A Charge to Both Men and Women. Moral purity, of course, was not just a problem for men. When Paul instructed the older women to train the younger women in his letter to Titus, he encouraged Titus to "admonish" these "young women to love their husbands" and "to be discreet" and "chaste" (Titus 2:5). The term "chaste" comes from the Greek word *hagnos* which literally means to be "pure."

Paul was concerned that all Christian women, young and old alike, maintain morally pure relationships with men. In many respects, women's attitudes and behaviors toward moral purity are more determinative than men's. History is filled with accounts of men, though rulers of kingdoms, who were often under the spell of beautiful and sensual women. For another woman's sexual favors and control many have given up fame, fortune, and position. And in our culture, I have seen men walk away from wives, children, and their church because of a sensual relationship with another woman.

Personal moral purity is to be a hallmark of the Christian faith. Since sex is a God-created gift, it is to be used within the guidelines of Scripture and the will of God. This is why Paul wrote specifically to the Thessalonians:

> For this is the will of God, your sanctification: that you should abstain from sexual immorality; that each of you should know how to possess his own vessel in sanctification and honor, not in passion of lust, like the Gentiles who do not know God; that no one should take advantage of and defraud his brother [or sister] in this matter, because the Lord is the avenger of all such, as we also forewarned you and testified. For God did not call us to uncleanness, but in holiness. (1 Thess. 4:3–7)

A Principle to Live By. No matter what culture we live in—and no matter what the direction of our culture morally—there is only one divine standard. When it comes to sexual intimacy, God created a man to have only one woman in his life—his wife. And He created a woman to have only one man in her life—her husband. Any other relationship that involves this kind of intimacy apart from a male-female marriage is immoral, adulterous, fornicative, and out of the will of God.

Again, we must take note that in both passages of Scripture (1 Tim. 3:2; Titus 1:6), being morally pure appears at the top of the list following "being blameless." Thus, one of the most important ways to build a good reputation—one that is trustworthy and respectable—is to be morally pure. If we cannot be trusted in our relationship with our mates, we cannot be trusted with *any* significant responsibility, either in business, politics, or as a leader in the church.

I have been a pastor for many years and have confronted immoral relationships on a number of occasions. As far as I can remember, I have never met a person who was unfaithful to his or her spouse who will not also lie. Deception and immorality always go together—unless the person is truly repentant. This is why Paul prioritized this quality in measuring spiritual maturity. Again, if we cannot be trusted morally, we cannot be trusted at all.

4. GUARDING OUR WORDS

Throughout Paul's ten profiles he warns against misusing the tongue. Interestingly, he is more specific with women. When addressing those who serve in the church, he warns them to avoid being "slanderers" (1 Tim. 3:11). When he told Titus what to teach "older women," he gave the same warning (Titus 2:3).

Something else is obvious—and curious. As we have seen, when Paul addressed the qualifications for men who were to be considered for spiritual leadership, he told both Timothy and Titus they should be "blameless"—that is, have "good reputations" (1 Tim. 3:2; Titus 1:6–7). The very next characteristic mentioned by Paul in both passages is being "a husband of one wife" (1 Tim. 3:2; Titus 1:6)—that is, maintaining moral purity.

However, when Paul addressed the marks of spiritual maturity for women, we see a similar pattern, but with a different issue. In Timothy's letter, Paul stated that women in serving positions should, first of all, be "reverent" in the way they live—*"not slanderers."* When Paul instructed Titus as to what to teach older women, he said they should "be reverent in behavior, *not slanderers"* (Titus 2:3).

What can we learn when we compare these two profiles? Notice the comparisons in the following graphic:

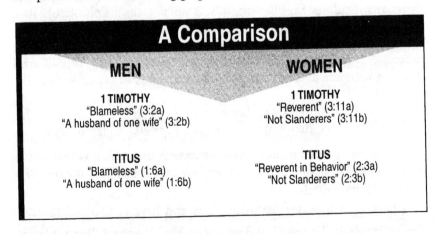

A Comparison

MEN	WOMEN
1 TIMOTHY "Blameless" (3:2a) "A husband of one wife" (3:2b)	**1 TIMOTHY** "Reverent" (3:11a) "Not Slanderers" (3:11b)
TITUS "Blameless" (1:6a) "A husband of one wife" (1:6b)	**TITUS** "Reverent in Behavior" (2:3a) "Not Slanderers" (2:3b)

This literary pattern is not accidental, but rather reflects a reality. Normally a man's area of vulnerability is sexual. On the other hand, a woman's area of vulnerability is often verbal. Nothing can destroy personal reputation faster than to fail God in these areas of our Christian lives. And nothing can devastate and destroy other people more than to be victims of either the sin of immorality or the sin of verbal abuse, false statements, rumors, and gossip.

There is another important lesson here. Nothing destroys the reputation of the church of Jesus Christ faster than these two sins. Think of the number of prominent Christian leaders who have committed adultery and hurt the reputation of the church before the watching world. And think of the number of churches that have been victims of splits and disunity because of inappropriate gossip and hurtful communication.

This does not mean that both men and women do not have problems in *both* areas. But experience verifies that Paul's point is well made. Men, particularly, must be on guard against sexual temptation (consider the words of Jesus in Matt. 5:27–28). And women must be especially on guard against inappropriate verbal communication (see 1 Tim. 5:13).

5. GUARDING OUR TEMPERS.

Here Paul zeroes in on men. Those chosen to be spiritual leaders were not to be "violent," "quarrelsome" (1 Tim. 3:3; Titus 1:7–8), "double tongued" (1 Tim. 3:2), "self-willed" or "quick-tempered" (Titus 1:7).

When discussing this mark of personal maturity, we must understand that the Bible nowhere classifies all anger as sin. In fact, writing to the Ephesians, Paul stated, "Be angry, and do not sin" (Eph. 4:26). Paul certainly did not encourage "anger"; rather, he was concerned that when Christians do get angry—and we all do—that we should not sin in the process. Anger, like love, is a part of the very nature of God Himself. And since we are made in God's image, we have an unusual capacity for both.

When Is Anger Sinful? Anger becomes sinful when it rises too soon. This is why Paul warned men not to be "quick tempered." As James says:

> So then, my beloved brethren, let every man be swift to hear, slow to speak, slow to wrath; for the wrath of man does not produce the righteousness of God. (James 1:19–20)

Anger also becomes sinful when we allow it to linger. After instructing the Ephesians to "be angry" and yet not to "sin," Paul said, "Do not let the sun go down on your wrath" (Eph. 4:26). If we do, we will give the devil an opportunity to take advantage of us and turn our natural and normal anger into sinful anger.

Sinful anger often becomes a "brooding" kind of anger, smoldering and seeking revenge. This kind of anger can lead an individual to pay back "evil for evil" (Rom. 12:17). When this happens, we take the law into our own hands; we try to play God; we become revengeful.

All Christians need to learn to express anger in nonjudgmental, nonhurtful, and nondestructive ways. It is always better to say, "I am feeling angry about this" rather than to say, "You make me angry when you do things like that." The first approach puts the focus on yourself, whereas the second approach puts the focus on the other person.

And remember, when you're handling anger in others, there is a powerful Proverb that we should practice:

A soft answer turns away wrath, But a harsh word stirs up anger. The tongue of the wise uses knowledge rightly, but the mouth of fools pours forth foolishness. (Prov. 15:1)

Once I was a visiting lecturer at a particular seminary. Those who invited me were kind enough to loan me a car with the name of the seminary painted on the door.

One morning as I was leaving my motel unit, I confused the edge of the parking lot with the berm of the main road and suddenly ended up in the middle of the street—still thinking I was in the parking lot. I discovered my error as I looked up and saw a car bearing down on me. I hit the brakes, but the driver coming at me made no effort to stop—until he was a few feet from my side door. He then hit his brakes and purposely did a 180-degree turn around my car. Stunned, I looked through his windshield at one of the angriest expressions I've ever seen. He threw open his door and came at me—eyes blazing and fists clenched.

As I saw him coming, I rolled down my window and did what I had to do—apologize profusely for being so stupid. I explained that I was from out of town and had made a serious error.

At that moment—and instantaneously—he dropped his head, lowered his eyes, and walked away mumbling "I'm sorry." He quickly got in his car and drove off.

In this case, I was clearly in the wrong, but confused. I imagine that he suddenly understood what had happened. Because of my apologetic attitude and "soft answer," his anger dissipated, especially when he realized I was a visiting professor.

Later, I concluded he no doubt had what he perceived to be some very unfortunate experiences with the seminary students or professors in this small town. When he saw the name of the seminary on the side of the car, it may have triggered his anger. In this case, I learned dramatically what the proverb really means—"A soft answer turns away wrath." Had I responded with harsh words and a defensive attitude, I would have been in serious trouble.

6. BEING TEMPERATE

Paul used this word to describe qualities of maturity for elders and pastors (1 Tim. 3:2), deaconesses (1 Tim. 3:11) and older men (Titus 2:2). He also used this same word in his letter to the Thessalonians when he discussed the coming day of judgment. "Therefore," Paul wrote, "let us not sleep, as others do, but let us watch and be sober [that is, temperate]" (1 Thess. 5:6).

A Christian who is "temperate" has a clear perspective on the Christian life. He understands how easy it is to be lulled into lethargy and to focus on life as it exists in the present. A temperate Christian—as Jesus exhorts— is seeking "first the kingdom of God and His righteousness," and trusting God to meet his material and spiritual needs. He doesn't "worry about tomorrow," because he knows that God is in charge of his life, as well as everything that is happening in the world.

Interestingly, Paul instructed the Thessalonians on how to develop this quality of temperance in their lives. He wrote:

> But let us who are of the day be *sober*[temperate], putting on the breastplate of faith and love, and as a helmet the hope of salvation. (1 Thess. 5:8)

Here Paul, presented a strategy to the whole church in Thessalonica. Together as a body, they were to put on "the breastplate of faith and love." Together as a body of believers, they were to also put on "as a helmet the hope of salvation." However, every Christian must personalize these quali- ties. For these characteristics to be reflected in a church, every Christian must contribute his own faith, love, and hope. In this sense, "every part must do its work."

Perhaps we could summarize this quality by saying it represents a Christian with a correct view regarding the "temporariness" of this life and everything in it. Temperate Christians don't get caught up in the "false security" of what appears to be human progress. They walk in the "light" of the Word of God and not in the "darkness" of the world of man (1 Thess. 5:4–5). They are certainly not pessimists, but realists. And their optimism is rooted in their eternal perspective, not in their earthly philosophy of life.

7. Being "Sober Minded"

The Greek word *sophron* which Paul used to describe this quality is translated in various ways: "being sensible", "being of sound mind and judgment", or "being prudent." Significantly, this quality appears primarily in Paul's exhortations to men—first, those who were being considered for pastoral leadership (1 Tim. 3:2; Titus 1:8); second, older men (Titus 2:2); and third, younger men (Titus 2:6).

Why is this true? I believe the Holy Spirit through Paul identified another one of man's major weaknesses and areas of vulnerability—the problem of ego and pride. Perhaps the best way to understand what Paul had in mind is to see how he used this word when he wrote to the Romans:

> For I say, through the grace given to me, to everyone who is among you, not to think of himself more highly than he ought to think, but to think *soberly*, as God has dealt to each one a measure of faith. (Rom. 12:3)

A sober-minded Christian is a humble Christian. When we reflect this characteristic, we have a proper view of ourselves. We are certainly not to "think less of ourselves" than we ought to think. Rather, when we reflect sober-mindedness, we demonstrate that our gifts, our abilities, and everything that we have is from God. Without His help, we are helpless.

When we demonstrate sober-mindedness, we also reflect that we have "a proper view of the grace of God." We realize that we were lost without Jesus Christ and that it was His boundless love that brought us eternal life. Sober-minded Christians realize every moment of every day that "by grace" they "have been saved through faith," not because of what they have done. Rather, their salvation "is the gift of God, not of works, lest anyone should boast" (Eph. 2:8–9).

Paul had this same concept in mind when he wrote to the Philippians:

> Let nothing be done through selfish ambition or conceit, but in lowliness of mind let each esteem others better than himself. Let each of you look out not only for his own interests, but also for the interests of others. (Phil. 2:3–4)

Meekness—the concept described here—is not weakness. It is possible to have a good self-image and to have confidence in our skills and abilities–and yet to realize that all we have is from Jesus Christ. It is possible to enjoy our achievements and to accept honor–and at the same time to glorify God. This is an intricate balance, but it can be maintained by mature Christians. This is, in essence, what Paul meant when he taught us to be "sober-minded."

8. Being Generous

Again, Paul's focus was on men who were in leadership roles in the church—and in their homes. Spiritual leaders were to be hospitable (1 Tim. 3:2; Titus 1:8)—using what they have materially to serve and help others. They were to be generous men.

This does not mean that a spiritual leader had to be wealthy, but if he was—as many elders in the New Testament church were—they were to use their resources to serve other Christians. Philemon certainly illustrates this kind of godly and generous man. However, even if an elder did not have much of this world's goods, he was still to be generous in the sight of God, since God measures generosity not by the quantity of our resources but by our heart attitude.

Paul became more specific when he indicated spiritual leaders should not be "greedy for money" (1 Tim. 3:1,8; Titus 1:7). To make his point clear, he accentuated this quality of generosity by stating that spiritual leaders must not be "covetous" (1 Tim. 3:3)—which literally means "not avaricious" or "a lover of money."

We must know that Paul was not teaching that "making money" *per se* is wrong or to be avoided. Rather, Christians who have these resources and have the capacity to even increase their resources must always be generous—as well as on guard (see 1 Tim. 6:9–10).

Why did Paul focus on men in emphasizing generosity? First, for men, "money" and "ego" often go together. Second, Paul was concerned that men take the leadership role in modeling generosity in their families. This is particularly true in cultures where men are the primary "breadwinners."

On the other hand, in cultures where women have the opportunity to earn substantial incomes along with their husbands, everything that Paul stated to men would apply to women, since they can be just as selfish as men when it comes to sharing their material possessions—and in some cases, more so, because of their natural tendency to seek security in their material possessions.

9. Free From Addictions

The addiction Paul dealt with in these New Testament passages involved "being addicted to wine." He included both men and women when mentioning this weakness (1 Tim. 3:3,8; Titus 1:7; 2:3).

Paul's specific concern in the culture of his day could be multiplied many times in various cultures of the world. Today we have a variety of alcoholic beverages, drugs, tobacco, delicious foods, beautiful clothing, health clubs—and the list goes on, including sexual activities. A Christian should not be addicted to anything; addictive behaviors demonstrate a lack of self-discipline in our lives. Addiction indicates that we are more preoccupied with the needs of our body and our flesh than with Jesus Christ and the things of the spirit.

Unfortunately, addictive behaviors are often difficult to overcome. This is where the body of Jesus Christ is so vital and so important. Addictive type people need to make themselves accountable to other Christians—for prayer, for encouragement as well as for confrontation when they fail.

If people could be freed from their addictions in the first century world through the power of God and the functioning body of Jesus Christ, the same can happen today. However, remember that these Christians also had to be held accountable.

I had the privilege of developing a close relationship with a former all-pro NFL football player—a man who earned two Super Bowl rings. However, he grew up in a seriously dysfunctional family and had been sexually abused as a young boy. Now, as an adult, he was seriously addicted in several areas of his life—alcohol, drugs, and sex. His marriage broke apart and his relationship with his children deteriorated which caused him a great deal of emotional pain.

He called me one day and said, "Gene, I need help." When we met to discuss his problem, I agreed to meet with him once a week to work through my book, *The Measure of a Man*, a chapter at a time.[6]

We had an agreement—that he would be totally honest with me each week in terms of his successes and failures in his areas of addiction. He was. And today this man is making significant progress in his spiritual life. Though he still has to maintain regular accountability to several trusted friends in the body of Christ, he is progressing in his spiritual walk with Christ.

Addictions are difficult to overcome, but with the power of God and His Holy Spirit—plus friends who care—it is possible.

10. ABLE TO TEACH

Though this quality of maturity appears only in Paul's profile for elders in his letter to Timothy (1 Tim. 3:2), it includes several other qualities outlined by Paul in the other profiles.

Actually, this phrase is only one word in the Greek language—*didaktikos*. There are hundreds of references in the New Testament to some form of the word having to do with "teaching," but Paul only used this word twice—and I believe for a unique reason.

The only other time Paul used this word is in his second letter to Timothy. And the context in which he used the word helps us understand why Paul included this phrase as a mark of spiritual maturity.

Following is the passage in which Paul used this word in his second letter to Timothy, which provides us with a mini-commentary on *didaktikos*:

> But avoid foolish and ignorant disputes, knowing that they generate strife. And a servant of the Lord must not quarrel but be gentle to all, able to teach [*didaktikos*], patient, in humility correcting those who are in opposition, if God perhaps will grant them repentance, so that they may know the truth. (2 Tim. 2:23–25)

The Rest Of The Story

I began this chapter by making reference to my good friend and fellow pastor and elder, Mike Cornwall. Confronted that Saturday morning by a crowd of angry people picketing his home, rather than getting angry and asking these people to leave, Mike invited all of them into his home. Naturally, the man at the door with the document in his hands was totally surprised—as was the entire group.However, in a few minutes, they laid down their placards in a pile on the front lawn and all marched into Mike's family room. Sharon served them coffee while Mike explained his personal concerns for minorities, as well as the history of his own involvement with minority groups in the city of Dallas.

At a certain point in time, Mike shifted his focus from his involvement in social activities to an experience that he had had several years before. Mike had come to know Jesus Christ as his personal Lord and Savior which, he told the group, even intensified his concern for helping others.

At that point, there was a decided change in the reactions of the group. He even began to get some affirmations from some of these strangers. Mike had won their hearts. They began to see more clearly his own perspective on what was happening in our society.

After a period of time together, the people stood up, thanked Mike and Sharon for their hospitality, and one by one walked out the door, got on the bus, and left—and were never heard from again.

When I heard Mike share this experience, I thought immediately of what Paul wrote to Timothy in his second letter. Mike and Sharon both demonstrated unusual maturity in that situation. Very quickly, a negative response on Mike's part could have led to a "dispute" and an argument. However, by being "gentle to all"—and I mean all—by being "patient" and "not resentful" toward people embarrassing him in front of his neighbors—he was given a wonderful opportunity to be "able to teach" and "with humility" to correct their thinking. Right there before his very eyes he began to see changes because this happens when people began to listen and to come to "know the truth."

What Mike did in no way justifies anything that may have been inappropriately done by the U.S. Government—or any organization. But Mike took this opportunity to share his desire to be fair, honest, and nonprejudiced in his dealings with people—both in his personal life and in his business. By practicing these qualities of life in a nondefensive and open way, he was able to communicate the truth, not only about his own Christian behavior but the truth about Jesus Christ. And that's what Christianity is all about (John 14:6).

Measuring Our Walk

1. Examine the ten characteristics of spiritual maturity. Identify the practical ways to make these a part of your life.

2. Which charactertistic do you struggle with the most? Find someone who can hold you accountable as you come "to the measure of the stature of the fullness of Christ."

3. Secure a copy of the *The Measure of a Man* or *The Measure of a Woman* (both published by Regal Books) and form a Bible discussion group. This will give you an opportunity to study all of the characteristics outlined by Paul in his letters to Timothy and Titus and to apply these qualities to your own life. This is also an excellent opportunity to be a part of a unique accountability group.

PAUL'S FINAL LETTER TO TIMOTHY

A Contemporary Paraphrase of 2 Timothy

My dear son Timothy:

I have such a longing to see you and to be with you, it hurts way down deep. I'm about to give my life for the cause of Christ. But I'm not fearful. I know I have fought a good fight. I have finished the race by keeping my eyes on Jesus Christ. And I thank God that I've kept the faith.

Before I depart, I want to share with you some final encouraging exhortations regarding your own personal walk with Christ.

- First, don't be intimidated by those who persecute you and make fun of you. Remember that God will strengthen you. Be strong in His grace.

- Endure hardship as a good soldier of Jesus Christ. You are in a battle. Keep your eyes focused on spiritual things and not on the things of this world.

- Be diligent in your study of God's Word. Interpret it carefully and accurately and faithfully communicate it to others.

- Don't be defensive and impatient with those who oppose you. Respond gently and with love as Jesus Christ has responded to you and to me.

Finally, if possible, come to see me. But, do so quickly because I sense my time as short. Others have forsaken me—but not Luke. What a faithful friend he is!

I look forward to seeing you my dear friend, Timothy. Be sure to bring those special books that have been such an encouragement to both of us.

If I don't see you, however, before my life is taken, I look forward to seeing you in heaven.

As I reminded you in my first letter, don't let anyone look down on you because you're young. Rather, be an example to all of the believers in word, in conduct, in love, in spirit, in faith, and in purity. My prayer for you is that you'll always be able to walk worthy of the great calling with which you have been called to serve Jesus Christ.

Your father in Christ,

Paul

NOTES

PREFACE: A PERSONAL JOURNEY

1. I personally use the term "vision" to describe spiritual wisdom, insight, or direction iin answer to prayer and in seeking God's will through the Scriptures (James 1:5). I'm not referring to "revelation" from God in the sense that God spoke directly to the New Testament authors and other first century personalities who had this unique experience. Nevertheless, I believe the kind of experience just described involves supernatural guidance.

2. This book was a result of the basic research and writing I did in preparation for the video series entitled, "The Measure of Spiritual Maturity." To discover how you can order this series, which corresponds with chapters 2–12, call 1-800-527-4014.

CHAPTER 1

1. Merrill C. Tenney, Interpreting Revelation (Grand Rapids, Michigan: Wm. B. Eerdmans Publishing Company, 1957), 87.

2. It is important to note that Paul used plural pronouns in this passage to indicate that he is addressing the church collectively in Corinth. "Together," they were Christ's "temple."

CHAPTER 2

1. In Paul's second letter to this church, he did not mention growth in their "hope." There's a reason, which we'll look at in detail in chapter 4.

2. In addition to using the term "grace" to refer to the free gift of salvation, scriptural writers frequently used the term "grace" to also refer to the gifts of the Spirit. For example, in Acts 4:33, Luke recorded—"With great power the apostles gave witness to the resurrection of the Lord Jesus and great grace was upon them all" (see also Acts 6:8, 11:23; Rom. 12:6; Eph. 4:7; 1 Peter 4:10).

3. Some of the Corinthians were denying Paul's apostolic calling. They did not trust him. Paul is reminding them that when there is no "trust," there is no love (See Cor. 1:12).

4. Some Bible interpreters believe Paul was referring here to the completion of the canon. However, the total context in the Corinthian letter does not seem to substantiate this interpretation. Rather, Paul seems to be referring to that aspect of Christ's second coming, commonly referred to as the "rapture of the church" (see 1 Cor. 15:50–57).

CHAPTER 3

1. Justification by faith apart from works also permeates the letter Paul wrote to the churches in Galatia. No doubt Paul's first letter reflects the law/grace controversy that was brewing in Antioch when Paul and Barnabas returned from their first missionary journey (Acts 15:1). Paul evidently received word that after he and Barnabas had left the churches they had established in southern Galatia, false teachers came in and confused these new believers, teaching particularly that they could not be saved apart from being circumcised. Paul was furious with these false teachers and very disappointed in the Galatian believers. In no uncertain terms, he wrote to them emphasizing that no one can ever "be justified by the works of the law." Rather, salvation comes by "faith in Jesus Christ" (Gal. 2:16; see also 3:8,24).

2. Another example involves the ministry of Paul and Silas on the second missionary journey. As they made a return trip to the churches that had been established on the first journey, they shared the conclusions that had been reached by the "apostles and elders at Jerusalem" (Acts 16:4). Consequently, Luke recorded. "The churches were strengthened in the faith and increased in numbers daily." (Acts 16:5). In other words, these believers were grounded in biblical truths, and as they were, more and more people experienced "saving faith."

3. The Philippians—who were also Macedonians—shared in this type of sacrificial service. Many of them gave to help Paul when they really had nothing to give. Speaking of their material gifts, Paul referred to their faith early in the letter (Phil. 2:17) and then called their help "a sweet-smelling aroma, an acceptable sacrifice, well pleasing to God" (Phil. 4:18).

James, too, made a powerful connection between faith and giving. He illustrated faith that produces works with a "material possessions" example (James 2:14–17).

4. Charles C. Ryrie, *Balancing the Christian Life* (Chicago: Moody Press, 1969), 84.

5. For an extensive treatment of why the biblical documents are reliable and trustworthy, see Josh McDowell, *Evidence that Demands a Verdict* (San Bernardino, California: Campus Crusade for Christ, Inc., 1972).

CHAPTER 4

1. Kefa Sempangi with Barbara R. Thompson, *A Distant Grief* (Glendale, California: Regal Books, 1979).

CHAPTER 5

1. Henry Dummond, *The Greatest Thing in the World* (Springdale, Pennsylvania: Whitaker House, 1981), 21, 22.

2. It should be recognized that the Greek words used to describe "love" in the New Testament can be overly categorized. They are overlapping and interrelated in meaning. However, used in the way they are described in this chapter can help us understand a very important reality in human relationships.

CHAPTER 6

1. See Gene A. Getz, *Praying for One Another* (Wheaton, Illinois: Victor Books, 1982).

2. For a very extensive study about what the Bible teaches regarding how Christians should use their material possessions, see Gene A. Getz, *Biblical Theology of Material Possessions*, (Chicago: Moody, 1990), and *Real Prosperity*, (Chicago: Moody, 1990).

CHAPTER 7

1. For a more in-depth study of these concepts, see Gene A. Getz, *Praying for One Another* (Wheaton, Illinois: Victor Books, 1982).

CHAPTER 8

1. For an in-depth study of the "One Another" concepts in Scripture, consult the following books by Gene A. Getz, *Building Up One Another* (Wheaton, Illinois: Victor Books, 1976); *Loving One Another* (Wheaton, Illinois: Victor

Books, 1979); *Praying for One Another* (Wheaton, Illinois: Victor Books, 1982); *Encouraging One Another* (Wheaton, Illinois: Victor Books, 1981); *Serving One Another* (Wheaton, Illinois: Victor Books, 1984).

CHAPTER 9

1. Joachim Jeremias, *Jerusalem in the Time of Jesus,* F.H. and C.H. Kay (London: SCM, 1969), 58.

2. It is not possible to know the exact number of people referred to in Acts 2:1. However, earlier in Luke's account, he made reference to the fact that the disciples who had gathered to listen to Peter numbered "about a hundred and twenty." If this indicates there were approximately this number of disciples in Jerusalem at this time, probably the number remained approximately the same until the Holy Spirit came on the Day of Pentecost.

3. Gene A. Getz, *A Biblical Theology of Material Possessions* (Chicago: Moody Press, 1990); and *Real Prosperity* (Chicago: Moody, Press, 1990).

4. Lyle Eggleston, "The Church That Learned to Give, *Moody Monthly* (July/August 1988), 31–32.

CHAPTER 10

1. Merrill Tenney, *John: The Gospel of Belief* (Eerdmans, 1953), 199.

2. Ibid, pp. 30–31.

3. Francis Schaeffer, *The Church at the End of the 20th Century* (Intervarsity Press, 1970), 139.

CHAPTER 11

1. "Rationale," *The Danvers Statement,* Council on Biblical Manhood and Womanhood.

2. George Peters, *Saturation Evangelism* (Zondervan, 1970), 160. [Peters here is in no way teaching salvation by baptism or as a result of a parent's faith. Salvation is personal. It results when an individual recognizes his need for Jesus Christ because of his sins. We can assume that those who were baptized in these households were all old enough to make an intelligent and personal decision to believe in the Lord Jesus Christ.]

3. The terms "elders" and "bishops" are used interchangeably by Paul in the New Testament. The term "elder" has its roots in Judaism. The term "bishop" has its roots in the Greek and Roman culture. An elder was a spiritual leader in Israel as far back as Moses. A bishop was a superintendent or leader of a Roman colony. Paul used these two terms interchangeably in connection with the church in Philippi, Ephesus and the churches in Crete since there was a strong mix of Christians with both Jewish and Gentile backgrounds. This demonstrates Paul's commitment to "freedom in form." Since language reflects structure, this illustrates what Paul meant when he told the Corinthians that he became "all things to all men" so that he "might by all means save some" (1 Cor. 9:22). Therefore, if he needed to change the form of language to get across biblical meaning, he did not hesitate to do so. In essence, then, elders and/or bishops were the pastors in the local church. Some Bible expositors correlate this with Paul's reference to "pastors and teachers" in Eph. 4:12.

4. Paul was evidently not referring here to small children or even teenagers. Again, we must understand the concept of the extended family. Many married children lived in the same household with their parents. If these grown children were guilty of immoral and unethical lifestyles and worshipped pagan gods rather than the true and living God, Paul simply said that this man was not qualified to be a spiritual leader in the church.

Furthermore, Paul was not teaching that an elder must have children old enough to be believers. If this were true, a husband who was childless could not be an elder. Again, Paul simply said that if a father and mother have grown children who are old enough to believe but they have chosen paganism over Christianity and have decided to live their lives in immoral and disrespectful ways, then this man should not consider spiritual leadership in the church—or be considered. He would not be above reproach—which simply means he would not have a good reputation in the community. Furthermore, his children's behavior would indicate weaknesses in his own leadership style as a father. Those same weaknesses would flow over into his leadership in the church. Furthermore, for this man to accept a spiritual leadership role in the church would create an even greater chasm between him and his children since they would be subject to criticism by the Christian community. Fortunately, geographical distances in our society today often make it easier for a godly man to become a spiritual leader when his children—once they leave home—choose not to follow the Lord and also leave the immediate community.

5. I do not believe that the qualifications of an elder in 1 Timothy 3 and Titus 1 restrict eldership to married men. Paul taught that if a man married, he must be loyal to one woman, and one woman alone; in other words, he must

be morally pure. As we've noted already, Paul did the same thing when he referred to having believing children. He did not say that a man must either have children or that his children must be old enough to believe. Rather, if a man has children who are old enough to believe and they choose to be pagan in their lifestyle, this then would disqualify the man from eldership.

CHAPTER 12

1. See chapter 11, endnote, 3.

2. I believe that deacons are men who assist the elders in carrying out the cultural needs of the church. The larger the church, the more need there will be for deacons. This explains why Paul and Barnabas only appointed elders on their return trip to visit the churches in Lystra, Iconium and Antioch (Acts 14:21-23). It further explains why Timothy was instructed to appoint elders and deacons in Ephesus while Paul instructed Titus to appoint only elders in the cities in Crete. Ephesus was an established growing church, whereas the churches in Crete were in an infant stage of growth.

3. It is my opinion that Paul referred not to the wives of deacons here, but to women who are in serving positions in the church—women like Phoebe whom Paul identified as "a servant of the church in Cenchrea" (Rom. 16:1). He also referred to a woman named Mary who, Paul stated—"Labored much for us" (16:6). Paul also included a reference to Tryphena and Tryphosa, women "who have labored in the Lord" (16:12).

4. There is no specific correlation between the ten profiles and the ten characteristics outlined in this chapter. Rather, the ten characteristics come from all ten profiles and have been determined by repetition and emphasis.

5. See chapter 11, endnote, 3.

6. Gene A. Getz, *The Measure of a Man* (Regal Books: Ventura, California, 1974). The book contains twenty chapters, each built on the twenty qualities of maturity that emerge from 1 Timothy 3 and Titus 1. It has been used extensively as a discipling tool.